BRITISH CINEMA

AN ILLUSTRATED GUIDE

BY

DENIS GIFFORD

PN
1998
.A2
G 48

A. ZWEMMER LIMITED, LONDON
A. S. BARNES & CO., NEW YORK

Acknowledgements

SPECIAL THANKS for rare stills and hitherto unpublished personal informa-
tion go to three great ladies of the early British screen, Miss Dorothy Bellew
(Mrs. Burke), Miss Chrissie White (Mrs. Edwards), and Miss Joan Morgan.
Other rare photographs came from Harold Dunham and Anthony Slide. Useful
material was loaned by Tony Hawes, John Kobal and Ray Selfe. Further stills
were generously supplied by F. Maurice Speed, also Peter Cowie, Allen
Eyles, Barrie Pattison, and the back cover still of Julie Christie by Warner
Pathe.

It is usual for an author of a work such as this to generously acknowledge his
sources of assistance and reference. So here goes. This book is based on
material gathered by a man who is so mad on movies that he has spent the
best twelve years of his life compiling the first complete filmography of
British productions listing details of over 15,000 entertainment films. So if
you find any errors and omissions, blame him. His name? Modesty forbids.
Seriously though, if you do find any mistakes, please send them to me c/o The
Tantivy Press, London W.I. There's always the chance of a revised edition.

FRONT COVER: Trevor Howard and Celia Johnson in *Brief Encounter*
BACK COVER: (top) Charles Laughton in *The Private Life of Henry VIII*;
(bottom) Julie Christie

Cover design by Allen Eyles

Introduction

IT IS accidentally fitting that the first entry in this alphabetical dictionary of British film personalities should be for the man who made the first successful film in this country. It is also accidentally fitting that the first film listed in the alphabetical Title Index should be for a British film directed by a German about a Turkish despot.

And that just about sums up the story of British cinema!

This book is a first attempt to put between handy covers at a handy price the complete story of British films in factual form. It is a kind of All Time Who's Who of stars and directors, 546 of them, selected for their contribution to the overall seventy year scene.

Pioneers and inventors like Acres, Paul and Smith; the first ever directors like Fitzhamon, Booth, and Aylott; the first stars, better known by their faces than their names, like the Misses Taylor, White and Bellew; the directors who progressed to features but fell away as sound came with Jolson, like Coleby, Paul (Fred) and Rooke; and stars who did the same, like the lovely Lilian Hall Davis and graceful Norah Baring; those who went from silence to greater strength in sound, like directors Hitchcock, Elvey and Saville, and stars John Stuart and Madeleine Carroll; stars who started here and then went to Hollywood, like Clive Brook, Gladys Cooper, Ray Milland; the new names of the Thirties, most of them from the stage: Jessie Matthews, Jack Buchanan, Cicely Courtneidge, and from a different form of stage, Formby and Fuller and Fields; the Gainsborough Girls of the Forties—Lockwood, Calvert, Kent and Roc, and the lovely lost ones, Crawford and Kendall; the Masons, the Grangers, the Harveys; and so to the swinging Christies. . . .

But quite possibly a person you expected to find has been left out, like that minor director of Merton Park mysteries or the cockney character who plays dustmen and drivers. The answer is that, knowing something had to go, I've chosen to deal only with stars and directors with a body of work in films. Writers and producers are generally omitted; but where a director springs from scripting or turns producer, I've usually included his writing and production credits. Perhaps one day we can do a Volume Two for all those creative people behind the screen, and include composers, cameramen, and clapperboys as well as the very backbone of British cinema, our character actors.

This book is for Pandora Jane.

D. G.

Abbreviations

AA   Academy Award
assoc. prod.   associate producer
asst.   assistant
B: birthplace
B.I.P.   British International Pictures
co-dir.   co-director
Co.   Company
C.O.I.   Central Office of Information
dir.   director
doc(s).   documentary film(s)
ed.   editor
E.M.B.   Empire Marketing Board

G.B.I.   Gaumont British Instructional
G.P.O.   General Post Office
M: married to
mgr.   manager
M.O.I.   Ministry of Information
prod.   producer
ph.   photographer
RN: real name
sc.   screenplay/script/scenario/story
tech.   technical
3D   stereoscopic

6

In the same
**INTERNATIONAL
FILM GUIDE SERIES**
edited by Peter Cowie

2,45

How to use the Filmographies

Each personality is given a number in alphabetical order from 1 (Birt Acres) to 546 (Mai Zetterling). The order of information given is: surname, Christian name; year of birth and year of death in brackets; profession within the film industry; birthplace; real name; original profession prior to films; year of entry into films and in what capacity; special family details such as parents, marriages, etc., where these are relevant to career; capsule comment describing work in cinema. Then follows a complete chronological filmography, with separate listing where necessary for Shorts, Documentaries, and Features, while silent and sound work is clearly differentiated. Where filmographies cannot be complete for reasons of space, only the most important titles are given following the words 'Main shorts' etc. Cross references are given in capital letters.

This is a book of British films, but certain films made abroad as co-productions are included. Many of the stars and directors listed have, of course, made films in Hollywood and elsewhere, but these titles are not included.

Films of a particular year are listed together with the year date following. This is given in abbreviated form: 00 for 1900, 67 for 1967. Numbers occurring in the biographical details are also year dates abbreviated in this fashion and never refer to the age of the person.

7

A

1 ACRES Birt (1854-1918) Inventor, director. B: Richmond, Va. 90: mgr. Elliot Dry Plate Co., Barnet. 93: invents camera with rapid plate exposure. 94: designs projector for series of photos in rapid succession; designs camera and takes first experimental movie of haycart at Hadley Green. 95: Feb. takes kinetoscope films outside his house, joins with Robert PAUL; Mar. 30 films Boat Race; May 25 patents Kinetic Lantern; Jun. films in Germany; Aug. projects at Barnet Assembly Hall. 96: Jan. 14 projects at Royal Photographic Society; Mar. 24 films included in Paul's show; May own show in Piccadilly; Jul. 21 first Royal show. 97: forms Northern Photographic Works. 98: invents home cine camera/projector. Main shorts: *Oxford and Cambridge Boat Race, The Derby, Inauguration of the Kiel Canal by Kaiser Wilhelm II, Charge of the Uhlans, Sea Waves at Dover, Shoeblack at Work in a London Street, Smith and Machinery at Work* 95; *Boxing Match, Three Burlesque Dancers, Boxing Kangaroo, Tom Merry Lightning Cartoonist, Golfing Extraordinary, The Arrest of a Pickpocket, Landing at Low Tide, The Miller and the Sweep* 96; *Pierrot and Pierrette* 97; *Briton v. Boer, Dan Leno's Cricket Match* 00.

2 AHERNE Brian (1902–   ) Actor. B: King's Norton. Stage: 13. Blond, blue-eyed hero of silents; main sound career in Hollywood. *The Eleventh Commandment* 24; *The Squire of Long Hadley,* King of the Castle 25; *Safety First* 26; *A Woman Redeemed* 27; *Shooting Stars, Underground* 28; sound: *The W Plan* 30; *Madame Guillotine* 31; *The Constant Nymph* 33; *Lancelot and Guinevere* 63.

3 AINLEY Henry (1879–1945) Actor. B: Morley. Stage: 00. First major stage star to become a film star. *A Bachelor's Love Story* (short), *Called Back, She Stoops to Conquer* 14; *Brother Officers, The Prisoner of Zenda, Rupert of Hentzau, Jelfs, Sweet Lavender, The Outrage, Iris, The Great Adventure* 15; *Sowing the Wind, The Marriage of William Ashe, The Manxman* 16; *Quinneys* 19; *Build Thy House* 20; *Money* 21; *The Royal Oak, Sally Bishop Inscrutable Drew Investigator* series 26; sound: *Armistice* (voice) (short) 29; *The First Mrs. Fraser* 32; *The Good Companions* (voice) 33; *As You Like It* 37; *Battle of the Books* (voice) (short) 41.

4 ALLAN Elizabeth (1908–   ) Actress. B: Skegness. Stage: 27. Slender heroine of early talkies, then in Hollywood. *Alibi, The Rosary, Rodney Steps In, Black Coffee, Chin Chin Chinaman, Michael and Mary, Many Waters* 31; *Service For Ladies, The Chinese Puzzle, Nine Till Six, Down Our Street, The Lodger, Insult* 32; *The Shadow, The Lost Chord* 33; *Java Head* 34; *Dangerous Medicine* 38; *The Girl Who Forgot* 39; *Inquest, Saloon Bar* 40; *The Great Mr. Handel, Went The Day Well* 42; *He Snoops To Conquer* 44; *That Dangerous Age* 49; *No Highway* 51;

Folly to be Wise 52; Twice Upon a Time,
The Heart of the Matter 53; Front Page
Story 54; The Brain Machine 55; Grip of the
Strangler 58.

ALLEN Chesney see CRAZY GANG.

5 AMES Gerald (1881–1933) Actor. B:
Blackheath. Stage: 05. Athletic mous-
tached hero of London Films, later
HEPWORTH films opposite Alma TAY-
LOR. Shorts: The Black Spot, The Cage,
The Kitchen Countess, A Highwayman's
Honour 14. Features: England's Menace,
The Difficult Way, On His Majesty's Service,
The Fringe of War, The Revenge of Mr.
Thomas Atkins 14; 1914, The Middleman,
Brother Officers, The King's Outcast, The
Prisoner of Zenda, Rupert of Hentzau, The
Sons of Satan, Whoso Diggeth a Pit, The
Shulamite, The Derby Winner, Jelfs, The
Christian, Love in a Wood 15; You, The
Game of Liberty, Paste, Me and My Moke,
The Morals of Weybury, When Knights
Were Bold, Arsene Lupin, The Greater
Need, The Princess of Happy Chance, The
King's Daughter 16; Masks and Faces, A
Gamble for Love, The Ragged Messenger 17;
Missing the Tide, Adam Bede, Red Pottage,
A Fortune at Stake, A Turf Conspiracy,
Boundary House, A Peep Behind the Scenes
18; Comradeship, The Irresistible Flapper,
The Nature of the Beast, Sunken Rocks,
Possession, Sheba, The Forest on the Hill 19;
Anna the Adventuress, Alf's Button, Aylwin,
The Amazing Quest of Mr. Ernest Bliss,
Helen of Four Gates, Once Aboard the
Lugger (also dir.), John Forrest Finds Him-
self, Mrs. Erricker's Reputation 20; Wild
Heather, Tansy, Mr. Justice Raffles (also
dir.) 21; A Royal Divorce, God's Prodigal,
The Woman Who Obeyed, The Loves of
Mary Queen of Scots 23; Fights Through the
Ages series 24; The Little People 26; The
King's Highway 27; The Rising Generation,
A Light Woman 28.

6 ANDERSON Lindsay (1923–   )
Director. B: Bangalore. 47: ed. Sequence
magazine. Also stage producer. After
Free Cinema shorts made one important
feature. Shorts: Meet the Pioneers (co-
dir.) 48; Idlers at work 50; Three Installa-
tions 57; The Pleasure Garden (prod.
only) 52; Wakefield Express 53; O Dreamland, Thursday's Children (co-dir.) (AA),
Trunk Conveyor, Green and Pleasant Land,
Children Upstairs, Henry 54; Foot and
Mouth, £20 a Ton 55; Together (ed. only)
56; Every Day Except Christmas 57;
March to Aldermaston (assoc. prod.) 58;
Let My People Go (prod. only) 61. Features: This Sporting Life 63; The White Bus
67; If 68.

7 ANDERSON Michael (1920–   )
Director. B: London. 35: office boy
Elstree. 36: asst dir. The Mill on the Floss.
37: actor, Housemaster. Polished adven-
ture films. Also U.S.A. Private Angelo (co-
dir.) 49; Waterfront 50; Hell Is Sold Out,
Night Was Our Friend 51; Will Any
Gentleman, House of the Arrow 52; The
Dambusters 53; 1984 56; Yangtse Incident
57; Chase a Crooked Shadow 58; Shake
Hands With the Devil 59; The Naked Edge
61; Operation Crossbow 65; The Quiller
Memorandum 66.

8 ANNAKIN   Ken   (1914–   )
Director. B: Beverley. Civil servant,
salesman, actor, journalist. 41: camera
asst. docs. Expert on family entertain-
ment. Also Hollywood. Shorts: London—
1942, A Ride With Uncle Joe 43; Combined
Cadets, The New Crop 44; Three Cadets,
Pacific Thrust, Fenlands, Make Fruitful the
Land 45; It Began on the Clyde, We of the
West Riding, English Criminal Justice 46.
Features: Holiday Camp 47; Miranda,
Broken Journey, Here Come the Huggetts,
Quartet (co-dir.) 48; Vote for Huggett, The
Huggetts Abroad, Landfall 49; Double

Confession, Trio 50; Hotel Sahara 51; The Planter's Wife, The Story of Robin Hood 52; The Sword and the Rose 53; You Know What Sailors Are, The Seekers 54; Value for Money 55; Three Men in a Boat, Loser Takes All 56; Across the Bridge 57; Nor the Moon by Night 58; Third Man on the Mountain 59; The Swiss Family Robinson 60; Very Important Person, The Hellions 61; Crooks Anonymous, The Fast Lady 62; The Informers 63; Those Magnificent Men in Their Flying Machines 65; The Long Duel 67.

9 ARGYLE John (1911–) Director, producer, writer. B: Staffordshire. 27: asst. ph. Gainsborough. Prod. & sc. That's His Weakness (short) (also dir.), Flames of Fear 30; The Last Tide (also dir.), A Game of Chance, Thoroughbred. Sound, prod, dir. & sc.: Paradise Alley 31; The Final Reckoning, Smiling Along 32; then prod. only: Variety 35; Happy Days Are Here Again 36; Kathleen Mavourneen, The Mutiny of the Elsinore, Old Mother Riley (sc. only) 37; My Irish Molly, Little Dolly Daydream 38; Dark Eyes of London 39; Traitor Spy, The Door With Seven Locks 40; This Man Is Dangerous, Tower of Terror 41; The Night Has Eyes 42; Thursday's Child 43; Send For Paul Temple (also dir.) 46; The Hills of Donegal (also dir.) 47; The Case of Charles Peace, The Girl Who Couldn't Quite 49; Once a Sinner 50; Holiday Island (short) (also dir.) 51; Sunshine in Attica (short) (also dir.) 52; The Land is Green (short) (also dir.) 58.

10 ARLISS Leslie (1901–) Director, writer. B: London. RN: Leslie Andrews. Journalist, critic. Co-wrote comedies in 30s, directed popular period pieces in 40s, mostly TV film series from 50s. Writer: Tonight's the Night, Innocents of Chicago, Strip Strip Hooray, Josser on the River, Holiday Lovers 32; Orders is Orders 33; Jack Ahoy, My Old Dutch, Road House 34; Heat Wave 35; Rhodes of Africa, Where There's a Will, Everybody Dance, All In, Windbag the Sailor 36; Said O'Reilly to McNab, Good Morning Boys 37; Too Dangerous to Live, Come On George, The Second Mr. Bush, For Freedom, Pastor Hall 40; The Saint Meets the Tiger, South American George 41; The Foreman Went to France 42; then director: The Farmer's Wife (co-dir.), The Team (short) 41; The Night Has Eyes 42; The Man in Grey 43; Love Story 44; The Wicked Lady 45; A Man About the House 47; Idol of Paris 48; Saint and Sinners 49; The Woman's Angle 52; See How They Run, Miss Tulip Stays the Night 55; Insomnia is Good for You (short), Dearth of a Salesman (short), Danger List (short) 57; Man with a Dog (short) 58.

11 ASHER Robert Director. B: London. Asst. dir. from 35. Comedies, many with Norman WISDOM. Follow a Star 59; Make Mine Mink, The Bulldog Breed 60; She'll Have to Go 61; On the Beat 62; A Stitch in Time 63; The Intelligence Men, The Early Bird 65; Press for Time 66.

12 ASKEY Arthur (1900–) Actor. B: Liverpool. Clerk; 24: Concert party. Small-sized, 'big-hearted' comedian of radio & TV. Band Wagon, Charley's Bighearted Aunt 40; The Ghost Train, I Thank You 41; Back Room Boy, King Arthur Was a Gentleman, The Nose Has It (short) 42; Miss London Ltd. 43; Bees in Paradise 44; The Love Match 55; Ramsbottom Rides Again 56; Make Mine a Million 58; Friends and Neighbours 59.

13 ASQUITH Hon. Anthony (1902– 1968) Director. B: London. 26: studied films in Hollywood, then asst. on Boadicea. Creative silents, stagey but tasteful talkies. Shooting Stars (co-dir.)

27; *Underground, The Runaway Princess* 28; sound: *A Cottage on Dartmoor* 29; *Tell England* (co-dir.) 30; *Dance Pretty Lady* 31; *Marry Me* (sc. only) 32; *Letting in the Sunshine* (sc. only), *Lucky Number* 33; *The Unfinished Symphony* 34; *Moscow Nights* 35; *Pygmalion* (co-dir.) 38; *Guide Dogs for the Blind* (short), *French Without Tears* 39; *Channel Incident* (short), *Rush Hour* (short), *Freedom Radio, Quiet Wedding* 40; *Cottage to Let* 41; *Uncensored* 42; *The Demi-Paradise, We Dive at Dawn, Welcome to Britain* 43; *Two Fathers* (short), *Fanny By Gaslight* 44; *The Way to the Stars* 45; *While the Sun Shines* 47; *The Winslow Boy* 48; *The Woman in Question* 50; *The Browning Version* 51; *The Importance of Being Earnest* 52; *The Net, The Final Test* 53; *The Young Lovers, Carrington V.C.* 54; *On Such a Night* (short) 56; *Orders to Kill* 58; *The Doctor's Dilemma, Libel* 59; *The Millionairess* 60; *Guns of Darkness* 62; *The V.I.Ps, An Evening With the Royal Ballet* 63; *The Yellow Rolls Royce* 64.

14 ASTELL Betty (1912–   ) Actress. B: London. Stage: 28. Pretty blonde queen of B features in the 30s. M: Cyril Fletcher. *Lead Kindly Light* (short) 28; sound: *Double Dealing, The Love Contract, A Tight Corner* 32; *Medicine Man, That's My Wife, The Lost Chord, Cleaning Up, Great Stuff, The Stickpin, I'll Stick to You, This is the Life, Strike It Rich* 33; *On the Air, Flat No. 3, The Man I Want, The Life of the Party, Josser on the Farm* 34; *Equity Musical Revue* series, *Strictly Illegal* 35; *The Vandergilt Diamond Mystery, A Wife or Two, Sunshine Ahead, Jack of All Trades* 36; *Behind Your Back* 37; *The Mind of Mr. Reeder* 39; *A Piece of Cake* 48.

15 ATTENBOROUGH Richard (1923–   ) Actor, also producer. B: Cambridge. Originally typecast as a coward or baby-faced crook; later many comedies and war films. Also Hollywood. M: Sheila Sim. *In Which We Serve* 42; *Schweik's New Adventures* 43; *The Hundred Pound Window* 44; *Journey Together* 45; *A Matter of Life and Death, School for Secrets* 46; *The Man Within, Dancing With Crime* 47; *Brighton Rock, London Belongs to Me* 48; *The Guinea Pig, The Lost People* 49; *Boys in Brown, Morning Departure* 50; *Hell is Sold Out, The Magic Box* 51; *The Gift Horse, Father's Doing Fine* 52; *Eight O'Clock Walk* 54; *The Ship That Died of Shame* 55; *Private's Progress, The Baby and the Battleship* 56; *Brothers in Law, The Scamp* 57; *Dunkirk, The Man Upstairs, Sea of Sand* 58; *Danger Within, Jet Storm, I'm All Right Jack, SOS Pacific* 59; *The Angry Silence* (also prod.), *League of Gentlemen* (also prod.) 60; *Whistle Down the Wind* (prod. only) 61; *Only Two Can Play, All Night Long, The Dock Brief, The L-Shaped Room* (prod. only) 62; *Seance on a Wet Afternoon* (also prod.), *The Third Secret, Guns at Batasi* 64; *The Bliss of Mrs. Blossom, Only When I Larf, Oh! What A Lovely War* (dir.) 68.

16 AYLOTT Dave (1885–   ) Director. B: London. Music Halls. Many early shorts in which he also appeared. Main shorts: *Mad Dog, The Pirates of Regent's Canal* 06; *The Pirate Ship, For His Child's Sake* 08; *Scouts to the Rescue, Muggins V.C.* 09; *Twixt Red Man and White, The Last of the Dandy, From Gipsy Hands, Prison Reform* 10; *Billy's Bible, Pirates of 1920* (co-dir.), *Scroggins Takes the Census, Charley Smiler Joins the Boy Scouts, The Adventures of Lt. Daring R.N. in a South American Port* 11; *Private Hector Gentleman, Paul Sleuth Investigator and the Burglary Syndicate* 12; *The Misadventures of Mike Murphy* 13; *The Sorrows of Selina, Lt. Geranium and the Stealed Orders, England's Call, War's Grim Reality* 14;

Toyland Topics series 28; Electrocord shorts 29. Features: For East Is East, The Gentleman Ranker 13; The Vengeance of the Air 14; The Crimson Triangle, The Second Lieutenant, The Jade Heart 15; The Price He Paid 16; The Man Who Made Good, A Shattered Idyll, Two Lancashire Lasses in London 17; It's Never Too Late to Mend 18; Gamblers All 19; The River of Light 21.

B

17 BAKER George (1931–   ) Actor. B: Bulgaria. Handsome hero. The Intruder 53; The Ship that Died of Shame, The Dambusters, The Woman for Joe 55; The Feminine Touch, The Extra Day, A Hill in Korea 56; These Dangerous Years, No Time for Tears 57; The Moonraker, Tread Softly Stranger 58; Lancelot and Guinevere 63; The Curse of the Fly 65; Mister Ten Per Cent 67.

18 BAKER Robert S. (1916–   ) Director. B: London. 37: asst. dir. 48: Production partnership with photographer Monty Berman as Tempean Films. Blackout 50; 13 East Street 52; The Steel Key 53; Passport to Treason 56; Jack the Ripper 59; The Siege of Sidney Street 60; The Hellfire Club, The Treasure of Monte Cristo 61.

19 BAKER Roy (1916–   ) Director. B: London. 34: asst. dir. Gainsborough. Also Hollywood. The October Man 47 The Weaker Sex 48; Paper Orchid, Morning Departure 49; Highly Dangerous 50; The House in the Square 51; Passage Home 55; Jacqueline, Tiger in the Smoke 56; The One That Got Away 57; A Night to Remember 58; The Singer Not the Song 60; Flame in the Streets 61; The Valiant 62; Two Left Feet (also prod.) 63; Quatermass and the Pit, The Anniversary 67.

20 BAKER Stanley (1927–   ) Actor (also producer). B: Rhondda Valley. One of our few he-men heroes. Undercover 43; All Over the Town 49; Your Witness 50; The Rossiter Case, Cloudburst, Home to Danger, Captain Horatio Hornblower R.N. 51; Whispering Smith Hits London 52; The Cruel Sea, The Red Beret, The Telltale Heart (short) 53; Hell Below Zero, The Good Die Young, Beautiful Stranger, Knights of the Round Table 54; Richard III, Child in the House, A Hill in Korea, Checkpoint 56; Hell Drivers, Campbell's Kingdom 57; Violent Playground, Sea Fury 58; The Angry Hills, Yesterday's Enemy, Jet Storm, Blind Date 59; Hell is a City, The Criminal 60; The Guns of Navarone 61; A Prize of Arms, The Man Who Finally Died 62; Zulu (also prod.) 63; Sands of the Kalahari (also prod.), One of them is Brett (short) (voice); Accident, Robbery (also prod.) 67; Where's Jack? (also prod.) 68.

21 BALFOUR Betty (1903–   ) Actress. Stage: 14. 24: Voted top British star in Daily News poll. 27: top world star

Daily Mirror poll. Bright, lively comedienne for George PEARSON and continental films. *Nothing Else Matters* 20; *Squibs* 21; *Mord Em'ly, The Wee MacGregor's Sweetheart, Squibs Wins the Calcutta Sweep* 22; *Love Life and Laughter, Squibs M.P., Squibs' Honeymoon* 23; *Reveille* 24; *Satan's Sister, Somebody's Darling* 25; *The Sea Urchin, Blinkeyes* 26; *A Little Bit of Fluff, Champagne, Paradise* 28; *Vagabond Queen* 29; sound: *Raise the Roof, The Nipper* 30; *Evergreen, My Old Dutch* 34; *Forever England, Squibs* 35; *Eliza Comes to Stay* 36; *29 Acacia Avenue* 45.

22 BANKS Leslie, C.B.E. (1890–1952) Actor. B: West Derby. Stage: 11. Strong character star, perhaps helped by paralysed profile. Also Hollywood. *Strange Evidence, The Fire Raisers* 33; *Night of the Party, The Red Ensign* 34; *Sanders of the River, The Man Who Knew Too Much, The Tunnel* 35; *Debt of Honour, The Three Maxims* 36; *Wings of the Morning, Fire Over England, Farewell Again, 21 Days* 37; *Jamaica Inn, Dead Man's Shoes, The Arsenal Stadium Mystery, Guide Dogs for the Blind* (short) 39; *Sons of the Sea, The Door With Seven Locks, Busman's Honeymoon, Neutral Port* 40; *Cottage to Let, Ships With Wings, Give Us More Ships* (short) 41; *The Big Blockade, Went the Day Well* 42; *Henry V* 45; *Mrs. Fitzherbert* 47; *The Small Back Room* 49; *Your Witness, Madeleine* 50.

23 BANKS Monty (1897–1950) Director, also actor. RN: Mario Bianchi. B: Italy. Dancer; silent film comic in Hollywood. To England to star in silent comedies, then direct. Played bits in most of his films. M: Gracie FIELDS. Actor: *Adam's Apple, Weekend Wives* 28; sound: *Atlantic*. Director: *Cocktails* 28; sound: *Amateur Night in London, Eve's Fall,*

The New Waiter, The Musical Beauty Shop, His First Car, The Jerry Builders, The Compulsory Husband (also acted), *Not So Quiet on the Western Front, Kiss Me Sergeant, Why Sailors Leave Home, Almost a Honeymoon, The Black Hand Gang* 30; *Old Soldiers Never Die, What a Night, My Wife's Family, Poor Old Bill* 31; *Tonight's the Night, Money for Nothing, For the Love of Mike* 32; *Leave It to Me, Heads We Go, You Made Me Love You* 33; *Falling in Love, The Girl in Possession* (also acted), *The Church Mouse* (also acted), *Father and Son* 34; *Hello Sweetheart, Man of the Moment, Eighteen Minutes, No Limit, So You Won't Talk* (acted only) 35; *Queen of Hearts, Keep Your Seats Please, Honeymoon Merry-go-round* (acted only), *We're Going to be Rich, Keep Smiling* 38; *Shipyard Sally* 39.

24 BANNEN Ian (1928–   ) Actor. B: Airdrie. *Private's Progress, The Long Arm* 56; *Miracle in Soho, Yangtse Incident, The Birthday Present* 57; *A Tale of Two Cities, Behind the Mask, She Didn't Say No* 58; *Carlton-Browne of the F.O.* 59; *Suspect, A French Mistress* 60; *Macbeth* 61; *Station Six Sahara* 62; *Psyche 59* 63; *Mister Moses* 64; *The Hill, Rotten to the Core* 65; *The Sailor from Gibraltar* 67; *Lock Up Your Daughters* 68.

25 BARING Norah (1907–   ) Actress. B: Newton Abbot. RN: Norah Baker. Doe-eyed, swan-necked silent star. *Underground* 28; *The Runaway Princess, The Celestial City* 29; sound: *Cottage on Dartmoor* 29; *At the Villa Rose, Two Worlds, Murder, Should a Doctor Tell* 30; *The Lyons Mail* 31; *Strange Evidence, The House of Trent* 33; *Little Stranger* 34.

26 BARNES Barry K. (1906–1965) Actor. B: Chelsea. RN: Nelson Barnes. Stage: 27. Stylish, sophisticated star. *Dodging the Dole* 36; *Return of the Scarlet*

Pimpernel 37; Who Goes Next, This Man is News, Prison Without Bars, You're the Doctor 38; The Ware Case, Spies of the Air, This Man in Paris 39; Two for Danger, The Midas Touch, Law and Disorder 40; The Girl in the News 41; Bedelia 46; Dancing with Crime 47.

27 **BARNES Binnie** (1906–   ) Actress. B: Sevenoaks. RN: Gertrude Barnes. Nurse, dancer, singer. Typed as Continental comedy vamp until Henry VIII. Later Hollywood. Phonofilm 29; A Night in Montmartre, Love Lies, Dr. Josser K.C., Out of the Blue 31; Murder at Covent Garden, Partners Please, Innocents of Chicago, Down Our Street, Strip Strip Hooray, The Last Coupon, Old Spanish Customers 32; Taxi to Paradise, Counsel's Opinion, Their Night Out, Heads We Go, The Private Life of Henry VIII 33; The Silver Spoon, The Lady is Willing, Nine Forty-five, No Escape, The Private Life of Don Juan, Forbidden Territory 34; The Divorce of Lady X 38; Shadow of the Eagle 50; Decameron Nights 53; Malaga 54.

28 **BARRY Joan** (1903–   ) Actress. Stage: 20. Blue-eyed blonde with brief talkie fame after dubbing cultured English to Anny Ondra in Blackmail. The Card 22; The Happy Ending 25; The Rising Generation 28. Sound: Blackmail (voice) 29; The Outsider, Man of Mayfair, Rich and Strange 31; Ebb Tide, Women Who Play, The First Mrs. Fraser, Sally Bishop, Rome Express 32; Mrs. Dane's Defence 34.

BATCHELOR Joy see HALAS & BATCHELOR.

29 **BATES Alan** (1934–   ) Actor. B: Allestree. Handsome young man with presence. Also Hollywood. The Entertainer 60; Whistle Down the Wind 61; A Kind of Loving 62; The Running Man, The Caretaker, Nothing but the Best 63; Georgy Girl 66; Far From the Madding Crowd 67.

30 **BATLEY Ernest G.** Actor, writer, director, in combination with wife **Ethyle** (1879–1917), actress, writer, director. Made approx 100 shorts and features, often starring daughter **Dorothy** (1902–   ). Main shorts: A Child's Strategy, Kleptomania Tablets, Peggy Gets Rid of the Baby, Through the Flames 12; The Child Mother, Two Father Christmasses, There's Good in the Worst of Us 13; Three Little Orphans, A Little Child Shall Lead Them, Out Of Evil Cometh Good, The Girl Boy Scout, Answering the Call, Christmas Without Daddy, Red Cross Pluck, One Shall Be Taken 14; Deliver the Goods, The Woman Pays, The Pressure of the Poster, Across the Wires, Those Children 15; Keep the Home Fires Burning, The Enemy Amongst Us, Into the Light, When the Germans Entered Loos, England's Future Safeguard 16. Features: Guy Fawkes and the Gunpowder Plot 13; The Tattooed Will, The Master Crook Outwitted by a Child, The Midnight Wedding, Charles Peace King of Criminals, The Master Crook Turns Detective, Revolution, When London Sleeps, An Englishman's Home 14; War Is Hell 15; The Great Red War, Boys of the Old Brigade 16.

31 **BAXTER Jane** (1909–   ) Actress. B: Germany. RN: Feodora Forde. Stage: 25. Pretty brunette of some character. Also Hollywood. Bedrock, Bed and Breakfast 30; Down River 31; Two White Arms, Flat No. 9 32; The Constant Nymph 33; The Night of the Party, The Double Event, Girls Please, Blossom Time 34; Royal Cavalcade, Drake of England, The Clairvoyant, Line Engaged 35; The Man Behind the Mask, Dusty Ermine 36; Second Best Bed, The Ware Case 38; Confidential Lady, Murder Will Out 39; The Chinese Bungalow, The Briggs Family 40; Ships With

Wings 41; The Flemish Farm 43; Death of an Angel 52; All Hallowe'en (short) 53.

32 BAXTER John (1896-) Director, also producer. B: Sidcup. Theatre mgr. 32: asst. dir. Reunion. Cheap quota quickies with a common touch of humanity. Director: Doss House, Song of the Plough, Taking Ways 33; Lest We Forget, Say It With Flowers, Kentucky Minstrels, Music Hall, Floodtide 34; A Real Bloke, The Small Man, Jimmy Boy, Birds of a Feather 35; Men of Yesterday, Hearts of Humanity 36. Producer: Sunshine Ahead 36; Overcoat Sam, Screen Struck 37. Director: The Academy Decides, Song of the Road, Talking Feet 37; Stepping Toes 38; Secret Journey, What Would You Do Chums 39; Laugh It Off, Old Mother Riley in Society, Crooks Tour, Old Mother Riley in Business 40. Producer: Old Mother Riley's Ghosts 41. Director: Love on the Dole, The Common Touch 41; Let the People Sing, We'll Smile Again 42. Producer: Old Mother Riley Detective, When We Are Married 43. Director: Theatre Royal, The Shipbuilders 43; Dreaming 44; Here Comes the Sun 45; The Grand Escapade 46; Fortune Lane, When You Come Home 47; Nothing Venture, The Last Load, Three Bags Full 48; The Dragon of Pendragon Castle 50; The Second Mate 51; Judgement Deferred 52; Ramsbottom Rides Again 56; The Heart Within (sc. only) 57. Producer: Make Mine a Million 59.

33 BEATTY Robert (1909-) Actor. B: Ontario. Cashier, salesman, radio actor. Rugged roles. Murder in Soho 38; Mein Kampf My Crimes 40; Dangerous Moonlight 41; 49th Parallel, One of Our Aircraft is Missing, Suspected Person 42; San Demetrio London 43; It Happened One Sunday 44; Appointment With Crime 46; Odd Man Out, Green Fingers 47; Against the Wind, Counterblast, Another

Shore, Portrait from Life 48; Twenty Questions Murder Mystery 49; Her Favourite Husband 50; Calling Bulldog Drummond, Captain Horatio Hornblower R.N., The Magic Box, Spotlight series (voice) 51; Wings of Danger, The Gentle Gunman, The Figurehead (voice) 52; The Net, The Oracle, The Square Ring, The Broken Horseshoe, Albert R.N. 53; Out of the Clouds 54; Portrait of Alison 55; Time Lock 57; Tarzan and the Lost Safari 58; The Shakedown 60; The Amorous Prawn 62; One Million B.C. (voice) 66; 2001 A Space Odyssey 68.

34 BEAUDINE William (1892-) Director. B: New York. Hundreds of films since joining Biograph 04, including many 'typically British' comedies. Dandy Dick 34; Two Hearts in Harmony, Boys Will Be Boys, So You Won't Talk, Get Off My Foot, Mr. Cohen Takes a Walk 35; Educated Evans, It's in the Bag, Where There's a Will, Windbag the Sailor 36; Said O'Reilly to McNab, Take It From Me, Feather Your Nest 37.

35 BELLEW Dorothy (1891-) Actress. B: Hampstead. RN: Falck. Clarendon's leading lady 1910–15. Main shorts: Father and Son, Lt. Rose and the Stolen Submarine, The Jealous Cavalier 10; Maud, A Miraculous Recovery, Her Guardian 11; At the Hour of Three, Foiled by a Girl, For Her Mother's Sake 12. Features: Saved by Fire, The Flooded Mine, Lorna Doone 12; A Strong Man's Love, Behind the Scenes, The House of Mystery, Face to Face, The Convent Gate, The Gardener's Daughter, King Charles 13; Secret Life, Southern Blood, The Love of an Actress, Wreck and Ruin, The Family Solicitor, In Peace and War 14; Under the German Yoke, Night and Morning, When East Meets West, The Master of Merripit, In the Blood, The Seventh Word, The Locket, Hard Times, The

Avenging Hand 15; The Treasure of Heaven, Disraeli 16; The Lost Chord, The Profligate, Master of Men 17; Lead Kindly Light 18.

36 BENNETT Compton (1900–   ) Director. B: Tunbridge Wells. RN: Robert Compton-Bennett. Electrician, artist, band leader. 32: ed. Also Hollywood. *Find Fix and Strike* (doc.) 42; *Men of Rochdale* (doc.) 44; *The Seventh Veil, Julius Caesar* (short) 45; *The Years Between* 46; *Daybreak* 47; *It Started in Paradise, So Little Time* 52; *Desperate Moment, The Gift Horse* 53; *That Woman Opposite, After the Ball, The Flying Scot* 57; *Beyond the Curtain* 60; *First Left Past Aden* (short) 61; *How to Undress in Public Without Undue Embarrassment* 65.

37 BENSON   Annette   Actress. Attractive silent star who disappeared with sound. *Love at the Wheel, The Temporary Lady, The Curse of Westacott* (short) 21; *Three Live Ghosts, The Man From Home, Squibs Wins the Calcutta Sweep, The Nonentity* 22; *Harbour Lights, Afterglow* 23; *The Money Habit, Lovers in Araby* 24; *Downhill, Confetti* 27; *Shooting Stars, A South Sea Bubble, The Ringer, Sir or Madam, Weekend Wives* 28; *The Inseparables* 29; sound: *Deadlock* 31.

38 BENTLEY John (1916–   ) Actor. B: Birmingham. Stage: 34. Low-budget hero of *Paul Temple* and *Toff* series. Also Hollywood and Africa. *The Hills of Donegal* 47; *Calling Paul Temple* 48; *The Happiest Days of Your Life* 49; *She Shall Have Murder, Torment* 50; *Paul Temple's Triumph* 51; *Salute the Toff, The Woman's Angle, Paul Temple Returns* 52; *Tread Softly, Black Orchid, Men Against the Sun* 53; *River Beat, The Scarlet Spear, Double Exposure, Profile, Final Appointment, Golden Ivory* 54; *Confession,*

The Flaw, Stolen Assignment, Dial 999 55; *Flight from Vienna, Escape in the Sun* 56; *The Singer not the Song, Mary Had a Little, The Sinister Man* 61; *The Fur Collar* 62.

39 BENTLEY Thomas (18 –195) Director. B: London. 01: Dickens character impersonator on Halls, became foremost Dickens exponent on silent/early-sound screen. 45: Tech. adviser British Council. *Leaves from the Books of Charles Dickens* (short); *Oliver Twist* 12; *David Copperfield* 13; *The Old Curiosity Shop, The Chimes* 14; *Barnaby Rudge, Hard Times, The Woman Who Dared* 15; *Beau Brocade, Milestones* 16; *The Labour Leader, Daddy, Les Cloches de Corneville* 17; *The Greatest Wish in the World, Once Upon a Time, The Divine Gift* 18; *The Lackey and the Lady* 19; *General Post, Beyond the Dreams of Avarice* 20; *The Adventures of Mr. Pickwick, The Old Curiosity Shop* 21; *A Master of Craft* 22; *Through Fire and Water, Jose Collins series* (6) 23; *Old Bill Through the Ages, Love and Hate* (short), *Wanted a Boy* (short), *After Dark* (short), *The Cavern Spider* (short), *Chappy That's All* 24; *Money Isn't Everything, A Romance of Mayfair* 25; *White Heat* 26; *The Silver Lining* 27; *Not Quite a Lady* 28; *Young Woodley* 29; sound: *The American Prisoner* 29; *Harmony Heaven, Young Woodley, Compromising Daphne* 30; *Keepers of Youth, Hobson's Choice* 31; *After Office Hours, The Last Coupon, Sleepless Nights* 32; *Hawleys of High Street, The Love Nest, The Scotland Yard Mystery* 33; *Those Were the Days, The Great Defender, The Old Curiosity Shop* 34; *Music Hath Charms* (co-dir.), *Royal Cavalcade* (co-dir.) 35; *She Knew What She Wanted* 36; *The Last Chance, Silver Blaze, The Angelus* 37; *A Night Alone, Marigold* 38; *Me and My Pal, Dead Man's Shoes, Lucky to Me* 39; *The Middle Watch, Three Silent Men, Cavalcade of Variety* 40; *Old Mother Riley's Circus* 41.

Top: Elizabeth Allan, Michael Anderson, Arthur Askey
Centre: Richard Attenborough, George Baker, Stanley Baker
Bottom: Betty Balfour, Ian Bannen, Binnie Barnes, Alan Bates

Top: Robert Beatty, Honor Blackman, Claire Bloom, Dirk Bogarde
Centre: Derek Bond, Chili/Dorothy Bouchier, Stephen Boyd, Clive Brook
Bottom: Langhorne Burton, Richard Burton, Anthony Bushell, Max Bygraves

40 BEST Edna (1900–   ) Actress. B: Hove. Romantic star of early talkies with her then husband Herbert Marshall. Later Hollywood. *Tilly of Bloomsbury* 21; *A Couple of Down and Outs* 23; sound: *Sleeping Partners, Loose Ends, Escape, Beyond the Cities* 30; *Michael and Mary, The Calendar* 31; *The Faithful Heart* 32; *The Man Who Knew Too Much* 34; *South Riding, Prison Without Bars* 38.

41 BIRT Daniel (1907–1955) Director. B: Mersham. 29: asst. ph. 31: ed. Fair thrillers. Prod.: *The Girl Who Forgot* 39. *Dai Jones* (short) 41; *Butterfly Bomb* (short) 43; *Three Weird Sisters, No Room at the Inn* 48; *Interrupted Journey* 49; *She Shall Have Murder* 50; *Circumstantial Evidence* 51; *The Night Won't Talk* 52; *Three Steps in the Dark, Background* 53; *Meet Mr. Malcolm* 54; *Third Party Risk* 55.

42 BISHOP Terry (1912–   ) Director. B: London. 32: sound asst. Twickenham. 39: docs. Seems unable to use his doc. background in features. Docs.: *Kill That Rat* 41; *Western Isles, More Eggs From Your Hens, Down Our Street* 42; *Out of the Box* 44; *Five Towns* 47; *Thee and Me* 48; *Daybreak in Udi* (AA) 49. Features: *You're Only Young Twice* 52; *Tim Driscoll's Donkey* 55; *Light Fingers* 57; *Life in Danger, Model for Murder* 59; *Cover Girl Killer, Danger Tomorrow, The Unstoppable Man* 60; *Hair of the Dog, Bomb in the High Street* 61.

43 BLACKMAN Honor (1926–   ) Actress. B: London. Rank starlet to 'Pussy Galore' via TV. *Fame Is the Spur* 47; *Daughter of Darkness, Quartet* 48; *A Boy a Girl and a Bike, Conspirator, Diamond City* 49; *So Long at the Fair* 50; *Green Grow the Rushes* 51; *The Rainbow Jacket, The Delavine Affair* 54; *Diplomatic Passport, The Glass Cage* 55; *Breakaway* 56;

Suspended Alibi, You Pay Your Money, Account Rendered, Danger List (short) 57; *A Night to Remember* 58; *The Square Peg* 59; *A Matter of Who* 61; *Serena, A Sense of Belonging* (short) 62; *Jason and the Argonauts* 63; *Goldfinger* 64; *The Secret of My Success, Life at the Top* 65; *A Twist of Sand, Shalako* 68.

44 BLAKELEY John E. (1889–1958) Director, also producer. B: Ardwick. 08: Renter. Founded several production companies: Song Films, Victoria Films. Sound: Mancunian Film Corporation. 47: Founded shortlived Manchester Film Studios. Comedies with Northern stars. Produced: *Boots Boots, Love Mirth and Melody* 34; *Off the Dole* 35; *The Penny Pool* 37; *Calling All Crooks* 38. Directed: *Dodging the Dole* 36; *Somewhere in England* 40; *Somewhere in Camp, Somewhere on Leave* 42; *Demobbed* 44; *Home Sweet Home* 45; *Cuptie Honeymoon, Holidays with Pay* 48; *Somewhere in Politics, What a Carry On, School for Randle* 49; *Over the Garden Wall, Let's Have a Murder* 50. Produced: *Love's a Luxury, Those People Next Door* 52. Directed: *It's a Grand Life* 53.

45 BLOOM Claire (1928–   ) Actress. B: London. Stage: 47. Cool, beautiful, intelligent. Also Hollywood. *The Blind Goddess* 48; *Innocents in Paris, The Man Between* 53; *Richard III* 56; *Look Back in Anger* 59; *The Haunting, 80,000 Suspects* 63; *The Spy Who Came in from the Cold* 65; *Three Into Two Won't Go* 68.

46 BOGARDE Dirk (1920–   ) Actor. B: Hampstead. RN: Derek Van Den Bogaerd. Handsome young hero to mature lead with added depth. Also Hollywood. *Esther Waters* 47; *Quartet* 48; *Once a Jolly Swagman, Dear Mr. Prohack, Boys in Brown, The Blue Lamp* 49; *So Long* at the Fair, The Woman in Question 50; Blackmailed 51; Hunted, Penny Princess, The Gentle Gunman 52; Appointment in London, Desperate Moment 53; They Who Dare, Doctor in the House, The Sleeping Tiger, For Better or Worse, The Sea Shall Not Have Them 54; Simba, Doctor at Sea, Cast a Dark Shadow 55; The Spanish Gardener 56; Ill Met by Moonlight, Doctor at Large 57; A Tale of Two Cities, The Wind Cannot Read 58; The Doctor's Dilemma, Libel 59; H.M.S. Defiant, The Password is Courage, The Mind Benders, We Joined the Navy, I Could Go On Singing 62; Doctor in Distress, The Servant, Hot Enough for June 63; King and Country, The High Bright Sun 64; Darling 65; Modesty Blaise 66; Accident, Our Mother's House 67; Sebastian 68.

47 BOND Derek (1919–   ) Actor.
B: Glasgow. Stage: 36. Rank contract hero. The Captive Heart 46; Nicholas Nickleby, The Loves of Joanna Godden, Uncle Silas 47; Broken Journey, The Weaker Sex 48; Scott of the Antarctic, Marry Me, Poet's Pub, Christopher Columbus 49; Tony Draws a Horse 50; The Quiet Woman 51; Distant Trumpet, Love's a Luxury, The Hour of 13 52; Trouble in Store 53; Stranger from Venus, Svengali 54; The High Terrace Behind the Screen (short) (voice) 56; Rogue's Yarn 57; Gideon's Day 58; The Hand 60; Saturday Night Out, Wonderful Life 64; Secrets of a Windmill Girl 65; Press for Time 66.

48 BOOTH Walter R. Director.
Conjurer. Trick films and comedies for R. W. PAUL, Charles Urban, etc. Main shorts: Upside Down or the Human Flies 99; Diving for Treasure, A Railway Collision, Chinese Magic 00; The Devil in the Studio, The Haunted Curiosity Shop, Cheesemites, Ora Pro Nobis, The Waif and the Wizard, Britain's Tribute to her Sons,

Scrooge, The Magic Sword 01; The Enchanted Cup, Father Thames' Temperance Cure 02; Pocket Boxers, The Adventurous Voyage of the Arctic 03; Topical Tricks 05; The '?' Motorist, The Hand of the Artist 06; Comedy Cartoons, The £1,000 Spook, Dreamland Adventures, When the Devil Drives, Diabolo Nightmare 07; The Chauffeur's Dream, The Star Globetrotter, The Guard's Alarum 08; The Wizard's Walkingstick, Prof. Puddenhead's Patents series, The Airship Destroyer 09; The Bewitched Boxing Gloves, The Electric Vitalizer 10; The Fakir's Fan, The Automatic Motorist, Mystic Manipulations 11; Clever Egg Conjuring, In Fairyland 12; Modelling Extraordinary, Artful Athletics 13; The Shirker's Nightmare 15; The Portrait of Dolly Grey 16.

49 BOUCHIER Chili/Dorothy (1910–
) Actress. B: Hammersmith. From mannequin to movies as a hot brunette, later more romantic as Dorothy (31–35). A Woman in Pawn 27; Shooting Stars, Maria Marten, Dawn, Palais de Danse, Chick, You Know What Sailors Are, Warned Off 28; The Silver King, City of Play, Downstream 29; sound: Enter the Queen, Call of the Sea, Kissing Cup's Race 30; Brown Sugar, Carnival 31; The Blue Danube, Ebb Tide 32; The King's Cup, Summer Lightning, Purse Strings 33; It's a Cop, To Be a Lady, The Office Wife 34; Death Drives Through, Royal Cavalcade, The Mad Hatters, Honours Easy, Lucky Days, Get Off My Foot, Mr. Cohen Takes a Walk 35; The Ghost Goes West, Faithful, Where's Sally, Southern Roses 36; Gypsy, Mayfair Melody, The Minstrel Boy, Change for a Sovereign 37; The Dark Stairway, Mr. Satan, The Singing Cop, The Return of Carol Deane, Everything Happens to Me 38; The Mind of Mr. Reeder 39; My Wife's Family, Facing the Music 41; Murder in Reverse 45; Laughing Lady 46; Mrs. Fitzherbert 47; The Case of Charles Peace, Old

Mother Riley's New Venture 49; The Wallet 52; The Counterfeit Plan 57; The Boy and the Bridge 59; Dead Lucky 60.

50 BOULTING John & Roy (1913–) Directors. B (twins): Bray. As Charter Films prod./dir. for each other. Early work morally superior to latterday farces. **John:** Journey Together 45; Brighton Rock 47; Seven Days to Noon 50; The Magic Box 51; Private's Progress 56; Lucky Jim 57; I'm All Right Jack 59; Heavens Above 63; Rotten to the Core 65. **Roy:** The Landlady, Consider Your Verdict (shorts) 38; Trunk Crime 39; Inquest, Pastor Hall 40; Dawn Guard (short) 41; Thunder Rock, They Serve Abroad (short) 42; Desert Victory (doc.) 43; Tunisian Victory (doc.) (co-dir.) 44; Burma Victory (doc.) 45; Fame Is the Spur 47; The Guinea Pig 48; Singlehanded, High Treason 51; Seagulls Over Sorrento 54; Josephine and Men 55; Happy Is the Bride, Brothers in Law 57; Carlton-Browne of the F.O. 59; Suspect, A French Mistress 60; The Family Way 66; Twisted Nerve 68.

51 BOX Muriel (1905–) Director, writer. B: Tolworth. 27: scriptgirl British Instructional. Wrote 65 short plays with husband Sydney Box, often her producer. Writer: Alibi Inn 35; 29 Acacia Avenue, The Seventh Veil 45; The Years Between, Girl in a Million 46; The Man Within, The Brothers, Daybreak, Dear Murderer, Holiday Camp 47; Good Time Girl, The Blind Goddess, Easy Money, Here Come the Huggetts, Portrait from Life 48; Christopher Columbus, The Lost People 49; The Astonished Heart, So Long at the Fair 50. Director: The Happy Family 52; Street Corner, A Prince for Cynthia (short) 53; To Dorothy a Son, The Beachcomber 54; Simon and Laura 55; Eyewitness 56; The Passionate Stranger 57; The Truth About Women 58; Subway in the Sky, This Other Eden 59; Too Young to Love 60; The Piper's Tune 62; Rattle of a Simple Man 64.

52 BOYD Dorothy (1907–) Actress. B: Sanderstead. Pretty B-picture blonde. The Ball of Fortune, The Veteran (short), Dream Faces (short) 26; Easy Virtue, Somehow Good 27; The Constant Nymph, Toni, Love's Option 28; Auld Lang Syne 29; sound: Knee Deep in Daisies (short) 26; The Sentence of Death (short), The Burglar and the Girl (short) 27; Too Many Crooks, Birds of Prey 30; Third Time Lucky, The Sport of Kings, The House of Unrest, Love Lies, The Girl in the Night, Rynox, The Love Race 31; The Iron Stair, Called Back, Two Wives for Henry, A Shot in the Dark 33; Lily of Killarney, Oh No Doctor, Important People, Get Your Man, Virginia's Husband 34; Ace of Spades, Inside the Room, It Happened in Paris 35; Ticket of Leave, A Touch of the Moon, Everything is Rhythm, Everything in Life 36; Pearls Bring Tears 37; Romance a la Carte 38; Shadowed Eyes 39.

53 BOYD Stephen (1928–) Actor. B: Belfast. International star. An Alligator Named Daisy 55; The Man Who Never Was, A Hill in Korea 56; Seven Waves Away, Island in the Sun, Seven Thunders 57; The Inspector 62; The Third Secret 64; Assignment K 67; Shalako 68.

54 BRAMBLE A. V. (18 –195) Director. B: Portsmouth. Stage: 04. Film actor: 13. The Boy and the Cheese (short) 14; Hearts that are Human 15; Jimmy, The Blind Man of Verdun, Fatal Fingers 16; When Paris Sleeps, The Laughing Cavalier, Profit and the Loss 17; Bonnie Mary 18; Her Cross, A Nonconformist Parson, The Smart Set, A Single Man 19; Her Benny, Mr. Gilfil's Love Story, Torn Sails, Wuthering Heights 20; The Will, The Old Country, The Prince and the Beggar-

maid, *The Bachelors' Club, The Rotters* 21; *The Card, The Little Mother* 22; *Shirley* 23; *Zeebrugge* (co-dir.) 24; *Bodiam Castle* (short) 26; *Shooting Stars* (co-dir.), *Chick* 28; *The Man Who Changed His Name* 29; sound: *A Veteran of Waterloo, A Lucky Sweep, Mrs. Dane's Defence* 33.

55 BRENON Herbert (1880–1958) Director. B: Dublin. 97: Theatre callboy. 09: writer/director in U.S. *Ivanhoe* 13; *The Secret of the Air* 14; *Victory and Peace* 18; *12-10* 19; sound: *Honours Easy* 35; *Living Dangerously, Someone at the Door* 36; *The Dominant Sex, Spring Handicap, The Live Wire* 37; *Housemaster, Yellow Sands* 38; *Black Eyes, The Flying Squad* 39.

56 BRISSON Carl (1895–1958) Actor. B: Copenhagen. RN: Pedersen. 15: Amateur middleweight champion Central Europe. 16: stage, musical comedy. Made a hero by Hitchcock. Also Hollywood. *The Ring* 27; *The Manxman* 29; sound: *Chelsea Nights* (short); *The American Prisoner* 29; *Song of Soho, Knowing Men* 30; *Prince of Arcadia* 33; *Two Hearts in Waltz Time* 34.

57 BRODY Estelle (1904–   ) Actress. B: Montreal. Stage: 24. Top British star of late silents, a few small parts since. *White Heat, Mademoiselle from Armentieres* 26; *Hindle Wakes, The Glad Eye, The Flight Commander, This Marriage Business* 27; *Sailors Don't Care, Mademoiselle Parley Voo, Weekend Wives* 28; sound: *Kitty, Me and the Boys* (short), *Plaything* 29; *They Were Not Divided* 50; *Lilli Marlene* 51; *Safari* 56; *The Story of Esther Costello* 57; *Breakout* 59; *Never Take Sweets From a Stranger* 60.

58 BROOK Clive (1891–   ) Actor. B: London. RN: Clifford Brook. Reporter, soldier. Stage: 19. First a villain,

then a hero, before long star career in Hollywood. Children: Lyndon & Faith Brook. Shorts: *Vanity Fair, A Tale of Two Cities, Whispering, The Sheik, Rigoletto, La Traviata, Sir Rupert's Wife, The Parson's Fight* 22; *The Reverse of the Medal* 23. Features: *Trent's Last Case, Kissing Cup's Race* 20; *Her Penalty, The Loudwater Mystery, Daniel Deronda, A Sportsman's Wife, Sonia, Christie Johnstone* 21; *Shirley, Married to a Mormon, Stable Companions, The Experiment, Debt of Honour, Love and a Whirlwind* 22; *Through Fire and Water, This Freedom, Out to Win, Royal Oak, Woman to Woman* 23; *The Money Habit, The White Shadow, The Wine of Life, The Passionate Adventure, Human Desires* 24; sound: *The Love Affair of the Dictator* 35; *Love in Exile* 36; *The Lonely Road* 37; *Action for Slander* 38; *The Ware Case, Return to Yesterday* 39; *Convoy* 40; *Freedom Radio* 41; *Breach of Promise* 42; *The Flemish Farm* 43; *Shipbuilders* 44; *On Approval* (also dir.) 45.

59 BROOK Peter (1925–   ) Director. B: London. Stage producer: 42. 44: Shorts for G.B.I. *The Beggar's Opera* 53; *Lord of the Flies* 63; *Marat/Sade, The Ride of the Valkyrie, Tell Me Lies* (also sc.) 67.

60 BRUNEL Adrian (1892–1958) Director; some scriptwriting. B: Brighton. Singer, actor. 15: film sales Moss Empires. Satirical and sensitive silents; quota quickies. Shorts: M.O.I. propaganda shorts 17; *The Bump, £5 Reward, Bookworms, Twice Two* 20; *Sheer Trickery, Moors and Minarets* (doc.), *The Shimmy Sheik, Two Chinned Chow, Yes We Have No—* 23; *Crossing the Great Sagrada, The Pathetic Gazette* 24; *Battling Bruisers, So This Is Jollygood, Cut It Out, The Blunderland of Big Game, A Typical Budget, Bonzo* cartoons (sc. only) 25; sound: *Food for*

Thought, Salvage With a Smile 40. Features: The Cost of a Kiss 17; A Temporary Lady 21; The Man Without Desire 23; Lovers in Araby 24; Land of Hope and Glory (sc. only), Blighty 27; The Constant Nymph, The Vortex, A Light Woman 28; The Crooked Billet 29; sound: Elstree Calling (co-dir.) 30; Taxi to Paradise, I'm an Explosive, Follow the Lady, Little Napoleon, Two Wives for Henry, The Laughter of Fools 33; Important People, Badger's Green 34; Cross Currents, Vanity, Variety, The City of Beautiful Nonsense, While Parents Sleep 35; Prison Breaker, Sabotage, Love at Sea, The Invader 36; The Return of the Scarlet Pimpernel (sc. only) 37; The Girl Who Forgot, The Lion Has Wings (co-dir.) 39.

61 BRYCE Alex (1905–   ) Director. B: Doune. 26: B.I.P. clapper boy; cameraman. Sexton Blake and the Mademoiselle 35; Wedding Group, Servants All, Big Noise, The End of the Road 36; The Black Tulip, Against the Tide, Macushlah 37; Londonderry Air, The Last Barricade 38; My Irish Molly 39. Shorts: Two Cooks and a Cabbage, Crumbs and Crusts 41; The Right Man 42; This Modern Age series 47.

62 BUCHANAN Jack (1891–1957) Actor. B: Glasgow. Stage: 12. Dashing, dancing, debonair lead. Also Hollywood. Auld Lang Syne 17; Her Heritage 19; The Audacious Mr. Squire 23; The Happy Ending, Settled Out of Court, Bulldog Drummond's Third Round 25; Confetti 27; Toni 28; sound: Man of Mayfair 31; Goodnight Vienna 32; Yes Mr. Brown 33; That's a Good Girl (also dir.), Brewster's Millions, Come Out of the Pantry 35; Limelight, When Knights Were Bold 36; This'll Make You Whistle, Smash and Grab 36; The Sky's the Limit (also prod.) 37; Sweet Devil (prod. only), Break the News (also prod.) 38; The Gang's All Here (also prod.) 39; The Middle Watch, Bulldog Sees It Through 40; Happidrome (prod. only) 43; Some Like It Rough (voice) (short) 44; A Boy and a Bike (short) (prod. only) 51; Giselle (voice) (short) 52; As Long As They're Happy, Josephine and Men 53.

63 BURDON Albert (1903–   ) Actor. B: South Shields. Stage: 16. Music Halls, revue. Northern knockabout comic; a star in the 30s for B.I.P. The Maid of the Mountains 32; Letting in the Sunshine, It's a Boy 33; Heat Wave 35; She Knew What She Wanted 36; Oh Boy, The Luck of the Navy 38; Jail Birds 39.

64 BURTON Langhorne (1872–19   ) Actor. B: Somersby. Handsome hero in his day. Turtle Doves (short), The Difficult Way, Bootles' Baby, The King's Minister, Liberty Hall 14; The Treasure of Heaven 16; The Profligate, Daddy, Tom Jones, Auld Robin Gray 17; God and the Man 18; The Impossible Woman, Sweet and Twenty 19; The Amateur Gentleman, At the Villa Rose, Little Dorrit, Two Little Wooden Shoes, By Berwen Banks, The Children of Gibeon, The Temptress, A Man's Shadow 20; Appearances, Moth and Rust, Beside the Bonnie Briar Bush 21; Who Is the Man 24; Sexton Blake series (6) 28; sound: Cross Roads 30.

65 BURTON Richard (1925–   ) Actor. B: Pontrhydyfen. RN: Jenkins. Dark, handsome, brooding; main work for Hollywood and with wife, Elizabeth Taylor. The Last Days of Dolwyn 48; Now Barabbas 49; Waterfront, The Woman With No Name 50; Green Grow the Rushes 51; Thursday's Children (voice) (short) 54; Seawife, Bitter Victory 57; Look Back in Anger 59; The V.I.P.s, Zulu (voice), The Inheritance (voice) (short) 63; Becket 64; The Spy Who Came In From The Cold 65;

Doctor Faustus (also prod. & co-dir.) 67; *Boom, Where Angels Dare* 68.

66 BUSHELL Anthony (1904–   ) Actor who has also directed. B: Westerham. Stage: 1924. Petulant, blue-eyed hero of early talkies; Hollywood. *The Silver Greyhound, Sally Bishop, The Midshipmaid* 32; *Soldiers of the King, The Ghoul, I Was a Spy, Channel Crossing, Crime on the Hill* 33; *Red Wagon, Love at Second Sight, Lilies of the Field, Forbidden Territory* 34; *The Scarlet Pimpernel, Admirals All* 35; *Dusty Ermine* 36; *Dark Journey, Farewell Again, The Angelus, The Return of the Scarlet Pimpernel* 37; *Rebel Son* 38; *The Lion Has Wings, The Arsenal Stadium Mystery* 39; *The Small Back Room* 48; *Angel with the Trumpet* (also dir.) 49; *The Miniver Story* 50; *The Long Dark Hall* (also dir.), *High Treason* 51; *Who Goes There* 52; *The Red Beret* 53; *The Black Knight, The Purple Plain* 54; *The Black Tent, Richard III* (co-dir.) 55; *The Battle of the River Plate* 56; *Bitter Victory* 57; *The Wind Cannot Read, A Night To Remember* 58; *Desert Mice* 59; *The Terror of the Tongs* (dir. only) 60; *A Woman's Privilege* (short) (dir. only) 62.

67 BUTLER Alexander Director. B: U.S.A. Silent features for Barker and

C

69 CAINE Michael (1933–   ) Actor. B: London. Tall blond cockney hero: the screen's 'Harry Palmer'. *A Hill in Korea* 56; *Zulu* 63; *The Ipcress File* 65; *Alfie, The Wrong Box, Funeral in Berlin* 66; *Billion*

SAMUELSON. *A Little Child Shall Lead Them, In London's Toils, The Passions of Men, The Anarchist's Doom, The Great Bullion Robbery, London by Night, Greater Love Hath No Man, In the Hands of the London Crooks* 13; *Nursie Nursie* (short), *Just a Girl, The Girl Who Loves a Soldier, A Fair Impostor* 16; *In Another Girl's Shoes, The Sorrows of Satan, Little Women, My Lady's Dress* 17; *Jo the Crossing Sweeper, On Leave* 18; *The Odds Against Her, The Beetle, The Thundercloud, The Disappearance of the Judge, The Life of a London Actress, Lamp of Destiny, Damaged Goods* 19; *Love in the Wilderness, Her Story, David and Jonathan, The Night Riders, The Ugly Duckling* 20; *For Her Father's Sake* 21; *A Royal Divorce, The Knockout, Should a Doctor Tell, Married Love* 23; *Twisted Tales* series (12), *Proverbs* series (12), *Milestone Melodies* series (6) 25.

68 BYGRAVES Max (1922–   ) Actor. B: Bermondsey. RN: Walter Bygraves. 46: stage comedian. From cockney comic to human character star. *Nitwits on Parade* (short), *Bless 'Em All, Skimpy in the Navy* 49; *Tom Brown's Schooldays* 51; *Harmony Lane* (3D) 54; *Charley Moon* 56; *A Cry From the Streets* 58; *Bobbikins* 59; *Spare the Rod* 61.

Dollar Brain, Tonite Let's All Make Love in London (doc.) 67; *Deadfall, Play Dirty* 68.

70 CALVERT Charles C. Director. Stage actor age 9, stage manager age 16.

22

09: film actor Clarendon. *Good for Evil, Paul Sleuth and the Mystic Seven, Snatched from Death* 13; *A Soldier's Honour, Wrecker of Lives, Temptation, His Country's Honour, Guarding Britain's Secrets, A London Mystery, Grip of the Past* 14; *The Avenging Hand* 15; *The Winner* (short), *The Test* (short), *The Cellar of Death, Ace of Hearts, Disraeli* 16; *Walls of Prejudice, The Edge of Youth, Branded* 20; *The Way of a Man, In His Grip, Roses in the Dust* 21; *The Prince of Lovers, Silent Evidence* 22; *The Lights o' London, Bonnie Prince Charlie, The Romance of Postal Telegraphy* (doc.) 23; *Children of the Night* series (3) 25; *Ashridge Castle* (short), *The Mistletoe Bough* (short) 26; *Oxford* (doc.) 28.

71 CALVERT Phyllis (1915–)
Actress. B: Chelsea. RN: Phyllis Bickle. Stage: 25. One of the Gainsborough girls in many forties romances. Also Hollywood. *Two Days to Live* 39; *They Came By Night, Let George Do It, Charley's Bighearted Aunt, Neutral Port* 40; *Inspector Hornleigh Goes To It, Kipps* 41; *The Young Mr. Pitt, Uncensored* 42; *The Man in Grey* 43; *Fanny By Gaslight, Two Thousand Women* 44; *Madonna of the Seven Moons, They Were Sisters* 45; *Men of Two Worlds, The Magic Bow* 46; *The Root of All Evil* 47; *Broken Journey* 48; *The Golden Madonna* 49; *The Woman With No Name* 50; *Mr. Denning Drives North* 51; *Mandy* 52; *The Net* 53; *It's Never Too Late, Child in the House* 54; *Indiscreet, A Lady Mislaid* 58; *The Young and the Guilty* 59; *Oscar Wilde* 60; *The Battle of the Villa Fiorita* 65; *Twisted Nerve* 68.

72 CAMPBELL Ivar (1904–)
Director. B: Otakike N.Z. Stock exchange. *Reunion* 32; *Side Streets, The Golden Cage, Eyes of Fate* 33; *Designing Women, How's Chances* (sc. only) 34;

Radio Pirates, The Mad Hatters, Expert's Opinion 35; *The Belles of St. Clement's, Grand Finale* 36; *Captain's Orders* 37; *Too Many Husbands* 38.

73 CARDIFF Jack (1914–)
Director. B: Yarmouth. 18: stage. 28: camera asst. *The Informer.* 46: ph. *A Matter of Life and Death.* 47: AA for best colour ph. *Black Narcissus.* Also Hollywood. *Intent to Kill* 58; *Beyond This Place* 59; *Sons and Lovers* 60; *The Lion* 62; *The Long Ships* 64; *Young Cassidy, The Liquidator* 65; *The Mercenaries* 67; *The Girl on the Motorcycle* 68.

74 CARMICHAEL Ian (1920–)
Actor. B: Hull. Revue. Natural successor to the 'Silly Ass' comedians of the 30s. *Bond Street* 48; *The Ghost Ship* 52; *Time Gentlemen Please, Meet Mr. Lucifer* 53; *Betrayed, The Colditz Story* 54; *Storm Over the Nile, Simon and Laura* 55; *Private's Progress* 56; *Brothers in Law, Lucky Jim* 57; *Happy is the Bride, The Big Money* 58; *I'm All Right Jack, Left Right and Centre* 59; *School for Scoundrels, Light Up the Sky* 60; *Double Bunk* 61; *The Amorous Prawn* 62; *Heavens Above, Hide and Seek* 63; *Smashing Time* 67.

75 CARRERAS Michael (1927–)
Director. Also producer, writer. B: London. 43: joined father James's Exclusive Films. 48: publicity mgr. 49: asst. prod. Hammer Films. Fast visual style. Shorts: *Cyril Stapleton and the Show Band, Eric Winstone Band Show, Just for You* 55; *Parade of the Bands, Eric Winstone's Stage Coach, Edmundo Ros Half Hour, Copenhagen* 56. Features: *The Steel Bayonet* 57; *Visa to Canton* 60; *Maniac* 62; *What a Crazy World* 63; *The Curse of the Mummy's Tomb* 64; *Slave Girls* 66; *The Lost Continent* 68.

76 CARROLL Madeleine (1906–) Actress. B: West Bromwich. Stage: 27. Lovely blonde star who soon went to Hollywood. *Guns of Loos, The First Born, What Money Can Buy* 28; *The Crooked Billet* 29; sound: *The American Prisoner, Atlantic* 29; *The W Plan, Young Woodley, French Leave, Escape, Kissing Cup's Race, School for Scandal, Madame Guillotine* 30; *Fascination, The Written Law* 31; *Sleeping Car, I Was a Spy* 33; *The Love Affair of the Dictator, The 39 Steps* 35; *Secret Agent, The Story of Papworth* (short) 36; *White Cradle Inn* 47.

77 CARSTAIRS John Paddy (1910–) Director & writer. B: London. RN: Keys. Father: Nelson Keys. 28: camera asst. *Dawn*. Efficient but old-fashioned comedies. Also painter, novelist. Scripted: *Honeymoon Adventure* 31; *The Water Gipsies, Nine Till Six, The Impassive Footman* 32; *It's a Boy* 33. Dir.: *Paris Plane.* Scripted: *It's a Cop, Boomerang, Lost in the Legion, Gay Love, Falling in Love* 34; *Where's George, While Parents Sleep* 35; *Two's Company* 36. Directed: *Holiday's End, Night Ride, Missing Believed Married, Incident in Shanghai, Double Exposures* 37; *Lassie from Lancashire* 38; *The Lambeth Walk* (sc. only), *The Second Mr. Bush, The Saint in London, Meet Maxwell Archer* 39; *Spare a Copper, All Hands* (short), *Dangerous Comment* (short), *Now You're Talking* (short), *Telefootlers* (short) 40; *He Found a Star* 41; *Dancing With Crime* 47; *Sleeping Car to Trieste* 48; *The Chiltern Hundreds, Fools Rush In* 49; *Tony Draws a Horse* 50; *Talk of a Million* 51; *Treasure Hunt, Made in Heaven, Little Big Shot* (sc. only) 52; *Top of the Form, Trouble in Store* 53; *Up to His Neck, One Good Turn, The Crowded Day* (sc. only) 54; *Man of the Moment, Jumping for Joy, A Yank in Ermine* (sc. only) 55; *The Big Money, Up in the World* 56; *Just My Luck* 57; *The Square Peg* 58; *Tommy the Toreador* 59; *Sands of the Desert, And the Same to You* (sc. only) 60; *A Weekend With Lulu* 61; *The Devil's Agent* 62.

78 CASS Henry (1902–) Director. B: London. Stage: actor 23, producer 34. Family films and minor thrillers. Shorts: *H.M.S. Minelayer* 41; *Ask C.A.B., Free House* 42; *Common Cause* 43; *Catholics in Britain, Danger Area, Jigsaw* 44; *Macbeth, The Great Game* 45. Features: *Lancashire Luck* 37; *29 Acacia Avenue* 45; *The Glass Mountain* 48; *No Place for Jennifer* 49; *Last Holiday* 50; *Young Wives' Tale* 51; *Father's Doing Fine, Castle in the Air* 52; *The Reluctant Bride, No Smoking* 55; *Bond of Fear, Breakaway, The High Terrace* 56; *Professor Tim, The Crooked Sky, Booby Trap* 57; *Blood of the Vampire* 58; *Boyd's Shop* 59; *The Man Who Couldn't Walk, The Hand* 60; *Mr. Brown Comes Down the Hill* 66; *Give a Dog a Bone* 68.

79 CAVALCANTI Alberto (1897–) Director. B: Rio de Janeiro. Architecture. 20: art dir. French films. 34: prod. G.P.O. Film Unit. 39: prod. Crown Film Unit. As a founder of French realist school, became key man in British docs. Also Brazil, Germany. Shorts: *Pett and Pott* (also sc.), *New Rates* 34; *Roadways, Coalface* 36; *A Midsummer Day's Work* (also sc.) 39; *Yellow Caesar* 41; *Watertight* 43. Features: *Went the Day Well* 42; *Champagne Charlie* 44; *Dead of Night* (co-dir.) 45; *Nicholas Nickleby* 46; *They Made Me a Fugitive* 47; *The First Gentleman* 48; *For Them That Trespass* 49; *The Monster of Highgate Ponds* 61.

80 CHAFFEY Don (1917–) Director. 44: art dept. Gainsborough. From children's films for C.F.F. to the same for Disney; saucy comedies and topical adults-only pictures en route. *The Mysterious Poacher* 50; *The Case of the Missing Scene* 51; *Skid Kids, Bouncer Breaks Up* (short), *A Good Pullup* (short), *Watch Out* (short) 53; *Time Is My Enemy* 54; *Dead on Time* (short) 55; *The Secret Tent* 56; *The Girl in the Picture, The Flesh is Weak* 57; *The Man Upstairs, A Question of Adultery* 58; *Danger Within* 59; *Dentist in the Chair* 60; *Nearly a Nasty Accident, Greyfriars Bobby, A Matter of WHO* 61; *The Prince and the Pauper, The Webster Boy* 62; *The Horse Without a Head, Jason and the Argonauts, A Jolly Bad Fellow* 63; *The Three Lives of Thomasina, The Crooked Road* 64; *One Million Years B.C., The Viking Queen* 66; *Twist of Sand* 68.

81 CHRISTIE Julie (1940–) Actress. TV: 62. Blonde swinging star; also Hollywood. Oscar for *Darling. Crooks Anonymous, The Fast Lady* 62; *Billy Liar* 63; *Young Cassidy, Darling* (AA) 65; *Fahrenheit 451* 66; *Far From the Madding Crowd, Tonite Let's All Make Love in London* (doc.) 67.

82 CHRYSTAL Belle (1910–) Actress. B: Fleetwood. Stage: 28. Dark-eyed brunette acclaimed for her naturalism. *A Warm Corner* 30; *Hindle Wakes, Hobson's Choice* 31; *The Frightened Lady* 32; *Friday the Thirteenth* 33; *The Scotland Yard Mystery, The Girl in the Flat, The Way of Youth* 34; *Key to Harmony* 35; *Edge of the World* 37; *Follow Your Star, Yellow Sands, Breakers Ahead, Anything to Declare* 38; *Poison Pen* 39; *House of the Arrow* 40.

83 CILENTO Diane (1933–) Actress. B: New Guinea. M: Sean CONNERY. Attractive blonde star. Also novelist. *Wings of Danger* 52; *All Hallowe'en* (short) 53; *The Passing Stranger* 54; *The Angel Who Pawned Her Harp, Passage Home, The Woman for Joe* 55; *The Admir-* able *Crichton, The Truth About Women* 57; *Jet Storm* 59; *The Full Treatment, The Naked Edge* 61; *I Thank a Fool* 62; *Tom Jones* 63; *The Third Secret, Rattle of a Simple Man* 64; *Negatives* 68.

84 CLARK Petula (1932–) Actress. B: West Ewell. Radio singer: 41. From child star to top pop singer. *Medal for the General* 44; *Murder in Reverse, I Know Where I'm Going, Trouble at Townsend* (short) 45; *London Town, Strawberry Roan* 46; *Easy Money, Vice Versa* 47; *Here Come the Huggetts* 48; *Vote for Huggett, The Huggetts Abroad, Don't Ever Leave Me, The Romantic Age* 49; *Dance Hall* 50; *White Corridors, Madame Louise, The Card* 51; *Made in Heaven* 52; *The Runaway Bus* 53; *The Gay Dog, The Happiness of Three Women* 54; *Track the Man Down* 55; *That Woman Opposite* 57; *The 6.5 Special* 58; *Goodbye Mr. Chips* 68.

85 CLAYTON Jack (1921–) Director. B: London. 35: asst. *Wings of the Morning*. Cannes award with first short. His features are polished and painstaking. *The Bespoke Overcoat* (short) 55; *Room at the Top* 58; *The Innocents* 61; *The Pumpkin Eater* 64; *Our Mother's House* 67.

86 CLEMENTS Sir John, C.B.E. (1910–) Actor. B: London. Stage: 30. Quota quickies to KORDA films. *Once in a New Moon, The Divine Spark* 35; *Things to Come, Ticket of Leave, Rembrandt* 36; *I Claudius, Knight Without Armour* 37; *South Riding, Star of the Circus* 38; *The Four Feathers* 39; *Convoy* 40; *This England, Ships With Wings* 41; *Tomorrow We Live* 42; *Undercover* 43; *They Came to a City* 44; *Call of the Blood* (also dir.) 48; *Train of Events* 49; *The Silent Enemy* 58; *The Mind Benders* 62; *Oh! What a Lovely War* 68.

25

87 CLIFT Denison (1892–)
Director. Some scriptwriting. B: San Francisco. Publicist. 15: scenarist for De Mille. In England prod., dir., and scripted 11 of the more polished productions of Ideal: *The Diamond Necklace, Demos, A Woman of No Importance, Sonia, The Old Wives' Tale* 21; *Bentley's Conscience, Diana of the Crossways, A Bill of Divorcement* 22; *This Freedom, Out to Win, The Loves of Mary Queen of Scots* 23; then *Paradise* 28; *City of Play, Taxi for Two, Power over Men* (sc. only) 29. Sound: *High Seas* 30; *The Mystery of the Mary Celeste* 35; *All That Glitters* (sc. only) 36; *The Last Adventurers* (sc. only) 37.

88 CLOSE Ivy (1893–) Actress. B: Stockton-on-Tees. 1911 *Daily Mirror* Beauty Contest winner in films directed by photographer husband Elwin Neame, then dramas; later comedies in Hollywood. Son: Ronald NEAME. Shorts: *Dream Paintings, The Lady of Shallot, Pygmalion and Galatea, The Legend of King Cophetua, The Sleeping Beauty* 12; *Mifanwy, La Cigale* 13; *The Girl from the Sky, Ghosts, The Hon. William's Donah, The Terrible Twins, Ivy's Elopement, Two Elderly Cupids, The Haunting of Silas P. Gould* 14. Features: *The Lure of London* 14; *Darkest London* 15; *The Ware Case, The House Opposite, Adventures of Dick Dolan* 17; *Missing the Tide, Adam Bede, A Peep Behind the Scenes, Nelson* 18; *The Irresistible Flapper, Her Cross, The Flag Lieutenant, Darby and Joan* 19; *The Worldlings* 20; *Expiation, Was She Justified* 22.

89 COLE George (1925–) Actor. B: London. Stage: 40. The 30s 'Silly Ass' with a middle class version for the 50s. *Cottage to Let* 41; *Those Kids From Town* 42; *The Demi-Paradise* 43; *Henry V* 45; *My Brother's Keeper, Quartet* 48; *Spider and the Fly* 49; *Morning Departure, Gone to Earth* 50; *Flesh and Blood, Laughter in Paradise, Scrooge, Lady Godiva Rides Again* 51; *The Happy Family, Who Goes There, Top Secret* 52; *Will Any Gentleman, The Intruder, Our Girl Friday* 53; *Happy Ever After, The Belles of St. Trinian's, The Clue of the Missing Ape* 54; *A Prize of Gold, Where There's a Will, The Constant Husband, The Adventures of Quentin Durward* 55; *It's a Wonderful World, The Weapon, The Green Man* 56; *Blue Murder at St. Trinian's* 57; *Too Many Crooks* 58; *Don't Panic Chaps, The Bridal Path* 59; *The Pure Hell of St. Trinians* 60; *Dr. Syn Alias the Scarecrow* 63; *One Way Pendulum* 64; *The Legend of Young Dick Turpin* 65; *The Great St. Trinian's Train Robbery* 66.

90 COLEBY A. E. (18 –1930) Director, writer, actor. Made and often acted in some 725 films. Began with knockabouts at Cricks & Martin, later many dramas noted for their human touch. Main shorts: *Serving a Summons* 07; *For Baby's Sake, The Guardian of the Bank, Brave Children* 08; *The Robber's Ruse, Saved by Carlo* 09; *The Terror and the Terrier, A Bolt From The Blue* 10; *Tatters a Tale of the Slums, Pirates of 1920, Topsy's Dream of Toyland* 11; *Peg Woffington, Battling Kelly, The Bloomsbury Burglars* 12. Features: *The Fate of a King, Grip, A Case of Arson* 13; *The Ghurka's Revenge, The Mysteries of London, Rogues of London, The Lure of Drink, The Blackmailers, The Cobbler* 15; *The Stolen Bride, Kent the Fighting Man, Chains of Bondage, The Wheel of Death, The Treasure of Heaven* 16; *The Will of the People, The Third Witness, A Pit Boy's Romance, A Just Deception, The Village Blacksmith, Holy Orders, For All Eternity* 17; *Thelma, Matt, The Secret Woman, World Power or Downfall* (doc.), *The Great Game* 18; *The Silver Lining, I Hear You Calling Me* 19; *The Pride of the North, The Hour of Trial, The*

Way of the World, The Call of the Road 20; The Right to Live, The Fifth Form at St. Dominics 21; Froggy's Little Brother, The Peacemaker, Long Odds 22; The Prodigal Son, The Mystery of Dr. Fu Manchu series (15), The Flying Fifty Five 23; The Rest Cure, The Great Prince Shan, The Pre-historic Man, Sen Yan's Devotion 24; Hints & Hobbies series (6), Fake Spiritualism Exposed (short) 26; Inscrutable Drew series (6), Il Trovatore (short) 27; Over the Sticks, Unto Each Other 29.

91 COLLEANO Bonar, Jr. (1923–1958) Actor. B: New York. RN: Sullivan. 29: Circus acrobat. 36: England; music halls, radio. Brilliant natural actor, usually wisecracking Yank or crook. M: Susan SHAW. Starlight Serenade 44; The Way to the Stars 45; Wanted for Murder, A Matter of Life and Death 46; While the Sun Shines, Merry-Go-Round 47; Good Time Girl, One Night With You, Sleeping Car to Trieste, Once a Jolly Swagman 48; Give Us This Day 49; Dance Hall, Pool of London 50; A Tale of Five Cities 51; Is Your Honeymoon Really Necessary 53; The Flame and the Flesh, Time is my Enemy, The Sea Shall Not Have Them 54; Joe Macbeth 55; Zarak, Stars in Your Eyes 56; Interpol, Fire Down Below 57; No Time to Die, Them Nice Americans, The Man Inside 58.

92 COLLINS Alf Director. Music hall comic who made many early chase comedies for Gaumont. Main shorts: Welshed a Derby Day Incident, Rip Van Winkle, Dotheboy's Hall, The Pickpocket, The Runaway Match 03; The Coster's Wedding, Behind the Scenes, The Haunted Houseboat 04; The Coster's Christening, How Brown Brought Home the Goose, The Burglar 05; Lost a Leg of Mutton, The Coster's Revenge, Dolly Varden, Curfew Shall Not Ring Tonight 06; Catch the Kid, The Ice Cream Jack, Father Buys a Lawn Roller 07; Black Eyed Susan, The Mechani-cal Legs, The Sloshton Quartette 08; Quicksilver Pudding 09; Algy Tries Physical Culture, The Coster's Phantom Fortune 10. Feature: A Maid of the Alps 12.

93 COLLINS Edwin J. Director. Acted in and made many shorts for Cricks & Martin, features mainly for Ideal and Master (PARKINSON). Main shorts: The Hunchback, Little Red Riding Hood 11; The Vengeance of Daniel Whid-den, The Masked Smuggler, The Bandit's Daughter, Nan in Fairyland 12; A Sporting Chance, The Scrapegrace, A Fishergirl's Love, The Newsboy's Christmas Dream 13. Features: A Daughter of Satan, Eugene Aram 14; £66.13.9 for Every Man Woman and Child, Blood Tells 16; Doing His Bit, Tom Jones 17; God and the Man, In the Gloaming 18; The Artistic Temperament, The Starting Point 19; Calvary, Foul Play, The Channings 20; The Single Life, Hard Cash, Stella, Miss Charity, The God in the Garden 21; The Green Caravan, Famous Songs of Long Ago series, Tense Moments with Great Authors series, Tense Moments from Great Plays series, Tense Moments from Operas series, The Sporting Twelve series, Famous Poems of George R. Sims series 22; A Gamble With Hearts 23.

94 COLLINS Joan (1933–   ) Act-ress. B: London. Darkly glamorous teenager; Hollywood star. M: (1) Max-well REED, (2) Anthony NEWLEY. I Believe in You, The Woman's Angle, Judgement Deferred, Decameron Nights 52; Cosh Boy, Turn the Key Softly, The Square Ring, Our Girl Friday 53; The Good Die Young 54; Island in the Sun, Sea-wife 57; The Road to Hong Kong 62; Subterfuge 68.

95 COMFORT Lance (1908–67) Director. B: Harrow. 26: ph./anim.

Community Service Films. 28: ph. Ealing. 34: tech. sup. John BAXTER. A few fair thrillers among many. *Sandy Steps Out* (short) 38; *Judy Buys a Horse* (short) 39; *Hatter's Castle, Penn of Pennsylvania* 41; *Those Kids From Town, Squadron Leader X* 42; *Escape to Danger, Old Mother Riley Detective, When We Are Married* 43; *Hotel Reserve* 44; *Great Day* 45; *Bedelia* 46; *Temptation Harbour* 47; *Daughter of Darkness* 48; *Silent Dust* 49; *Portrait of Clare* 50; *Home to Danger* (prod. only) 51; *Girl on the Pier* 53; *Bang You're Dead, Eight O'Clock Walk* 54; *Man in the Road* 56; *Face in the Night, At the Stroke of Nine, The Man from Tangier* 57; *The Ugly Duckling, Make Mine a Million* 59; *The Breaking Point* 60; *Rag Doll, Pit of Darkness* 61; *The Break, The Painted Smile, Tomorrow at Ten, Touch of Death* 62; *Live It Up, Blind Corner* 63; *Devils of Darkness* 64; *Be My Guest* 65.

96 COMPTON Fay (1894–) Actress. B: London. Stage: 06. Star of silents and early talkies, later character parts. *She Stoops to Conquer* 14; *One Summer's Day, The Labour Leader* 17; *Judge Not* 20; *A Woman of No Importance, The Old Wives' Tale* 21; *House of Peril, Diana of the Crossways, A Bill of Divorcement* 22; *This Freedom, The Loves of Mary Queen of Scots* 23; *Claude Duval, The Eleventh Commandment* 24; *The Happy Ending, Settled Out of Court* 25; *London Love* 26; *Robinson Crusoe, Somehow Good* 27; *Zero* 28; sound: *Cape Forlorn, Uneasy Virtue, Tell England* 31; *Waltzes From Vienna* 33; *Autumn Crocus, Song at Eventide* 34; *Wedding Group* 36; *The Mill on the Floss* 37; *So This is London* 39; *The Prime Minister* 41; *Odd Man Out* 46; *Nicholas Nickleby* 47; *London Belongs to Me, Esther Waters* 48; *Britannia Mews* 49; *Blackmailed* 50; *Laughter in Paradise* 51; *Aunt Clara* 54; *Doublecross* 55; *Town on Trial* 56; *The Story of Esther Costello* 57; *The Haunting* 63.

97 CONNERY Sean (1930–) Actor. B: Edinburgh. Handsome hero who leapt to fame as James Bond. M: Diane CILENTO. Also Hollywood. *No Road Back* 56; *Action of the Tiger, Time Lock, Hell Drivers* 57; *Another Time Another Place* 58; *Tarzan's Greatest Adventure* 59; *The Frightened City, On the Fiddle* 61; *Dr. No* 62; *From Russia With Love* 63; *Woman of Straw, Goldfinger* 64; *The Hill, Thunderball* 65; *You Only Live Twice* 67; *Shalako* 68.

98 CONYERS D'Arcy (1919–) Director. B: Tanganyika. 47: Film actor. Children's films and Brian Rix farces. *Ha'penny Breeze* (prod. only) 50; *Secret of the Forest* 56; *The Devil's Pass* (also sc.) 57; *The Soapbox Derby, Gateway to Adventure* (short) 58; *The Night We Dropped a Clanger* 59; *The Night We Got the Bird* 60; *Nothing Barred, In the Doghouse* 61.

99 CONYNGHAM Fred (1909–) Actor. B: Sydney. Dancer: 25. Britain's B-picture Fred Astaire. *The Indiscretions of Eve* 32; *Radio Parade of 1935* 34; *Key to Harmony, School for Stars, The Crouching Beast* 35; *Ball at Savoy, Beloved Imposter, She Knew What She Wanted, Chick* 36; *Wake Up Famous, Rose of Tralee, The Minstrel Boy* 37; *Sam Small Leaves Town* 38; *When You Come Home* 47.

100 COOPER Arthur Melbourne (1872–1962) Director, producer. B: St. Albans. Photographer. 92: worked for Birt ACRES, later staging his films. 03: formed Alpha Trading Co.; puppet films for Butcher's. Main shorts: *The Village Blacksmith* 98; *Soldier Policeman and Cook, The Fireman's Snapshot, Fight Between a Miller and a Sweep* 99; *It's No Use Crying Over Spilt Milk, Farmer Giles and his Portrait* 00; *Ducks on Sale or Return* 04; *The Death of the Iron Horse, The Motor*

Highwayman, McNab's Visit to London 05; *The Motor Valet, Robbing H.M. Mails, The Guinea Entertainer, Held to Ransom, The Modern Pirates, Oh That Molar* 06; *The Poet's Bid for Fame, The Luck of Life* 07; *Dreams of Toyland, In the Land of Nod, Animated Matches, The Curate's Honeymoon* 08; *The Tale of the Ark* 09; *The Toymaker's Dream* 10; *Road Hogs in Toyland* 11; *The Cats' Cup Final* 12; *Larks in Toyland* 13.

101 COOPER George A. (1894–1947)
Director; some scriptwriting. Also journalist, actor, playwright. 20: ed. Unione Cinetografica Italia. Taut two-reelers and quota quickies for Julius Hagen. Shorts: *The White Rat, A Question of Principle, Fallen Leaves, The Thief, Geraldine's First Year, The Big Strong Man, Poetic License, The Cunninghame's Economise, Keeping Man Interested, The Letters, Her Dancing Partner, Pearl for Pearl, His Wife's Husband* 22; *Finished, Darkness, The Reverse of the Medal, The Man Who Liked Lemons, Constant Hot Water, Three to One Against* 23; *The Mystery of the Silent Death, Silken Threads* 28. Features: *Claude Duval, The Eleventh Commandment* 24; *The Happy Ending, Settled Out of Court, Somebody's Darling* 25; *If Youth But Knew* 26; *The Fake* (sc. only) 27; *Master and Man* 29; *The Woman From China* (sc. only) 31; sound: *DeForest Phonofilms* 27; *The World the Flesh and the Devil* 32; *Puppets of Fate, The Shadow, The Man Outside, His Grace Gives Notice, Home Sweet Home, The Roof, Mannequin* 33; *The Black Abbot, Tangled Evidence, Anything Might Happen, The Case for the Crown* 34; *Sexton Blake and the Bearded Doctor* 35; *Royal Eagle* 36; *Down Our Alley* 39. Scripted: *Men Without Honour* 39; *What Do We Do Now, Old Mother Riley at Home* 45; *Loyal Heart* 46.

102 CORBETT Harry H. (1925–)
Actor. B: Rangoon. Stage. Small tough guy parts until TV made him a comedy star. *The Passing Stranger* 54; *Floods of Fear, Nowhere to Go* 58; *In the Wake of a Stranger, Shake Hands With the Devil* 59; *Shakedown, Cover Girl Killer, The Big Day, The Unstoppable Man, Marriage of Convenience* 60; *Wings of Death* (short) 61; *Time to Remember* 62; *Sparrows Can't Sing, Sammy Going South, Ladies Who Do, What a Crazy World* 63; *The Bargee, Rattle of a Simple Man* 64; *Joey Boy* 65; *Carry on Screaming, The Sandwich Man* 66.

103 CORNELIUS Henry (1913–1958)
Director. B: S. Africa. 33: stage prod. Berlin. 34: Film ed. Studios de Montrouge. 35: asst. ed. *The Ghost Goes West.* Made two of the best and most British of comedies. *It Always Rains on Sunday* (sc. only) 47; *Passport to Pimlico* 49; *The Galloping Major* 51; *Genevieve* 53; *I Am a Camera* 55; *Next to No Time, Law and Disorder* (co-dir.) 58.

104 COURT Hazel (1926–)
Actress. B: Sutton Coldfield. Red-headed lovely of the 40s who never quite attained the status of the other Gainsborough girls. Also Hollywood. *Champagne Charlie* 44; *Dreaming* 45; *Gaiety George, Carnival, Meet Me at Dawn* 46; *The Root of All Evil, Dear Murderer, Holiday Camp* 47; *My Sister and I, Bond Street* 48; *Forbidden* 49; *Ghost Ship* 52; *Counterspy* 53; *Devil Girl from Mars* 54; *The Narrowing Circle* 56; *The Curse of Frankenstein, The Hour of Decision* 57; *Woman of Mystery, Model for Murder, Breakout* 58; *The Man Who Could Cheat Death* 59; *The Shakedown, The Man Who Was Nobody* 60; *Dr. Blood's Coffin, Mary Had a Little* 61; *The Masque of the Red Death* 64.

105 COURTENAY Tom (1937–)
Actor. B: Hull. Lean and hungry-looking star of British neo-naturalism. Stage: 59. Also Hollywood. *The Loneliness of the Long Distance Runner, Private Potter* 62; *Billy Liar* 63; *King and Country* 64; *Operation Crossbow* 65; *Night of the Generals* 66; *The Day the Fish Came Out* 67; *A Dandy in Aspic, Otley* 68.

106 COURTNEIDGE Cicely, C.B.E. (1893–) Actress. B: Sydney. Stage: 01. M: Jack HULBERT. Dancer, comedienne. Eccentric leading characters and adept at donning even more eccentric disguises. *Elstree Calling* 30; *The Ghost Train* 31; *Jack's the Boy, Happy Ever After* 32; *Soldiers of the King, Falling for You* 33; *Aunt Sally* 34; *Things Are Looking Up, Me and Marlborough* 35; *Everybody Dance* 36; *Take My Whip* 37; *Under Your Hat* 40; *The Spider's Web* 60; *The L-shaped Room* 62; *Those Magnificent Men in Their Flying Machines* 65; *The Wrong Box* 66.

107 COWARD Noël (1899–)
Director, producer, writer, actor. B: Teddington. Stage: 11; playwright: 20. Many plays filmed, also by Hollywood; latterly playing splendid character cameos. *Hearts of the World* (acted) 18; *The Queen Was in the Parlour* (sc.), *Easy Virtue* (sc.), *The Vortex* (sc.) 27; sound: *Bitter Sweet* (sc.) 33; *In Which We Serve* (prod., dir., sc. & acted) 42; *This Happy Breed* (prod. & sc.) 44; *Blithe Spirit* (prod. & sc.), *Brief Encounter* (prod. & sc.) 45; *The Astonished Heart* (sc. & acted) 50; *Meet Me Tonight* (sc.) 52; *Our Man In Havana* (acted), *Surprise Package* (acted) 60; *Bunny Lake is Missing* (acted) 65; *Pretty Polly* (sc.) 67; *Boom* (acted) 68.

108 CRABTREE Arthur (1900–)
Director. B: Shipley. 23: still photographer. 29: asst. ph. B.I.P. 35: ph.

Wedding Group. Dir. several typical Gainsborough romances and too-typical thrillers. *Madonna of the Seven Moons* 44; *They Were Sisters* 45; *Caravan* 46; *Dear Murderer* 47; *The Calendar, Quartet* (co-dir.) 48; *Don't Ever Leave Me* 49; *Lilli Marlene* 50; *Hindle Wakes* 51; *The Wedding of Lilli Marlene* 53; *Death Over My Shoulder, West of Suez* 57; *Morning Call, Fiend Without a Face* 58; *Horrors of the Black Museum* 59.

109 CRAIG Michael (1928–)
Actor. B: India. Merchant seaman; stage: 49. Hidden depths to this handsome hero. *Malta Story, Love Lottery, Svengali* 54; *Passage Home, The Black Tent* 55; *Eyewitness, Yield to the Night, House of Secrets, High Tide at Noon* 56; *Campbell's Kingdom, The Silent Enemy* 57; *Nor the Moon by Night, Sea of Sand* 58; *Life in Emergency Ward 10, Sapphire, Upstairs and Downstairs, The Angry Silence* (also sc.) 59; *Cone of Silence, Doctor in Love* 60; *Payroll, No My Darling Daughter* 61; *A Pair of Briefs, The Mysterious Island, Life for Ruth, The Iron Maiden* 62; *Stolen Hours* 63; *Life at the Top* 65; *Modesty Blaise* 66.

110 CRAWFORD Anne (1920–1956)
Actress. B: Haifa. RN: Imelda Crawford. Stage: 40. Well-bred blonde with a sense of humour. *They Flew Alone, The Peterville Diamond* 42; *The Dark Tower, Millions Like Us, The Night Invader, Headline* 43; *The £100 Window, 20,000 Women* 44; *They Were Sisters* 45; *Caravan, Bedelia* 46; *Master of Bankdam, Daughter of Darkness* 47; *Night Beat, The Blind Goddess, It's Hard to be Good* 48; *Tony Draws a Horse, Trio* 50; *Street Corner* 53; *Knights of the Round Table, Mad About Men* 54.

111 CRAWFORD Michael (1942–) Actor. Light comedy lead. *Soap Box Derby, Blow Your Own Trumpet* 58;

Two Left Feet 62; The War Lover 63; The Knack 64; A Funny Thing Happened on the Way to the Forum 65; The Jokers 66; How I Won the War 67.

112 THE CRAZY GANG Three music hall double acts working as a team. Okay for Sound 37; Alf's Button Afloat 38; The Frozen Limits 39; Gasbags 40; Life Is A Circus 59. Teams also starred individually. **Bud Flanagan and Chesney Allen:** The Bailiffs (short) 32; They're Off (short), The Dreamers (short) 33; Wild Boy 34; A Fire Has Been Arranged 35; Underneath the Arches 37; We'll Smile Again 42; Theatre Royal 43; Dreaming 44; Here Comes the Sun 45; Judgement Deferred (Flanagan only) 52; Dunkirk 57; The Wild Affair (Flanagan only) 63. **Charlie Naughton and Jimmy Gold:** Sign Please (short), My Lucky Star 33; Cock o' the North 35; Highland Fling 36; Wise Guys 37. **Jimmy Nervo and Teddy Knox:** Phonofilm 26; The Rising Generation (silent) 28; Alf's Button 30; It's in the Bag, Skylarks 36.

113 CRICHTON Charles (1910–   )
Director. B: Wallasey. Prospector. 35: ed. Sanders of the River. 42: assoc. prod. Nine Men. Stalwart of the Ealing School (14 films), less happy since. Young Veterans (short) 41; For Those In Peril 44; Painted Boats, Dead of Night (co-dir.) 45; Hue and Cry 47; Against the Wind, Another Shore 48; Train of Events (co-dir.) 49; Dance Hall 50; The Lavender Hill Mob 51; Hunted 52; The Titfield Thunderbolt 53; The Love Lottery, The Divided Heart 54; The Man in the Sky 57; Floods of Fear, Law and Disorder (co-dir.) 58; Battle of the Sexes 59; The Boy Who Stole a Million 60; The Third Secret 64; He Who Rides a Tiger 65.

114 CUMMINS Peggy (1925–   )
Actress. B: Prestatyn. Stage: 38. Pretty pint-sized teenagers and comedy wives. Also Hollywood. Dr. O'Dowd 40; Salute John Citizen 42; Old Mother Riley Detective 43; Welcome Mr. Washington, English Without Tears 44; Escape 48; That Dangerous Age 49; My Daughter Joy 50; Who Goes There 52; Street Corner, Always a Bride, Meet Mr. Lucifer 53; The Love Lottery, To Dorothy a Son 54; The March Hare 56; Carry On Admiral, Hell Drivers, Night of the Demon 57; The Captain's Table 58; Your Money or Your Wife 59; Dentist in the Chair 60; In the Doghouse 61.

115 CUSHING Peter (1913–   )
Actor. B: Kenley. 35: stage. Hollywood: 38. Cool king of Hammer horror films. Hamlet 49; Moulin Rouge 53; The Black Knight 54; The End of the Affair 55; Time Without Pity 56; The Curse of Frankenstein, The Abominable Snowman, Violent Playground 57; Dracula, The Revenge of Frankenstein 58; Hound of the Baskervilles, The Mummy 59; Cone of Silence, Flesh and the Fiends, The Brides of Dracula, The Sword of Sherwood Forest, Suspect 60; The Hellfire Club, Fury at Smugglers Bay, The Naked Edge, Cash on Demand 61; Captain Clegg, The Man Who Finally Died 62; The Evil of Frankenstein, The Gorgon, Dr. Terror's House of Horrors 64; She, Dr. Who and the Daleks, The Skull 65; Island of Terror, Daleks Invasion Earth A.D. 2150 66; Frankenstein Created Woman, Some May Live, Night of the Big Heat, Torture Garden 67; Blood Beast Terror, Corruption 68.

116 CUTTS Graham (1885–1958)
Director. B: Brighton. Marine engineer. 09: exhibitor. Top British box-office director of silents; eclipsed by sound until he came back with comedy. While London Sleeps, The Wonderful Story,

Flames of Passion 22; Paddy the Next Best Thing, Woman to Woman 23; The White Shadow, The Prude's Fall, The Passionate Adventure 24; The Blackguard, The Rat 25; The Sea Urchin, The Triumph of the Rat 26; The Rolling Road, The Queen Was in the Parlour, Confetti 27; God's Clay 28; Glorious Youth, The Return of the Rat 29; sound: The Temperance Fete, The Sign of Four, Love on the Spot, Looking on the Bright Side 32; As Good as New, Three Men In A Boat 33; Oh Daddy, Car of Dreams (co-dir.) 35; Aren't Men Beasts, Let's Make a Night of It, Over She Goes 37; Just William, She Couldn't Say No 39; Miss Knowall (short) 40; Air Transport Support (doc.) 45; Combined Operations (doc.), Our Daily Bread (short) 46.

117 CZINNER Paul (1890–   )
Director. B: Hungary. 24: Dir. Germany. Romantic films with wife Elisabeth Bergner and film reproductions of stage productions. The Woman He Scorned 30; The Loves of Ariane 31; Catherine the Great 34; Escape Me Never 35; As You Like It 36; Dreaming Lips 37; Stolen Life 39; Don Giovanni 55; Kings and Queens (short), Salzburg Pilgrimage (short) 56; The Bolshoi Ballet 57; The Royal Ballet 59; Der Rosenkavalier 62; Romeo and Juliet 66.

D

118 DALRYMPLE Ian (1903–   )
Director, writer, producer. B: Johannesburg. 32: ed. G.B.–Gainsborough. Wrote many of the better films in the 30s and as Wessex Films prod. good ones in the 40s. Scripted: The Good Companions 33; Her Last Affaire 35; Jury's Evidence, The Brown Wallet, Radio Lover 36; Storm in a Teacup, Action for Slander 37; South Riding, The Divorce of Lady X, Pygmalion, The Citadel 38; Q Planes, French Without Tears, The Lion Has Wings (also prod.), A Window in London 39; Old Bill and Son (also dir.), Sea Fort (short) (dir.) 40; Pimpernel Smith 41. Produced: London Can Take It (doc.) 40; Christmas Under Fire (doc.), Listen to Britain (doc.), Target for Tonight (doc.) 41; Coastal Command (doc.), Ferry Pilot (doc.), Wavell's 30,000 (doc.) 42; Close Quarters (doc.) 43; Perfect Strangers 45; The Woman in the Hall (also sc.) 47; Esther Waters (also dir.), Once a Jolly Swagman 48; All Over the Town, Dear Mr. Prohack (also sc.) 49; The Wooden Horse 50; The Changing Face of Europe (doc.) 51; The Heart of the Matter (also sc.) 52; Three Cases of Murder (also sc.) 54; Raising a Riot (also sc.) 55; A Hill in Korea (also sc.) 56; The Admirable Crichton 57; A Cry from the Streets 58; Hunted in Holland (also sc.) 61; Mix Me a Person (sc. only) 62; Calamity the Cow 67.

119 DAMPIER Claude (1879–1955)
Actor. B: Clapham. RN: Cowan. Music Halls. 25: Australian films. Bucktoothed, bespectacled 'silly ass' comedian. Claude Deputises (short) 30; Radio

Top: Michael Caine, Phyllis Calvert, Ian Carmichael
Centre: John Paddy Carstairs, Diane Cilento, Petula Clark, George Cole
Bottom: Joan Collins, Sean Connery, Tom Courtenay

Top: Michael Craig, Peggy Cummins, Peter Cushing
Centre: Robert Donat, Diana Dors, Basil Dearden
Bottom: Ivy Duke, Shirley Eaton, Henry Edwards

Parade of 1935 34; So You Won't Talk, White Lilac, Boys Will Be Boys, No Monkey Business, She Shall Have Music 35; King of the Castle, Public Nuisance No. 1, She Knew What She Wanted, Such Is Life, All In 36; Wanted, Mr. Stringfellow Says No, Sing As You Swing, Riding High 37; The Backyard Front (short) 40; Don't Take It To Heart 44; Meet Mr. Malcolm 54.

120 **DAUMERY John** (1898–1934) Director. B: Brussels. Asst. Rex Ingram in Nice; made French versions of Warner's early talkies. Teddington quickies for Warner. Meet My Sister, Help Yourself, Postal Orders (short), A Letter of Warning, Blind Spot 32; Naughty Cinderella, Mr. Quincey of Monte Carlo, Little Miss Nobody, The Thirteenth Candle, Call Me Mame, Head of the Family, This Acting Business 33; Over the Garden Wall, Without You 34.

121 **DAVIS Desmond** (1928–) Director. B: London. Stage: 28. TV: 38. Camera operator on some Tony RICHARDSON prods. Stylish films. Julius Caesar (short), Antony and Cleopatra (short) 50; The Girl with Green Eyes, The Uncle 64; I Was Happy Here 65; Smashing Time 67.

122 **DAVIS Redd** (1896–) Director. B: Canada. RN: Herbert Davis. Films: actor with Edison. Dir. 1920. To England with Monty BANKS, 28. Quota comedies. The Bells of St. Mary's 29; sound: Here's George 32; Medicine Man, Send 'Em Back Half Dead, Excess Baggage, The Umbrella, Ask Beccles 33; Seeing is Believing, The Girl in the Flat, Easy Money 34; Handle With Care, Say It With Diamonds 35; Excuse My Glove, On Top of the World, King of the Castle 36; Underneath the Arches, Sing as You Swing, The Biter Bit, Variety Hour 37; Anything to Declare, Special Edition 38; Discoveries 39; That's the Ticket 40; The Balloon Goes Up 42.

123 **DAY Robert** (1922–) Director. B: Sheen. 39: asst. Warners. 48: ph. Noose. Crisp comedies and thrillers; also Hollywood. The Green Man 56; Stranger's Meeting 57; Grip of the Strangler, Corridors of Blood 58; First Man into Space, Life in Emergency Ward 10, Bobbikins 59; Two Way Stretch, Tarzan the Magnificent 60; The Rebel 61; Operation Snatch 62; She 65.

124 **DEAN Basil**, O.B.E. (1888–) Producer (also director and writer). B: Croydon. Stage producer. Formed Associated Talking Pictures in conjunction with Radio (U.S.A.) as quality quota outfit—later became Ealing Studios. Discovered and built up Victoria HOPPER, Gracie FIELDS, George FORMBY etc. Scripted: The Constant Nymph 28. Sound, produced: Escape (also dir.), Birds of Prey (also dir.) 30; Sally in Our Alley, A Honeymoon Adventure 31; Water Gipsies, Nine Till Six (also dir.), The Sign of Four, The Impassive Footman (also dir.), Love on the Spot, Looking on the Bright Side (also dir.) 32; Loyalties (also dir.), Three Men in a Boat, The Constant Nymph (dir. & sc. only) 33; Autumn Crocus (also dir.), Love Life and Laughter, Java Head, Sing As We Go (also dir.) 34; Lorna Doone (also dir.), Look Up and Laugh (also dir.), Midshipman Easy, No Limit 35; Queen of Hearts, Whom the Gods Love (also dir.), Laburnum Grove, The Lonely Road, Keep Your Seats Please 36; Feather Your Nest, The Show Goes On (also dir.), 21 Days (dir. only), Keep Fit 37; I See Ice, Penny Paradise (also sc.), It's In The Air 38.

125 **DEARDEN Basil** (1911–) Director. B: Westcliff. Actor; stage mgr. to Basil DEAN; then his asst. at Ealing. Many comedies with George FORMBY

and Will HAY; both serious and topical work later with producer Michael Relph. Scripted: *This Man is News* 38; *Let George Do It* 40; *Turned Out Nice Again* 41. Co-directed: *The Black Sheep of Whitehall* 41; *The Goose Steps Out* 42; *My Learned Friend* 43. Directed: *The Bells Go Down* 43; *Halfway House, They Came to a City* 44; *Dead of Night* (co-dir.) 45; *The Captive Heart* 46; *Frieda* 47; *Saraband for Dead Lovers* 48; *Train of Events* (co-dir.) 49; *The Blue Lamp, Cage of Gold* 50; *Pool of London* 51; *I Believe in You, The Gentle Gunman* 52; *The Square Ring* 53; *The Rainbow Jacket* 54; *Out of the Clouds, The Ship That Died of Shame* 55; *Who Done It?* 56; *The Smallest Show on Earth* 57; *Violent Playground* 58; *Sapphire* 59; *The League of Gentlemen, Man in the Moon* 60; *The Secret Partner, Victim* 61; *All Night Long, Life For Ruth* 62; *The Mind Benders, A Place to Go, Woman of Straw* 63; *Masquerade* 64; *Khartoum* 66; *Only When I Larf, The Assassination Bureau* 68.

126 De COURVILLE Albert (1887–19) Director. B: London. Prod. Spectacular stage revues in the 20s but nothing spectacular in films. *Wolves* 30; *77 Park Lane, Night Shadows* 31; *There Goes the Bride, The Midshipmaid* 32; *This Is the Life* 33; *Wild Boy* 34; *Things Are Looking Up, The Case of Gabriel Perry, Charing Cross Road* 35; *Seven Sinners, Strangers on a Honeymoon* 36; *Clothes and the Woman* 37; *Oh Boy, Star of the Circus, Crackerjack* 38; *The Lambeth Walk, An Englishman's Home, Rebel Son* 39.

127 DENHAM Reginald (1894–) Director (also writer). B: London. Stage actor/producer. Made middle-bracket movies in the 30s. Scripting: *Stamboul, These Charming People* 31; *Ebb Tide* 32. Directed: *The Jewel, Called Back* 33; *Brides to Be, The Primrose Path, Borrow a* Million, *Death at Broadcasting House* 34; *The Silent Passenger, The Price of Wisdom, The Village Squire, Lucky Days, Lucky Loser, Lieut. Daring R.N.* 35; *The Crimson Circle, Dreams Come True, Calling the Tune, The House of the Spaniard* 36; *Kate Plus Ten* 38; *Blind Folly, The Flying Fifty Five* 39.

128 DENISON Michael (1915–) Actor. B: Doncaster. Stage: 37. M: Dulcie GRAY. Gentlemanly lead. *Tilly of Bloomsbury* 40; *Hungry Hill* 46; *My Brother Jonathan* 47; *The Blind Goddess, The Glass Mountain* 48; *Landfall* 49; *The Franchise Affair* 50; *The Magic Box* 51; *The Tall Headlines, Angels One Five, The Importance of Being Earnest* 52; *There Was a Young Lady* 53; *Contraband Spain* 55; *The Truth About Women* 57; *Faces in the Dark* 60.

129 DEWHURST George Director, producer, writer, actor. Stage. *The Home Maker* (prod., dir.) 19; *Her Benny* (sc.), *The Shadow Between* (dir.), *A Great Coup* (dir.), *Helen of Four Gates* (acted) 20; *The Lunatic at Large* (sc., acted), *The Tinted Venus* (acted), *The Narrow Valley* (sc., acted), *Wild Heather* (sc., acted), *Dollars in Surrey* (dir., sc.), *Tansy* (sc., acted). Directed: *A Sister to Assist 'Er* (also sc.) 22; *The Uninvited Guest* (also prod.), *Little Door into the World* (also prod.), *What the Butler Saw* (also prod.), *Doubles* (short) 23; *Bright Young Things* (short), *A Sister to Assist 'Er* (also sc.), *Motoring* 27. Sound, scripting: *A Sister to Assist 'Er* (also dir.) 30; *Never Trouble Trouble* (acted) 31; *Get Your Man, Adventure Ltd.* 34; *The Price of Wisdom* 35; *King of the Castle, Wednesday's Luck* (acted only) 36; *A Sister to Assist 'Er* (also dir.) 38; *A Sister to Assist 'Er* (also dir.), *Crime Reporter* (acted only) 47.

130 DICKINSON Thorold (1903–) Director. B: Bristol. 25: asst. *Mr. Preedy and the Countess*. 26: Co-sc. *The Little People*. 33: ed. *Perfect Understanding*. 35: prod. *Midshipman Easy*. With only 8 features he is the major lost talent of British cinema. Now Professor of Film at London University (Slade School). *The High Command* 37; *Spanish ABC* (doc.) 38; *The Arsenal Stadium Mystery* 39; *Gaslight, Yesterday Is Over Your Shoulder* (short) 40; *The Prime Minister* 41; *The Next of Kin* 42; *Men of Two Worlds* 46; *Queen of Spades* 49; *The Secret People* 52.

131 DICKSON Paul (1920–) Director. Ph. with Army Film Unit. Asst. Paul ROTHA. His docs. more successful than his Danziger features. *The Undefeated* (doc.) 50; *David* (doc.) 51; *The Story of an Achievement* (doc.) 52; *Star of my Night* 54; *Satellite in the Sky, Look This Way* (short) 56; *The Depraved, Fun at the Movies* (short) 57; *Enquiry into General Practice* (doc.) 59; *Stone into Steel* (doc.) 61.

132 DONAT Robert (1905–1958) Actor. B: Withington. Stage: 21. Despite chronic asthma gave some of the best performances in British films. Also Hollywood. *Men of Tomorrow, That Night in London* 32; *Cash, The Private Life of Henry VIII; The 39 Steps* 35; *The Ghost Goes West* 36; *Knight Without Armour* 37; *The Citadel* 38; *Goodbye Mr. Chips* (A.A.) 39; *The Young Mr. Pitt* 42; *The Adventures of Tartu* 43; *Perfect Strangers* 45; *Captain Boycott* 47; *The Winslow Boy* 48; *The Cure for Love* (also dir.) 49; *The Magic Box* 51; *Lease of Life* 54; *Stained Glass at Fairford* (short) (voice) 56; *The Inn of the Sixth Happiness* 58.

133 DONNER Clive (1926–) Director. B: London. 40: Asst. ed. Den-ham. 51: ed. *Scrooge*. Films with children and teenagers led to a 60s stylishness. Also Hollywood. *The Secret Place* 57; *Heart of a Child* 58; *Marriage of Convenience* 60; *The Sinister Man* 61; *Some People* 62; *The Caretaker, Nothing But The Best* 63; *Here We Go Round the Mulberry Bush* 67; *Alfred the Great* 68.

134 DORS Diana (1931–) Actress. B: Swindon. RN: Fluck. Britain's only Blonde Bombshell. Also Hollywood. *The Shop at Sly Corner* 46; *Holiday Camp, Dancing With Crime* 47; *Good Time Girl, The Calendar, My Sister and I, Oliver Twist, Penny and the Pownall Case, Here Come the Huggetts, Vote for Huggett* 48; *It's Not Cricket, A Boy a Girl and a Bike, Diamond City* 49; *Dance Hall* 50; *Worm's Eye View, Lady Godiva Rides Again* 51; *The Last Page, My Wife's Lodger* 52; *The Great Game, Is Your Honeymoon Really Necessary, The Weak and the Wicked, It's a Grand Life* 53; *As Long As They're Happy* 54; *A Kid For Two Farthings, Value For Money, An Alligator Named Daisy* 55; *Yield to the Night* 56; *The Long Haul* 57; *Tread Softly Stranger* 58; *Passport to Shame* 59; *Mrs. Gibbon's Boys* 62; *West 11* 63; *Allez France* 64; *The Sandwich Man* 66; *Berserk, Danger Route* 67; *Hammerhead, Baby Love* 68.

135 DUKE Ivy (1895–) Actress. B: Kensington. Popular silent star romantically teamed with Guy NEWALL, whom she married. *I Will, The Double Life of Mr. Alfred Burton, The March Hare, Fancy Dress, The Garden of Resurrection* 19; *The Lure of Crooning Water, Duke's Son, Testimony* 20; *The Bigamist* 21; *Beauty and the Beast* (short), *The Persistent Lovers, Boy Woodburn, Fox Farm, Maid of the Silver Sea* 22; *The Starlit Garden* 23; *The Great Prince Shan, Decameron Nights* 24; *A Knight in London* 29.

136 DUPONT E. A. (Ewald Andreas) (1891–1956) B: Zeitz. 11: film critic. 18: films. 23: director. 27: to Elstree as prod.-dir. Expressionistic silent style too ponderous for talkies. *Madame Pompadour* 27; *Moulin Rouge* 28; *Piccadilly* 29. Sound: *Atlantic* 29; *Two Worlds* 30; *Cape Forlorn* 31.

E

137 EATON Shirley (1937–   ) Actress. B: Middlesex. Stage: 54. Bright brassy blonde of British comedies. *You Know What Sailors Are, Doctor in the House* 54; *The Love Match* 55; *Charley Moon, Sailor Beware* 56; *Doctor at Large, Three Men in a Boat, The Naked Truth* 57; *In the Wake of a Stranger, Carry On Sergeant, Further Up the Creek* 58; *Carry On Nurse* 59; *Life is a Circus, Carry On Constable* 60; *A Weekend With Lulu, Nearly a Nasty Accident, Dentist on the Job, What a Carveup* 61; *The Girl Hunters* 63; *Goldfinger* 64; *Ten Little Indians* 65; *Sumuru* 67.

138 EDWARDS Henry (1883–1952). Actor, director. B: Weston-super-Mare. 00: stage. HEPWORTH's dreaming hero; wed his co-star Chrissie WHITE. Star in 20s, director in 30s, character actor in 40s. Actor: *Clancarty* (short), *A Bachelor's Love Story* (short) 14; *The Man Who Stayed At Home, Alone in London, My Old Dutch, Lost and Won, Far From the Madding Crowd* 15. Actor-director: *A Welsh Singer, Doorsteps* 15; *Grim Justice* (acted only), *East is East* 16; *The Cobweb* (acted only), *Merely Mrs. Stubbs, Dick Carson Wins Through, Nearer My God To Thee* (acted only), *Broken Threads* 17; *The Touch of a Child* (acted only), *The Hanging Judge, Film Tags* series, *The Refugee* (short) (acted only), *Tares* (short) (acted only), *Towards the Light* 18; *Broken in the Wars* (short) (acted only), *His Dearest Possession, The Kinsman, Possession, The City of Beautiful Nonsense* 19; *A Temporary Vagabond, The Amazing Quest of Mr. Ernest Bliss, Aylwin, John Forrest Finds Himself* 20; *The Lunatic at Large, The Bargain* 21; *Simple Simon, Tit for Tat* 22; *Lily of the Alley, Boden's Boy, The Naked Man* 23; *The World of Wonderful Reality* 24. Director: *Owd Bob* 24; *King of the Castle, A Girl of London* 25; *One Colombo Night, The Island of Despair* 26. Actor: *The Flag Lieutenant* 26; *The Fake, The Further Adventures of the Flag Lieutenant* 27; *The Three Kings, Ringing the Changes* 29. Sound: *The Call of the Sea* (also prod.) 30; *The Girl in the Night* (also prod. & dir.), *Stranglehold* (also prod. & dir.) 31; *The Flag Lieutenant* (also dir.) 32. Director: *The Barton Mystery, Brother Alfred* 32; *General John Regan, Discord, One Precious Year, Lord of the Manor, Anne One Hundred, Purse Strings* 33; *The Man Who Changed His Name, The Lash, Lord Edgware Dies, Are You a Mason* 34; *D'Ye Ken John Peel, The Rocks of Valpre, The Lad, Vintage Wine, Squibs, Scrooge, The Private Secretary* 35; *In the Soup, Eliza Comes to Stay, Juggernaut* 36; *Beauty and the Barge, The Vicar of Bray, The Song of the Forge* 37. Actor: *Captain's Orders* 37; *East of Piccadilly,*

Spring Meeting 41; The Magic Bow, Green for Danger 46; Take My Life 47; London Belongs to Me, Oliver Twist, Woman Hunter, Quartet, All Over the Town, Lucky Mascot 48; Dear Mr. Prohack, Madeleine 49; Double Confession, Trio, The Rossiter Case 50; White Corridors, The Lady With the Lamp, The Magic Box 51; Never Look Back, Something Money Can't Buy, The Long Memory, Trent's Last Case 52.

139 EGGAR Samantha (1940–)
Actress. B: London. Attractive star; also Hollywood. The Wild and the Willing 61; Dr. Crippen 62; Doctor in Distress, Psyche 59 63; Return From the Ashes 65.

140 ELLIOTT Denholm (1922–)
Actor. B: London. Stage: 45. Gentlemanly lead now skilfully adding a touch of mannered decay to character parts. Also Hollywood. Dear Mr. Prohack 49; The Sound Barrier, The Holly and the Ivy, The Ringer 52; The Cruel Sea, The Heart of the Matter, They Who Dare 53; Lease of Life, The Man Who Loved Redheads 54; The Night My Number Came Up 55; Pacific Destiny 56; Station Six Sahara, Nothing But the Best 63; The High Bright Sun 64; You Must Be Joking 65; Alfie, Maroc 7, The Spy With a Cold Nose 66; Here We Go Round the Mulberry Bush 67.

141 ELSOM Isobel (1893–) Actress. B: Cambridge. Stage: 11. M: Maurice ELVEY. Silent star for SAMUELSON; character roles in Hollywood. A Prehistoric Love Story (short) 15; Milestones 16; The Way of an Eagle, Tinker Tailor Soldier Sailor, The Elder Miss Blossom, God Bless Our Red White and Blue, Onward Christian Soldiers, The Man Who Won 18; Quinneys, In Bondage, Linked by Fate, A Member of Tattersalls, Edge o' Beyond, Mrs. Thompson 19; Nance,

Aunt Rachel 20; For Her Father's Sake 21; The Game of Life, Dick Turpin's Ride to York, Debt of Honour 22; Harbour Lights, The Sign of Four, The Wandering Jew 23; The Love Story of Ailette Brunton, Who is the Man 24; The Last Witness 25; Glamis Castle, The Tower of London (shorts), Human Law 26. Sound: The Other Woman, Stranglehold 31; The Crooked Lady, Illegal 32; The Thirteenth Candle 33; The Primrose Path 34.

142 ELVEY Maurice (1887–1967)
Director. B: Darlington. RN: William Folkard. 05: Actor, stage prod. Record run as feature dir. of 44 years: films competent, many above average, several big box-office successes. Also Hollywood and Continent. M: (2) Isobel ELSOM. The Fallen Idol (short), Bridegrooms Beware (short), Popsy Wopsy (short), The Great Gold Robbery, Maria Marten, Inquisitive Ike (short) 13; The Cup Final Mystery, Black-eyed Susan, The Suicide Club, The Loss of the Birkenhead, Beautiful Jim, Lest We Forget (short), The Bells of Rheims, The White Feather (short), Her Luck in London, It's a Long Long Way to Tipperary, The Sound of Her Voice (short), The Idol of Paris 14; There's Good in Everyone (short), A Honeymoon For Three, Gilbert Gets Tiger-itis (short), Gilbert Dying to Die (short), Midshipman Easy, London's Yellow Peril, Florence Nightingale, From Shopgirl to Duchess, Her Nameless Child, Grip, Home, A Will of Her Own, Charity Ann, Fine Feathers, Love in a Wood 15; Meg the Lady, Esther, Driven, Money for Nothing (short), Vice Versa, Motherlove, When Knights Were Bold, Trouble for Nothing (short), The Princess of Happy Chance, The King's Daughter 16; Smith, The Grit of a Jew, The Woman Who Was Nothing, Flames, Mary Girl, Goodbye, Justice, The Gay Lord Quex, Dombey and Son 17; Hindle Wakes, Adam Bede, Nelson,

The Life Story of David Lloyd George 18; Bleak House, Comradeship, Keeper of the Door, The Rocks of Valpre, The Victory Leaders, God's Good Man, Mr. Wu, The Swindler 19; The Elusive Pimpernel, The Amateur Gentleman, At the Villa Rose, The Hundredth Chance, A Question of Trust, The Tavern Knight 20; Innocent, The Tragedy of a Comic Song (short), A Gentleman of France, The Hound of the Baskervilles, The Fruitful Vine, A Romance of Wastdale, Man and His Kingdom, The Adventures of Sherlock Holmes series (15) 21; The Passionate Friends, Debt of Honour, Dick Turpin's Ride to York, Running Water 22; The Sign of Four, The Wandering Jew, Guy Fawkes, Royal Oak, Sally Bishop, Don Quixote 23; Henry King of Navarre, Slaves of Destiny, The Love Story of Ailette Brunton 24; Baddesley Manor, Windsor Castle, Glamis Castle, Kenilworth Castle, Tower of London (last five shorts), Woman Tempted, Human Law, The Flag Lieutenant, Mademoiselle From Armentieres 26; Hindle Wakes, Roses of Picardy, The Glad Eye, The Flight Commander, Quinneys 27; Mademoiselle Parley Voo, Palais de Danse, You Know What Sailors Are 28. Sound: High Treason 29; The School for Scandal, Balaclava (co-dir.) 30; Sally in our Alley, Honeymoon Adventure, Potiphar's Wife, The Water Gipsies, Diamond Cut Diamond (co-dir.), Frail Women, In a Monastery Garden, The Marriage Bond, The Lodger 32; The Lost Chord, I Lived With You, This Week of Grace, The Wandering Jew, Soldiers of the King 33; Princess Charming, My Song for You, Road House, Love Life and Laughter, Lily of Killarney 34; Heat Wave, Clairvoyant, The Tunnel 35; Spy of Napoleon, The Man in the Mirror 36; Change for a Sovereign, Who Killed John Savage, A Romance in Flanders, Melody and Romance 37; Who Goes Next, The Return of the Frog, Lightning Conductor 38; Sword of Honour, The Spider, Sons of the Sea 39;

Room for Two, Under Your Hat, For Freedom, Goofer Trouble (short) 40; Salute John Citizen 42; The Lamp Still Burns, The Gentle Sex (co-dir.) 43; Medal for the General 44; Strawberry Roan 45; Beware of Pity 46; The Late Edwina Black, The Third Visitor 51; My Wife's Lodger 52; House of Blackmail, The Great Game, Is Your Honeymoon Really Necessary 53; What Every Woman Wants, The Happiness of Three Women, The Harassed Hero, The Gay Dog 54; You Lucky People, Room in the House 55; Fun at St. Fanny's, Stars in Your Eyes, Dry Rot, Last Man to Hang (sc. only) 56; Second Fiddle 57.

143 ENDFIELD Cy/C. Raker (1914–) Director, producer, writer. B: America. Drama teacher, stage prod., radio writer. 42: Passing Parade shorts. In England since McCarthy. Hard, brisk adventures. The Limping Man 53; The Master Plan 54; The Secret, Impulse 55; Child in the House 56; Hell Drivers 57; Sea Fury 58; Jet Storm 59; Mysterious Island 60; Hide and Seek 62; Zulu 63; Sands of the Kalahari 65.

144 EVANS Dame Edith (1888–) Actress. B: Pimlico. Stage: 12. Brilliant character studies. A Welsh Singer 15; East is East 16; sound: The Queen of Spades 48; The Last Days of Dolwyn 49; The Importance of Being Earnest 52; Look Back in Anger 59; Tom Jones 62; The Chalk Garden 63; Young Cassidy 65; The Whisperers 67; Prudence and the Pill 68.

145 EVANS Fred ('Pimple') (1889–1951) Actor, director. 1893: circus. 10: acrobatic extra for Cricks & Martin, then Charley Smiler series. 12: as Pimple (U.S.: Flivver) in weekly burlesques by and with brother **Joe Evans** (1891–1967). Top British silent slapstick star, an extra in sound. Main shorts: The Last of the Dandy

10; *Charley Smiler Joins the Boy Scouts* 11; *Pimple Does the Turkey Trot* 12; *Pimple's Battle of Waterloo, Pimple's Ivanhoe, Lieut. Pimple on Secret Service* 13; *The House of Distemperley, The Battle of Gettysownback, How Lieut. Pimple Captured the Kaiser* 14; *Sexton Pimple,* *Pimple's Million Dollar Mystery, Pimple's Three Weeks, Pimple's Royal Divorce* 15; *Pimple's Midsummer Night's Dream, Pimple as Hamlet, Pimple's Clutching Hand* 16; *Rations, Pimple's Better 'Ole* 18; *Pimple's Topical Gazette* 20; *Pimple's Three Musketeers* 22.

F

146 FAIRCHILD William (1918–)
Writer and director. B: Cornwall. Sailor, author. Scripting: *Penny and the Pownall Case, A Song for Tomorrow, Colonel Bogey* 48; *Badger's Green* 49; *Morning Departure, The Long Dark Hall* 50; *Outcast of the Islands* 51; *The Gift Horse, The Net* 52; *Malta Story* 53; *The Seekers* 54; *Passage Home, Value for Money* 55. Writer-director: *John and Julie* 55; *The Extra Day* 56; *The Silent Enemy* 58; *The Horsemasters* 61.

147 FARR Derek (1912–) Actor.
B: Littlehampton. Stage: 37. M: Muriel PAVLOW. Small parts pre-Army service; typecast as a hero on the run. *The Outsider, Black Eyes* 39; *Spellbound* 40; *Freedom Radio, Quiet Wedding* 41; *Quiet Weekend* 45; *Wanted for Murder, The Shop at Sly Corner* 46; *Teheran* 47; *Bond Street, Noose, Silent Dust* 48; *Man on the Run, The Story of Shirley Yorke* 49; *Double Confession, Murder Without Crime* 50; *Young Wives' Tale, Reluctant Heroes* 51; *Little Big Shot* 52; *Front Page Story* 53; *Bang You're Dead, Eight O'Clock Walk* 54; *The Dambusters, Value For Money* 55; *The Man in the Road, Town on Trial* 56; *Doctor at Large, Vicious Circle* 57; *The Truth About Women* 58; *Attempt to Kill* 61;

The Projected Man 66; *30 Is A Dangerous Age Cynthia* 67.

148 FARRAR David (1908–) Actor.
B: Forest Gate. Journalist; stage: 32. Handsome, masculine star at his prime in pictures 46–50; later Hollywood. *Return of a Stranger* 37; *Silver Top, Sexton Blake and the Hooded Terror, A Royal Divorce* 38; *Danny Boy, Penn of Pennsylvania, Sheepdog of the Hills* 41; *Suspected Person, Went the Day Well* 42; *The Dark Tower, They Met in the Dark, The Night Invader, Headline* 43; *The £100 Window, For Those in Peril, Meet Sexton Blake* 44; *The Echo Murders, The Trojan Brothers* 45; *Lisbon Story, The World Owes Me a Living* 46; *Black Narcissus, Frieda* 47; *Mr. Perrin and Mr. Traill, The Small Back Room* 48; *Diamond City* 49; *Cage of Gold, Gone to Earth* 50; *Night Without Stars, The Late Edwina Black* 51; *Duel in the Jungle, Lilacs in the Spring* 54; *Lost* 55; *I Accuse, Son of Robin Hood* 58; *Beat Girl* 60; *The Webster Boy* 62.

149 FAYE Randall Writer and director
(also producer). B: America. Scripting: *Song of Soho, Harmony Heaven* 30; *High Society, Lucky Ladies* 32; *As Good as New, Call Me Mame* 33; *Murder at the Inn, The Office Wife, Father and Son, Hyde Park*

(also dir.) 34. Writer-producer: *Handle With Care, Maria Marten* (sc. only), *Lend Me Your Husband, Windfall, The Man Without a Face, Gay Old Dog* 35. Producer-director: *The Vandergilt Diamond Mystery, This Green Hell* (also sc.), *If I Were Rich, Born that Way, The Luck of the Turf, Such is Life* (dir. only) 36; *Mr. Stringfellow Says No* 37; *Scruffy* (dir. only) 38; *The Face at the Window* (sc. only) 39.

150 **FIELD Mary** (1896–   ) Director. B: Wimbledon. Teacher. 26: education mgr. British Instructional Films. 27: asst. ed., writer, then dir. docs. with H. Bruce Woolfe and Percy Smith. 34: G.B.-Instructional with same team. 44: Exec. prod. Children's Entertainment Films, later Children's Film Foundation. Main shorts: *Secrets of Nature* series 28; *The King's English, The Changing Year* 32; *Secrets of Life* series 34; *This Was England* 35; *They Made the Land* 38; *The Mediaeval Village* 40; *Winged Messengers* 41. Feature: *Strictly Business* (co-dir.) 32.

151 **FIELD Shirley Ann** (1936–   ) Actress. B: London. Model, rep actress. Developed depth after pretty bit parts. *It's Never Too Late, Lost, It's a Wonderful World, Dry Rot, Loser Takes All, Yield to the Night* 56; *The Good Companions, Seven Thunders, The Flesh is Weak, The Silken Affair* 57; *Horrors of the Black Museum, Upstairs and Downstairs, And the Same to You* 59; *Peeping Tom, The Entertainer, Beat Girl, Saturday Night and Sunday Morning, Man in the Moon* 60; *The Damned* 61; *The War Lover, Lunch Hour* 62; *Doctor in Clover* 65; *Alfie* 66.

152 **FIELDS Gracie**, C.B.E. (1898–   ) Actress. B: Rochdale. RN: Grace Stansfield. Stage: 11. Singer, comedienne; starred by Basil DEAN, became top box-office and world's highest paid star. M:

(2) Monty BANKS. Also Hollywood. *Sally in Our Alley* 31; *Looking on the Bright Side* 32; *This Week of Grace, Love Life and Laughter* 33; *Sing as We Go* 34; *Look Up and Laugh* 35; *Queen of Hearts* 36; *The Show Goes On* 37; *We're Going to Be Rich, Keep Smiling* 38; *Shipyard Sally* 39.

153 **FINCH Peter** (1916–   ) Actor. B: London. 36: Stage in Australia. Popular star of some strength. Also Hollywood. *Eureka Stockade* 48; *Train of Events* 49; *The Wooden Horse, The Miniver Story* 50; *The Story of Robin Hood* 51; *The Story of Gilbert and Sullivan, The Heart of the Matter* 53; *Father Brown* 54; *Make Me an Offer, Passage Home, The Dark Avenger, Simon and Laura, Josephine and Men* 55; *A Town Like Alice, The Battle of the River Plate* 56; *The Shiralee, Robbery Under Arms, Windom's Way, Operation Amsterdam* 57; *A Far Cry* (short) (voice) 58; *The Trials of Oscar Wilde, Kidnapped* 60; *No Love for Johnnie, The Day* (short) (prod., dir., & sc.) 61; *I Thank a Fool* 62; *In the Cool of the Day* 63; *The Girl with Green Eyes, The First Men in the Moon, The Pumpkin Eater* 64; *Far From the Madding Crowd* 67.

154 **FINNEY Albert** (1936–   ) Actor. B: Salford. Stage: 58. Forceful star expressing the rebellion of 60s youth. *The Entertainer, Saturday Night and Sunday Morning* 60; *Tom Jones, The Victors* 63; *Night Must Fall* 64; *Two for the Road, Charlie Bubbles* (also dir.) 67.

155 **FISHER Terence** (1904–   ) Director. B: London. Merchant seaman. 33: asst. ed. to Ian DALRYMPLE. 36: Ed. *Tudor Rose*. Graduated from glossy Gainsboroughs to Hammer horrors. *A Song For Tomorrow, Colonel Bogey, To the Public Danger, Portrait From Life* 48; *Marry Me* 49; *The Astonished Heart, So*

Long at the Fair, Home to Danger 50; A Distant Trumpet, The Last Page, Stolen Face, Wings of Danger 52; Mantrap, The Four Sided Triangle, Spaceways, Blood Orange 53; Face the Music, Mask of Dust, The Stranger Came Home, Final Appointment, Children Galore 54; Murder by Proxy, The Flaw, Stolen Assignment 55; The Last Man to Hang 56; Kill Me Tomorrow, The Curse of Frankenstein 57; Dracula, The Revenge of Frankenstein 58; The Hound of the Baskervilles, The Man Who Could Cheat Death, The Mummy, The Stranglers of Bombay 59; The Brides of Dracula, The Two Faces of Dr. Jekyll, Sword of Sherwood Forest 60; The Curse of the Werewolf 61; The Phantom of the Opera 62; The Horror of It All, The Earth Dies Screaming, The Gorgon 64; Dracula Prince of Darkness 65; Island of Terror 66; Frankenstein Created Woman, Night of the Big Heat 67; The Devil Rides Out 68.

156 FITZGERALD Geraldine (1914–) Actress. B: Dublin. Dark-eyed Irish star, mainly Hollywood. Blind Justice, Open All Night 34; The Lad, Ace of Spades, Three Witnesses, Department Store, Lieut. Daring R.N., Turn of the Tide 35; Debt of Honour, Café Mascot 36; The Mill on the Floss 37; The Late Edwina Black 51.

157 FITZHAMON Lewin (1869–1961) Director. B: Aldingham. Steeplechase rider. 89: actor-producer, sketch writer. First film for R. W. PAUL; 04–12 contract writer-director-actor to HEPWORTH making 600 shorts. 07: started annual location trip to coast. 08: discovered Chrissie WHITE, 09: Alma TAYLOR. 12: as Fitz Films starring Pathe beauty contest winner Constance Somers-Clarke, whom he wed. Specialised in children and animals (Tiger the dog, Tariff the pony). Main shorts: Briton v.

Boer 00; The Great Servant Question, The Press Illustrated, Lady Plumpton's Motor, A Race for a Kiss, A Den of Thieves, For the Hand of a Princess 04; Children v. Earthquakes, Rescued by Rover, Prehistoric Peeps, The Death of Nelson, The Aliens' Invasion, Babes in the Wood 05; The Voters' Guide, Dick Turpin's Ride to York, The Squatter's Daughter, Black Beauty, The Dollmaker's Daughter 06; That Fatal Sneeze, The Ghost's Holiday, A Seaside Girl, Dying of Thirst, Cinderella 07; The Dog Outwits the Kidnapper, Baby's Playmate, Saved from a Terrible Death, John Gilpin's Ride, The Fairy Sword 08; The Cabman's Good Fairy, The Race for the Farmer's Cup, The Little Milliner and the Thief, The Girl who Joined the Bushrangers 09; The Burglar and Little Phyllis, Lord Blend's Love Story, The Detective's Dog, Tilly the Tomboy plays Truant, The Sheriff's Daughter 10; The Dog's Devotion, Harry the Footballer, Rover the Peacemaker, Tilly and the Mormon Missionary, Jim of the Mounted Police, Tiger the Tec 11; The Blind Man's Dog, A Fisherman's Love Story, The Mermaid, The Children of the Forest, Saving the Royal Mail, The Flapper and the Curates, The Pony Who Paid the Rent 12; While Shepherds Watched, The Flappers and the Nuts, Her Pony's Love 13; A Hateful Bondage, The Scallywag, Her Faithful Companions, The Hurricane Kids series 14.

FLANAGAN Bud see CRAZY GANG

158 FLEMYNG Gordon (1934–) Director. B: Glasgow. 55: TV. Solo for Sparrow 62; Five to One, Just For You 63; Dr. Who and the Daleks 65; Daleks Invasion Earth 2150 A.D. 66; Great Catherine 68.

159 FOGWELL Reginald Writer, director, producer. B: Dartmouth. Bank clerk. 21: Fox publicist. Scripting: *The Price of Divorce, Warned Off* 28; *Dick Turpin* series (also dir.), *The Warning* (also prod. & dir.), *The Return of the Rat* 29; sound: *Such is the Law* 30. Prod., dir. & sc.: *Cross Roads* 30; *Guilt, Madame Guillotine, The Written Law* 31; *The Temperance Fete* (not dir.), *Betrayal, The Wonderful Story* 32; *Prince of Arcadia* (not dir.) 33; *Two Hearts in Waltztime* (not dir.) 34; *Murder at the Cabaret, Terror on Tiptoe* (prod. only) 36.

160 FORBES Bryan (1926–   )

Director, writer, actor. B: Stratford-atte-Bow. Stage: 42. M: Nanette Newman. From juvenile parts to adult scripts and direction. Also Hollywood. Actor: *The Small Back Room, All Over the Town* 48; *Dear Mr. Prohack* 49; *The Wooden Horse* 50; *Green Grow the Rushes* 51; *Appointment in London* 52; *Sea Devils, Wheel of Fate, The Million Pound Note* 53; *An Inspector Calls, Up to the Neck, The Colditz Story* 54; *Passage Home, Now and Forever, The Quatermass Xperiment, The Last Man to Hang* 55; *The Extra Day, It's Great to be Young, The Baby and the Battleship, Satellite in the Sky* 56; *Quatermass II* 57; *The Key, I Was Monty's Double* 58; *Yesterday's Enemy* 59; *League of Gentlemen* 60; *Guns of Navarone* 61; *Shot in the Dark* 64. Scripting: *Cockleshell Heroes* 55; *The Baby and the Battleship, The Black Tent, House of Secrets* 56; *I Was Monty's Double* 58; *The Captain's Table* 59; *The Angry Silence, League of Gentlemen, Man in the Moon* 60; *Only Two Can Play, Station Six Sahara* 62; *Of Human Bondage, The High Bright Sun* 64. Directed: *Whistle Down the Wind* 61; *The L-Shaped Room* (also sc.) 62; *Seance on a Wet Afternoon* (also sc.) 64; *The Wrong Box* (also prod.) 66; *The Whisperers* (also sc.), *Deadfall* (also sc.) 67.

161 FORDE Walter (1897–   )

Director. B: Bradford. RN: Tom Seymour. Pianist, music hall comic. Made and starred in slapstick shorts and 3 features as Britain's only major silent film comedian. 23: Hollywood: ed. and dir. Universal. Became our best comedy director and second best for thrillers. Shorts: *The Handy Man, Fishing for Trouble, Never Say Die, Walter's Winning Ways, Walter Finds a Father* 21; *Walter Wins a Wager, Walter's Trying Frolics, Walter Makes a Movie, Walter Wants Work* 22; *Walter's Paying Policy, Walter's Worries, Walter the Sleuth, Walter's Day Out, Walter Tells the Tale, Walter the Prodigal* 26. Features: *Wait and See, What Next* 28; *Would You Believe It, The Silent House* 29. Sound: *Red Pearls, You'd Be Surprised, The Last Hour, Lord Richard in the Pantry, Bed and Breakfast* 30; *The Ringer, Splinters in the Navy, Third Time Lucky, The Ghost Train* 31; *Lord Babs, Jack's The Boy, Rome Express, Condemned to Death* 32; *Orders Is Orders* 33; *Chu Chin Chow, Jack Ahoy* 34; *Bulldog Jack, Forever England* 35; *King of the Damned, Land Without Music* 36; *Kicking the Moon Around, The Gaunt Stranger* 38; *Inspector Hornleigh on Holiday, Let's Be Famous, The Four Just Men, Cheer Boys Cheer* 39; *Saloon Bar, Sailors Three, Charley's Big-hearted Aunt, Neutral Port, Gasbags* 40; *The Ghost Train, Inspector Hornleigh Goes To It, Atlantic Ferry* 41; *Flying Fortress, The Peterville Diamond, Go to Blazes* (short) 42; *It's That Man Again* 43; *Time Flies* 44; *Master of Bankdam* (also prod.) 47; *Cardboard Cavalier* 49.

162 FORMBY George (1904–1961)

Actor. B: Wigan. Music Hall comic, all teeth and a ukelele, who became the top box-office star thanks to Basil DEAN. *By the Shortest of Heads* 15. Sound: *Boots Boots* 34; *Off the Dole, No Limit* 35; *Keep*

Your Seats Please 36; Feather Your Nest, Keep Fit 37; I See Ice, It's in the Air 38; Trouble Brewing, Come on George 39; Let George Do It, Spare a Copper 40; Turned Out Nice Again, South American George 41; Much Too Shy 42; Get Cracking, Bell Bottom George 43; He Snoops to Conquer 44; I Didn't Do It 45; George in Civvy Street 46.

163 FOSS Kenelm (1885–1963) Actor, writer, director. Stage career as actor, producer and playwright. Major writer of originals for the screen 17–19; thereafter director, adaptor and designer. Acted: Fine Feathers 15; Arsene Lupin, Odd Charges, The Persecution of Bob Pretty, The Skipper of the Osprey, A Marked Man, The Manxman 16; The Top Dog, The Wages of Sin 18; Whosoever Shall Offend, Not Guilty, Damages for Breach, Till Our Ship Comes In series, The Double Life of Mr. Alfred Burton 19; The Joyous Adventures of Aristide Pujol (also prod.) 20. Scripting: The Shulamite, Love in a Wood 15; The Morals of Weybury, Motherlove, Arsene Lupin, The Man Without a Soul, The Mother of Dartmoor, A Mother's Influence, The Manxman 16; The Labour Leader, The Gift of a Jew, Asthore, Daddy, If Thou Wert Blind, Auld Robin Gray 17; The Admirable Crichton, The Slave, Adam Bede, My Sweetheart, Once Upon a Time, Man and the Moment, All the Sad World Needs, Consequences, Rock of Ages, Tinker Tailor Soldier Sailor, The Divine Gift, The Top Dog, The Woman Wins, The Wages of Sin, Peace Perfect Peace (short), Not Negotiable 18; A Soul's Crucifixion, Whosoever Shall Offend, Not Guilty, The Romance of Lady Hamilton, Damages for Breach, Under Suspicion, Till Our Ship Comes In series, The Double Life of Mr. Alfred Burton, Fettered, When It Was Dark 19. Scripted and directed: A Peep Behind the Scenes 18; A Little Bit of Fluff, I Will, Fancy Dress 19;

The Glad Eye, The Breed of the Treshams, A Bachelor Husband 20; The Headmaster, The Double Event, Cherry Ripe, The Street of Adventure, The Wonderful Year, Number 5 John Street, All Roads Lead to Calvary 21; House of Peril, Dicky Monteith, Romance of Old Bagdad 22.

164 FRANCIS Freddie (1917–   ) Director. B: London. 34: stills; 35: asst. ph. B.I.P. 48: ph. Night Beat. Makes stylish and mobile horror films. Two and Two Make Six, Vengeance 62; Paranoiac, Nightmare 63; The Evil of Frankenstein, Hysteria, Dr. Terror's House of Horrors, Traitor's Gate 64; The Skull 65; Psychopath, The Deadly Bees, They Came from Beyond Space 66; Torture Garden 67; Dracula Has Risen from the Grave 68.

165 FRANKEL Cyril (1921–   ) Director. 47: asst. dir.; docs. incl. Eagles of the Fleet. First opportunity with Group 3. Man of Africa, The Nutcracker (short) 53; Devil on Horseback, Make Me an Offer 54; It's Great to Be Young 55; No Time For Tears 57; She Didn't Say No, Alive and Kicking 58; Never Take Sweets From a Stranger 60; Don't Bother to Knock, On the Fiddle 61; The Very Edge 63; The Witches 66; The Trygon Factor 67.

166 FREELAND Thornton (1898–   ) Director. B: Hope N.D. 16: asst. Vitagraph; 29: dir. United Artists. Several fast, lively comedies and musicals in England. Brewster's Millions 35; Skylarks, The Amateur Gentleman, Accused 36; Paradise for Two, Jericho 37; Hold My Hand 38; Over the Moon, So This Is London, The Gang's All Here 39; Meet Me At Dawn 46; Lucky Mascot 47; Dear Mr. Prohack 49.

167 FRENCH Harold (1897–   ) Actor, writer, director. B: London. At his best with good actors and dialogue.

Actor: *Hypocrites* 23; sound: *East Lynne on the Western Front, The Officer's Mess, Jealousy, The Star Reporter* 31; *The Callbox Mystery, A Safe Proposition, When London Sleeps, Tight Corner* 32; *Yes Madam, Night of the Garter, The Umbrella, I Adore You, Mannequin* 33; *Faces, Murder at the Inn, How's Chances* 34; *Radio Pirates, The Girl in the Crowd, A Fire Has Been Arranged* 35; *Two on a Doorstep* 36. Writer: *Accused, Crime Over London* 36; *Jump for Glory* 37. Director: *Cavalier of the Streets* 37; *Dead Men Are Dangerous* 39; *House of the Arrow* 40; *Jeannie, Major Barbara* (co-dir.) 41; *Secret Mission, Unpublished Story, The Day Will Dawn* 42; *Dear Octopus* 43; *English Without Tears, Mr. Emmanuel, Quiet Weekend* 46; *White Cradle Inn* 47; *The Blind Goddess, Quartet* (co-dir.), *My Brother Jonathan* 48; *Adam and Evelyne* 49; *The Dancing Years, Trio* (co-dir.) 50; *Encore* (co-dir.) 51; *The Man Who Watched Trains Go By* 52; *Isn't Life Wonderful, The Hour of 13, Rob Roy the Highland Rogue* 53; *Forbidden Cargo* 54; *The Man Who Loved Redheads* 55.

168 FREND Charles (1909–)
Director. B: Pulborough. 31: asst. ed. B.I.P. 33: ed. Gaumont. An Ealing man at his best with war and action. *The Big Blockade* 41; *The Foreman Went to France* 42; *San Demetrio London* 43; *Johnny Frenchman, Return of the Vikings* (doc.) 45; *The Loves of Joanna Godden* 47; *Scott of the Antarctic* 48; *A Run For Your Money, The Magnet* 49; *The Cruel Sea* 53; *Lease of Life* 54; *The Long Arm* 56; *Barnacle Bill* 57; *Cone of Silence* 60; *Girl on Approval* 62; *The Sky Bike* (also sc.) 67.

169 FULLER Leslie (1889–1948) Actor. B: Hackney. Singer, concert party comic. Built up into big box-office star by B.I.P. in cheap comedies, dir. Monty BANKS. *Not So Quiet on the Western Front, Kiss Me Sergeant, Why Sailors Leave Home* 30; *Old Soldiers Never Die, What a Night, Poor Old Bill, Bill's Legacy* 31; *Tonight's the Night, The Last Coupon, Old Spanish Customers* 32; *Hawleys of High Street, The Pride of the Force* 33; *A Political Party, The Outcast, Lost in the Legion, Doctor's Orders* 34; *Strictly Illegal, The Stoker, Captain Bill* 35; *One Good Turn* 36; *Boys Will Be Girls* 37; *The Middle Watch, Two Smart Men* 40; *My Wife's Family* 41; *Front Line Kids* 42; *What Do We Do Now* 45.

170 FURIE Sidney J. (1933–   )
Director. B: Toronto. 54: dir.-sc. features in Canada. Visual films, stylish and youthful. To Hollywood. *Dr. Blood's Coffin, The Snake Woman* 60; *During One Night, The Young Ones* 61; *The Boys* 62; *The Leather Boys* 63; *Wonderful Life* 64; *The Ipcress File* 65; *The Naked Runner* 67.

171 FYFFE Will (1885–1947) Actor. B: Dundee. Stage: 1891. Music hall singer/comedian who became one of our finest character actors. Also Hollywood. *Elstree Calling* 30; *Happy* 34; *Rolling Home* 35; *King of Hearts, Debt of Honour, Love in Exile, Men of Yesterday, Annie Laurie* 36; *Well Done Henry, Spring Handicap, Cotton Queen, Said O'Reilly to McNab* 37; *Owd Bob* 38; *The Mind of Mr. Reeder, The Missing People* 39; *They Came By Night, For Freedom* 40; *Neutral Port, The Prime Minister* 41; *Heaven is Round the Corner* 43; *Give Me the Stars* 45; *The Brothers* 47.

44

G

172 GARRICK John (1902–)
Actor. B: Brighton. RN: Reginald Dandy.
Bank clerk. 20: singer. 29: Hollywood
films. Handsome singing star. *Lily of
Killarney* 33; *The Broken Melody, Chu Chin
Chow, Too Many Millions, Anything Might
Happen, D'Ye Ken John Peel, The Rocks of
Valpre, His Majesty and Co.* 34; *Street
Song, The Turn of the Tide* 35; *A Touch of
the Moon, Royal Eagle, Shipmates o' Mine,
To Catch a Thief, A Woman Alone, Live
Again* 36; *Knights for a Day, Sunset in
Vienna, Riding High* 37; *Special Edition* 38.

173 GENN Leo (1905–) Actor. B:
London. Barrister; stage: 30. Sympa-
thetic lead. Also Hollywood. *Immortal
Gentleman* 35; *Dream Doctor* 36; *Cavalier
of the Streets, Jump for Glory, The Rat* 37;
*Governor Bradford, Kate Plus Ten, Danger-
ous Medicine, The Drum* 38; *Ten Days in
Paris* 39; *Law and Disorder, Contraband* 40;
The Way Ahead, Tunisian Victory (doc.)
(voice) 44; *Henry V, Julius Caesar* (short)
45; *Caesar and Cleopatra* 46; *Green For
Danger* 47; *No Place for Jennifer* 49; *The
Wooden Horse, The Miniver Story* 50; *The
Magic Box* 51; *24 Hours of a Woman's Life*
52; *The Red Beret, Personal Affair* 53; *The
Green Scarf* 54; *Beyond Mombasa, Moby
Dick* 56; *The Steel Bayonet* 57; *No Time to
Die, I Accuse* 58; *Too Hot to Handle* 60;
Ten Little Indians 65; *Circus of Fear,
Khartoum* (voice) 66.

174 GERRARD Gene (1892–)
Actor (also director). B: Clapham. RN:

Eugene O'Sullivan. Music Halls: 1911.
Middle-class 'Jack Buchanan' in musicals
and comedies, some of which he directed
quite well. *Let's Love and Laugh, My Wife's
Family, Out of the Blue* (also dir.) 31;
Brother Alfred, Lucky Girl (also dir.), *Let
Me Explain Dear* (also dir.) 32; *Leave It To
Me, The Love Nest* 33; *There Goes Susie* 34;
*It's a Bet, Royal Cavalcade, Joy Ride, The
Guvnor, No Monkey Business* 35; *Faithful,
Where's Sally, Such Is Life* 36; *Wake Up
Famous* (dir. only) 37; *Glamour Girl, It's
In The Blood* (dir. only) 38; *Dumb Dora
Discovers Tobacco* 45.

175 GIELGUD Sir John (1904–)
Actor. B: London. Stage: 21. Distin-
guished stage star with a few memorable
film roles. Also Hollywood. *Who Is The
Man* 24; *The Clue of the New Pin* 29;
sound: *Insult* 32; *The Good Companions*
33; *Secret Agent* 36; *The Prime Minister* 41;
Richard III 55; *The Barretts of Wimpole
Street* 56; *Saint Joan* 57; *Becket* 64;
Sebastian 67; *The Charge of the Light
Brigade, Oh! What a Lovely War* 68.

176 GILBERT Lewis (1920–)
Director. B: London. 37: actor *Over the
Moon*. 40: asst. dir. R.A.F. Film Unit.
Some of our best films about World War
Two. Shorts: *Sailors Do Care* 44; *Ten
Year Plan* 45; *Arctic Harvest* 46. Features:
The Little Ballerina 47; *Marry Me* (sc.
only) 49; *Once a Sinner* 50; *There Is
Another Sun, Scarlet Thread* 51; *Emergency
Call, Time Gentlemen Please* 52; *Cosh Boy,*

Johnny on the Run, Albert R.N. 53; The Sea Shall Not Have Them, The Good Die Young 54; Cast a Dark Shadow 55; Reach for the Sky 56; The Admirable Crichton 57; Carve Her Name with Pride, A Cry from the Streets 58; Ferry to Hong Kong 59; Sink the Bismarck, Light Up the Sky 60; The Greengage Summer 61; H.M.S. Defiant 62; The Seventh Dawn 64; Alfie 66; You Only Live Twice 67.

177 GILL Basil (1877–1955) Actor. B: Birkenhead. Stage: 97. Star of silents, then character actor. Henry VIII II; Chains of Bondage, On the Banks of Allan Water 16; The Ragged Messenger, Adventures of Dick Dolan (short) 17; Missing the Tide, Spinner o' Dreams, What's the Use of Grumbling (short) 18; A Soul's Crucifixion, The Irresistible Flapper, Keeper of the Door, The Rocks of Valpre, God's Good Man 19; The Worldlings 20. Sound: Julius Caesar (short), Santa Claus (short) 26; High Treason 29; School for Scandal, Should a Doctor Tell 30; Glamour 31; The Wandering Jew, Mrs. Dane's Defence 33; The Immortal Gentleman, Royal Cavalcade, The Divine Spark 35; Gaolbreak, The Crimson Circle, His Lordship, Rembrandt 36; I Claudius, Knight Without Armour 37; Saint Martin's Lane, Dangerous Medicine, The Citadel 38.

178 GILLIAT Sidney (1908–) Writer, director, producer. B: Edgeley. 27: asst. to Walter MYCROFT. Partnership with Frank LAUNDER began as writers, then own co. Individual Pictures (45). His prime period for comedies & thrillers: 38–48. Scriptwriting: Rome Express 32; Facing the Music, Falling for You, Orders Is Orders, Friday the Thirteenth 33; Jack Ahoy, Chu Chin Chow, My Heart Is Calling 34; Bulldog Jack 35; King of the Damned, Twelve Good Men, Where There's a Will, Seven Sinners, The Man Who

Changed His Mind 36; Take My Tip 37; A Yank at Oxford, Strange Boarders, The Lady Vanishes, The Gaunt Strangers 38; Jamaica Inn, Ask a Policeman, Inspector Hornleigh on Holiday 39; They Came by Night, Night Train to Munich, Girl in the News 40; Kipps 41; The Young Mr. Pitt 42; The Pure Hell of St. Trinian's 60. Writer-director: Partners in Crime (short) (co-dir.) 42; Millions Like Us (co-dir.) 43; Waterloo Road 44; The Rake's Progress 45; Green for Danger 46; London Belongs to Me 48; State Secret 50; The Story of Gilbert and Sullivan 53; The Constant Husband 55; Fortune Is a Woman 57; Left Right and Centre 59; Only Two Can Play 61; The Great St. Trinian's Train Robbery (co-dir.) 66.

179 GILLIE Jean (1915–1949) Actress. B: Kensington. Dancer, stage: 31. Also Hollywood. His Majesty and Co., Smith's Wives, Brewster's Millions, School for Stars, It Happened in Paris, While Parents Sleep 35; This'll Make You Whistle 36; The Girl in the Taxi, The Live Wire 37; Sweet Devil 38; What Would You Do Chums?, The Middle Watch 39; The Spider, Tilly of Bloomsbury, Sailors Don't Care, A Call to Arms (short) 40; The Saints Meets the Tiger 41; The Gentle Sex 43; Tawny Pipit 44; Flight From Folly 45.

180 GILLING John (1912–) Writer, director. 33: asst. dir. B.I.P. Brisk, efficient low-budget thrillers and middle-budget adventures. Scripting: Black Memory 47; The Greed of William Hart, House of Darkness, A Gunman Has Escaped, Escape from Broadmoor (also dir.) 48; The Man from Yesterday, A Matter of Murder (also dir.), The Man in Black, Room to Let 49; The Lady Craved Excitement, No Trace (also dir.), Blackout (also dir.), Dark Interval 50; The Rossiter Case, The Quiet Woman (also dir.), Chelsea Story 51; Blind Man's Bluff, Whispering

Smith Hits London, Thirteen East Street, The Frightened Man (also dir.), Wings of Danger, King of the Underworld, Mother Riley Meets the Vampire (prod. & dir. only), The Lost Hours, The Voice of Merrill (also dir.), Murder at Scotland Yard 52; Deadly Nightshade (dir. only), The Steel Key 53. Dir. & sc.: Recoil, Three Steps to the Gallows, Escape by Night 53; Double Exposure, The Embezzler, Profile (sc. only) 54; The Gilded Cage (dir. only), Tiger by the Tail, Windfall (sc. only) 55; The Gamma People, Bond of Fear (sc. only), Odongo 56; High Flight (dir. only), Interpol (dir. only) 57; The Man Inside (dir. only) 58; Idle on Parade (dir. only), Bandit of Zhobe 59; Flesh and the Fiends, Challenge 60; Fury at Smugglers Bay, Shadow of the Cat (dir. only) 61; Pirates of Blood River 62; The Scarlet Blade, Panic 63; The Gorgon (sc. only), Secret of Blood Island (sc. only) 64. Director: Brigand of Kandahar, Plague of the Zombies, The Reptile 65; Where the Bullets Fly 66; The Mummy's Shroud, The Night Caller 67.

181 GLENVILLE Peter (1913–   ) Director, former actor. B: Hampstead. Stage: 34. Parents: Shaun Glenville, Dorothy Ward. Highly regarded stage producer, his few films are equally respected. Also Hollywood. Acted: Two for Danger 40; Uncensored 42; Heaven is Round the Corner 43; Madonna of the Seven Moons 44; Good Time Girl 48. Directed: The Prisoner 55; Term of Trial 62; Becket 63; Hotel Paradiso 66.

GOIMBAULT Odette see Mary ODETTE.

GOLD Jimmy see CRAZY GANG.

182 GRAHAME Margot (1911–   ) Actress. B: Canterbury. Stage: 26. Voluptuous blonde glamour star, later in Hollywood. Rookery Nook, Compromising Daphne 30; The Love Habit, Uneasy Virtue, The Rosary, Glamour, Creeping Shadows, Stamboul 31; Postal Orders (short), Letter of Warning, Innocents of Chicago, Illegal 32; Yes Mr. Brown, Forging Ahead, Timbuctoo, Prince of Arcadia, I Adore You, Sorrell and Son 33; Without You, The Broken Melody, Falling in Love 34; Crime Over London 36; Broken Journey 48; The Romantic Age 49; Venetian Bird, The Crimson Pirate 52; The Beggar's Opera 53; Orders are Orders 55; Saint Joan 57.

183 GRANGER Stewart (1913–   ) Actor. B: London. RN: James Stewart. 33: Extra: A Southern Maid. Suave romantic star of the 40s in Gainsborough, Spain, West Germany etc. Give Her a Ring 34; So This is London 39; Convoy 40; Secret Mission 42; Thursday's Child, The Lamp Still Burns, The Man in Grey 43; Fanny By Gaslight, Love Story, Madonna of the Seven Moons 44; Waterloo Road 45; Caravan, Caesar and Cleopatra, The Magic Bow 46; Captain Boycott, Blanche Fury 47; Saraband for Dead Lovers, Woman Hater 48; Adam and Evelyne 49; Footsteps in the Fog 55; Bhowani Junction 56; The Whole Truth, Harry Black 58; The Secret Partner 61; The Crooked Road 64; The Trygon Factor, The Last Safari 67.

184 GRAY Dulcie (1919–   ) Actress. B: Kuala Lumpur. Stage: 36. M: Michael DENISON. Somewhat sweet leading lady. 2,000 Women, Victory Wedding (short), Madonna of the Seven Moons 44; A Place of One's Own, They Were Sisters 45; Wanted for Murder, The Years Between, A Man About the House 46; Mine Own Executioner, My Brother Jonathan 47; The Glass Mountain 48; The Franchise Affair

50; *Angels One Five* 52; *There Was a Young Lady* 53.

185 GRAY Eve (1904–   ) Actress. B: Birmingham. Stage in Australia: 22. *Daughter of the Night* (short), *Poppies of Flanders, The Silver Lining, One of the Best* 27; *Moulin Rouge, Smashing Through* 28; sound: *The Lovers of Robert Burns, Why Sailors Leave Home, Night Birds* 30; *Midnight, The Wickham Mystery, The Flaw, Smithy, The Bermondsey Kid* 33; *The Crimson Candle, Guest of Honour, Big Business, Womanhood, What's in a Name* 34; *Murder at Monte Carlo, Death on the Set, Three Witnesses, Just for Tonight* (short), *Department Store, Scrooge, The Last Journey* 35; *Twice Branded, Jury's Evidence, They Didn't Know, The Happy Family, Such Is Life* 36; *Pearls Bring Tears, When the Devil Was Well, The Vicar of Bray, The Strange Adventures of Mr. Smith, Fifty Shilling Boxer, The Angelus, Silver Blaze* 37; *His Lordship Regrets* 38.

186 GRAY Sally (1916–   ) Actress. B: Holloway. RN: Constance Stevens. Stage: 28. Gay pre-war blonde who turned into a sultry star of the 40s. *School for Scandal* 30; *Marry the Girl, Radio Pirates, Cross Currents, Lucky Days, Checkmate* 35; *Cheer Up, Calling the Tune, Honeymoon Merrygoround* 36; *Cafe Colette, Over She Goes, Saturday Night Revue* 37; *Mr. Reeder in Room 13, Hold My Hand, Lightning Conductor* 38; *The Lambeth Walk, Sword of Honour, The Saint in London, A Window in London* 39; *The Saint's Vacation, Dangerous Moonlight* 41; *Carnival, Green For Danger* 46; *They Made Me a Fugitive, The Mark of Cain* 47; *Silent Dust* 48; *Obsession* 49; *Escape Route* 52.

187 GRAYSON Godfrey (1913–   ) Director. 34: asst. ed. Warner Bros. Class B thrillers for early Hammer and Danzigers. *Dick Barton Strikes Back, Dr. Morelle, The Adventures of P.C.49, Meet Simon Cherry* 49; *Dick Barton at Bay, Room to Let, What the Butler Saw* 50; *To Have and to Hold* 51; *The Fake* 53; *Black Ice* 57; *Innocent Meeting, High Jump, A Woman's Temptation* 59; *Date at Midnight, An Honourable Murder, The Spider's Web, Escort for Hire* 60; *So Evil So Young, The Pursuers* 61; *The Battleaxe, Design for Loving, She Always Gets Their Man, The Durant Affair, Lamp in Assassin Mews* 62.

188 GREEN Guy (1913–   ) Director. B: Somerset. 29: asst. B.I.P. 44: ph. *The Way Ahead.* Some well-photographed thrillers and at least two triumphs (*The Angry Silence, The Mark*). Also Hollywood. *River Beat* 54; *Portrait of Alison* 55; *Lost* 56; *House of Secrets* 57; *The Snorkel, Sea of Sand* 58; *S.O.S. Pacific* 59; *The Angry Silence, The Mark* 60; *Pretty Polly* 67.

189 GREENWOOD Joan (1921–   ) Actress. B: Chelsea. Stage: 38. Petite seductress with a deliciously distinctive voice. *John Smith Wakes Up* 40; *My Wife's Family, He Found a Star* 41; *The Gentle Sex* 42; *They Knew Mr. Knight* 44; *Latin Quarter* 45; *Girl in a Million, The Man Within* 46; *The October Man, The White Unicorn* 47; *Saraband for Dead Lovers, The Bad Lord Byron* 48; *Whisky Galore, Kind Hearts and Coronets, Flesh and Blood* 50; *The Man in the White Suit, Young Wives Tale* 51; *The Importance of Being Earnest* 52; *Knave of Hearts, Father Brown* 54; *The Mysterious Island, The Amorous Prawn* 62; *Tom Jones* 63; *The Moon Spinners* 64.

190 GREGSON John (1919–   ) Actor. B: Liverpool. Stage: 47. Dry Scots leading man. *Saraband for Dead Lovers, Scott of the Antarctic* 48; *Whisky Galore, Train of Events* 49; *Treasure Island,*

Top: Samantha Eggar, Denholm Elliott, Edith Evans
Centre: Derek Farr, Albert Finney & Shirley Ann Field, Peter Finch
Bottom: Bud Flanagan, Bryan Forbes, George Formby

Top: Margot Grahame, Stewart Granger, Joan Greenwood
Centre: John Gregson, Alec Guinness, Edmund Gwenn, Greta Gynt
Bottom: Lilian Hall Davis, Kay Hammond, Jimmy Hanley

Cairo Road 50; The Lavender Hill Mob 51; Angels One Five, The Brave Don't Cry, The Venetian Bird, The Holly and the Ivy 52; The Titfield Thunderbolt, Genevieve, The Weak and the Wicked 53; Conflict of Wings, To Dorothy a Son, The Crowded Day 54; Above Us the Waves, Value for Money 55; Jacqueline, The Battle of the River Plate, True as a Turtle 56; Miracle in Soho, Rooney 57; Sea of Sand, The Captain's Table 58; S.O.S. Pacific 59; Faces in the Dark, Hand in Hand 60; The Treasure of Monte Cristo, The Frightened City 61; Live Now Pay Later, Tomorrow at Ten 62.

191 GREY Anne (1907–   ) Actress.
B: Lincoln. RN: Aileen Ewing. M: Lester MATTHEWS. Stage: 25. Classy charmer of early talkies. To Hollywood. The Constant Nymph 27; What Money Can Buy, The Warning 28; Master and Man, Taxi for Two 29; sound: The Nipper, The Squeaker, Cross Roads, School for Scandal 30; Guilt, Other People's Sins, The Man at Six, The Happy Ending, The Calendar, The Old Man 31; Murder at Covent Garden, Lily Christine, The Faithful Heart, Number Seventeen, Arms and the Man, Leap Year 32; One Precious Year, She Was Only a Village Maiden, The Golden Cage, The Blarney Stone, The Lost Chord, The Lure, The Fire Raisers, Just Smith, The Wandering Jew, The House of Trent 33; Colonel Blood, Borrowed Clothes, Scoop, Lady in Danger, Road House, The Poisoned Diamond 34; Dr. Sin Fang, Chinatown Nights 37.

192 GRIERSON John (1898–   )
Director. B: Deanstown, N.B. 28: E.M.B. Film Unit. 33: G.P.O. Film Unit. 37: Film Centre. 39: Canadian Film Commissioner (established National Film Board of Canada). 46: UNESCO. 48: Film Controller C.O.I. 51: Exec. prod. Group Three. 57: Scottish TV. Mainly a producer, rightly dubbed Father of British Doc. Drifters 29; sound: Industrial Britain (short) (co-dir.) 32; The Fishing Banks of Skye (short), So This Is London (short) (co-dir.) 34.

193 GUEST Val (1911–   ) Writer,
director, producer. B: London. Journalist Film Pictorial, etc. Actor, 31: Warners Hollywood, 32: Innocents of Chicago (B.I.P.). Expert comedy man (Will HAY, Arthur ASKEY, CRAZY GANG etc.), near-expert with thrillers; apart from two bad failures, has maintained a highly competent standard. M: his star Yolande Donlan. Scripting: No Monkey Business 35; Public Nuisance No. I, A Star Fell From Heaven, All In, Windbag the Sailor 36; Good Morning Boys, Okay for Sound, Oh Mr. Porter 37; Convict 99, Alf's Button Afloat, Hey Hey U.S.A., Old Bones of the River 38; Ask a Policeman, Where's That Fire, The Frozen Limits 39; Band Wagon, Charley's Bighearted Aunt, Gasbags 40; The Ghost Train, Inspector Hornleigh Goes To It, I Thank You, Hi Gang 41; Back Room Boy 42. Writer-director: The Nose Has It (short) 42; Miss London Ltd. 43; Bees in Paradise, Give Us the Moon 44; I'll Be Your Sweetheart 45; London Town (sc. only) 46; Just William's Luck 47; William Comes to Town, Paper Orchid (sc. only) 48; Murder at the Windmill 49; Miss Pilgrim's Progress, The Body Said No, Happy Go Lovely (sc. only), Another Man's Poison (sc. only) 50; Mr. Drake's Duck 51; Penny Princess (also prod.) 52; Life With the Lyons 53; The Runaway Bus (also prod.), Men of Sherwood Forest, Dance Little Lady 54; They Can't Hang Me, The Lyons in Paris, Break in the Circle, The Quatermass Xperiment 55; Men Without Women (sc. only), It's A Wonderful World, The Weapon 56; Carry On Admiral, Quatermass II, The Abominable Snowman 57; The Camp on Blood Island, Up the Creek,

Further Up the Creek 58; Life is a Circus, Yesterday's Enemy, Expresso Bongo (also prod.) 59; Hell Is a City, The Full Treatment (also prod.), Dentist in the Chair (sc. only) 60. Writer-director-producer: The Day the Earth Caught Fire 61; Jigsaw 62; 80,000 Suspects 63; The Beauty Jungle 64; Where the Spies Are 65; Casino Royale (co-dir. only), Assignment K (not prod.).

194 GUILLERMIN John (1925–)
Director. B: London. 47: docs. in France. From lowest Bs to biggest A features. Scripting: Melody in the Dark, High Jinks in Society 49. Director: Torment (also sc.) 49; Smart Alec, Two on the Tiles, Four Days 51; Song of Paris, Miss Robin Hood 52; Operation Diplomat 53; Adventure in the Hopfields, The Crowded Day 54; Thunderstorm 55; Town on Trial 57; The Whole Truth, I Was Monty's Double 58; Tarzan's Greatest Adventure 59; The Day They Robbed the Bank of England, Never Let Go 60; Waltz of the Toreadors, Tarzan Goes to India 62; Guns at Batasi 64; The Blue Max 66.

195 GUINNESS Sir Alec (1914–)
Actor. B: London. Stage: 33. Distinguished actor originally acclaimed for his multi-character studies and his make-up. Evensong 33; Great Expectations 46; Oliver Twist 48; Kind Hearts and Coronets, A Run For Your Money 49; Last Holiday, The Mudlark 50; The Lavender Hill Mob, The Man in the White Suit 51; The Card 52; The Captain's Paradise, The Malta Story 53; Father Brown, To Paris With Love 54; The Prisoner, The Ladykillers, Rowlandson's England (short) (voice) 55; Barnacle Bill, The Bridge on the River Kwai (AA) 57; The Scapegoat, The Horse's Mouth 58; Our Man in Havana 59; Tunes of Glory 60; H.M.S. Defiant, Lawrence of Arabia 62; The Quiller Memorandum, Hotel Paradiso 66.

196 GUNN Gilbert (19–)
Director. B: Glasgow. Stage producer, playwright. 37: scenarist B.I.P. 41: extra The Farmer's Wife. From docs., has made several comedies in the pre-war style. Main shorts: Royal Observer Corps 41; The Owner Goes Aloft 42; Canteen Command 43; Tyneside Story 44; Star in the Sand 45; Routine Job 46; Country Policeman 47. Features: Landfall (sc. only) 49; Elstree Story (compilation) 52; Valley of Song, The Good Beginning 53; My Wife's Family 56; Accused (co-dir.) 57; Girls at Sea, The Strange World of Planet X 58; Operation Bullshine 59; What a Whopper 61; Wings of Mystery 62; The Young Detectives 63.

197 GWENN Edmund (1875–1959)
Actor. B: Glamorgan. Stage: 96. Popular character star; also Hollywood. The Real Thing at Last (short) 16; Unmarried, The Skin Game 20. Sound: How He Lied to Her Husband, The Skin Game, Hindle Wakes 31; Money for Nothing, Frail Women, Condemned to Death, Love on Wheels, Tell Me Tonight 32; The Good Companions, Cash, Early to Bed, I Was a Spy, Channel Crossing, Smithy, Marooned, Friday the 13th 33; Waltzes from Vienna, The Admiral's Secret, Passing Shadows, Warn London, Java Head, Father and Son, Spring in the Air 34; Laburnum Grove 36; South Riding, A Yank at Oxford, Penny Paradise 38; Cheer Boys Cheer, An Englishman's Home 39.

198 GYNT Greta (1916–) Actress.
B: Oslo, RN: Woxholt. Stage: 34. Bright blonde glamour girl. Boys Will Be Girls, The Last Curtain 37; Second Best Bed, Sexton Blake and the Hooded Terror, The Last Barricade 38; Too Dangerous to Live, Dark Eyes of London, She Couldn't Say No, The Arsenal Stadium Mystery, The

Middle Watch 39; *Two for Danger, Bulldog Sees It Through, Room for Two, Crooks' Tour* 40; *The Common Touch* 41; *It's That Man Again, Tomorrow We Live* 42; *Mr. Emmanuel* 44; *London Town, Take My Life* 46; *Dear Murderer, Easy Money* 47; *The Calendar, Mr. Perrin and Mr. Traill* 48; *Shadow of the Eagle, I'll Get You For This* 50; *Whispering Smith Hits London* 51; *I'm a Stranger, The Ringer* 52; *Three Sreps in the Dark* 53; *Forbidden Cargo, Devil's Point* 54; *See How They Run, Blue Peter, Dead on Time* (short) 55; *My Wife's Family, Fortune is a Woman* 56; *Morning Call* 58; *Witness, Bluebeard's Ten Honeymoons* 59.

H

199 HAGGAR William (1851–1924) Director, producer. B: Dedham. 62: docker. 68: travelling showman. 97: fairground exhibitor. Made sensational and slapstick shorts featuring his family. Main shorts: *The Maniac's Guillotine, Duel Scene from The Two Orphans, The Wild Man of Borneo, True as Steel* 02; *Mirthful Mary series, A Desperate Poaching Affray, A Dash for Liberty* 03; *The Sign of the Cross* 04; *The Squire's Daughter, Charles Peace, The Salmon Poachers, A Message from the Sea* 05; *Desperate Footpads* 07; *Maria Marten, The Maid of Cifn Ydfa, The Dumb Man of Manchester* 08.

200 HALAS AND BATCHELOR Cartoon producers/directors. **John Halas** (1912–) B: Budapest. 28: asst. Georg Pal. 34: prod. cartoons. 41: Halas & Batchelor cartoon films with wife **Joy Batchelor** (1914–). B: London. 35: anim. *Robin Hood.* Together over 200 shorts for M.O.I./C.O.I. and 750 commercials. Main shorts: *The Pocket Cartoon* 41; *Dustbin Parade* 42; *Abu series* (4) 43; *Six Little Jungle Boys* 45; *Old Wives' Tales* 46; *Heave Away My Johnny* 47; *Charley series* (7) 48; *First Line of Defence* 49; *Magic Canvas* 50; *Poet and Painter series* (4) 51; *The Figurehead* (puppet) 52; *The Owl and the Pussycat* (3D) 53; *Power to Fly* 54; *Speed the Plough* 55; *The History of the Cinema* 56; *All Lit Up* 57; *The Christmas Visitor* 58; *The Energy Picture* 59; *The History of Inventions* 60; *For Better For Worse* 61; *Hamilton the Musical Elephant* 62; *Automania 2000* 63; *Men in Silence* 64. Features: *Handling Ships* (doc.) 45; *Animal Farm* 54; *The Monster of Highgate Ponds* (live) 61; *Is There Intelligent Life on Earth* (Living Screen) 63; *Ruddigore* 67.

201 HALDANE Bert Director. Fred Karno stage mgr. 10–12: a film a week for HEPWORTH usually starring Flora Morris. Made approx. 325 films. Main shorts: *A Flower Girl's Romance, Woman v. Woman* 10; *A Girl's Love Letter, The Silver Lining, The Convict's Sister, For Better or Worse, The Foreign Spy* 11; *A Brother's Sacrifice, For Baby's Sake, The Draughtsman's Revenge* 12. Features: *In the Toils of the Blackmailer, Zaza the Dancer, East Lynne, Younita, Sixty Years a Queen* 13; *Jim the Fireman, The Lights o' London, The Last Round, As a Man Sows* 14; *Tommy Atkins, Jane Shore, Jack Tar, By the Shortest of Heads, Brigadier Gerard* 15; *On Leave, The Ticket of Leave Man* 18; *The Romance of Lady Hamilton* 19; *The Grip of*

Iron, The Winding Road, Mary Latimer Nun 20.

202 HALE Sonnie (1902–1959) Actor (also director). B: London. RN: John Hale-Monro. Stage: 21. Playwright as Robert Munro. M: (1) Evelyn Laye; (2) Jessie MATTHEWS, 3 of whose films he directed. Comedian in mostly musicals. *The Parting of the Waves* (short), *On With the Dance* (short) 27. Sound: *Happy Ever After, Tell Me Tonight* 32; *Early to Bed, Friday the Thirteenth* 33; *Evergreen, Wild Boy, Are You a Mason, My Song for You, My Heart is Calling* 34; *Marry the Girl, First a Girl* 35; *It's Love Again* 36; *The Gaunt Stranger* 38; *Let's Be Famous* 39; *Fiddlers Three* 44; *London Town* 46. Directed: *Head Over Heels, Gangway* 37; *Sailing Along* 38.

203 HALL DAVIS Lilian (1901–1933) Actress. B: Hampstead. Elegant blonde star of SAMUELSON silents. Also Continentals. *The Admirable Crichton, The Better 'Ole* 18; *The Honeypot, Ernest Maltravers* 20; *Love Maggy* 21; *Wonderful Story, Stable Companions, The Game of Life, Brown Sugar, The Faithful Heart, If Four Walls Told, Let's Pretend* 22; *A Royal Divorce, The Right to Strike, The Knockout, Married Love, The Hotel Mouse, Should a Doctor Tell, I Pagliacci, Afterglow* 23; *Unwanted, The Passionate Adventure, The Eleventh Commandment, If Youth But Knew* 24; *Boadicea* 26; *Blighty, Roses of Picardy, The Ring* 27; *The White Sheik, The Farmer's Wife, Tommy Atkins* 28; sound: *As We Lie* (short) 27; *Her Reputation, Many Waters* 31.

204 HAMER Robert (1911–1963) Director, writer. B: Kidderminster. 35: asst. ed. KORDA. 38: ed. *Vessel of Wrath*. His writing and direction added stylish sophistication to Ealing comedy. Scripting: *San Demetrio London* 43; *Dead of*

Night (also co-dir.) 45. Directed: *Pink String and Sealing Wax* 45; *It Always Rains on Sunday* (also sc.) 47; *Kind Hearts and Coronets* (also sc.), *The Spider and the Fly* 49; *His Excellency* (also sc.) 52; *The Long Memory* (also sc.) 53; *Father Brown* 54; *To Paris With Love* 55; *The Scapegoat* 59; *School for Scoundrels* 60; *A Jolly Bad Fellow* (sc. only) 63.

205 HAMILTON Guy (1922–   ) Director. B: Paris. 39: apprentice Victorine, Nice. 40: British Paramount News. 47: asst. dir. *They Made Me a Fugitive*. The financial failure of his one personal film has caused him to turn to costly crime pictures. *The Ringer* 52; *The Intruder* 53; *An Inspector Calls* 54; *The Colditz Story* 55; *Charley Moon* 56; *Manuela* 57; *The Devil's Disciple* 58; *A Touch of Larceny* 59; *The Man in the Middle, The Party's Over* 63; *Goldfinger* 64; *Funeral in Berlin* 66; *The Battle of Britain* 68.

206 HAMMOND Kay (1909–19   ) Actress. B: London. RN: Dorothy Standing. Father: Sir Guy Standing. M: John CLEMENTS. Stage: 27. Tongue-in-cheek, plum-in-mouth acting style plus great beauty. *Children of Chance* 30; *Fascination, A Night in Montmartre, Almost a Divorce, Out of the Blue, Carnival, Chance of a Night-time* 31; *The Third String, A Night Like This, Nine Till Six, Money Means Nothing, Sally Bishop* 32; *Yes Madam, Sleeping Car, Britannia of Billingsgate, Bitter Sweet, The Umbrella* 33; *Bypass to Happiness* 34; *Two on a Doorstep* 36; *Jeannie* 41; *Blithe Spirit* 45; *Call of the Blood* 48; *Five Golden Hours* 61.

207 HAMPSHIRE Susan (1941–   ) Actress. B: London. Stage. Pretty young star, more successful on TV. *Upstairs and Downstairs* 59; *During One Night, The*

Long Shadow 61; Night Must Fall, Three Lives of Thomasina, Wonderful Life 64; The Fighting Prince of Donegal 66; The Trygon Factor 67.

208 HANBURY W. Victor (1897–1954) Director; producer. B: London. 19: salesman Stoll. 28: prod. mgr. Whitehall. Dir. most of John Stafford's productions. Dir.: Where Is This Lady (co-dir.) 32; No Funny Business, Dick Turpin 33; There Goes Susie, Spring in the Air 34; Admirals All, The Crouching Beast 35; Ball at Savoy, Beloved Impostor, The Avenging Hand, Second Bureau 36; Return of a Stranger 37. Prod.: Gentleman of Venture 40; They Flew Alone, Squadron Leader X 42; Escape to Danger 43; Hotel Reserve 44; Great Day 45; Daughter of Darkness 49; Noose for a Lady, Glad Tidings, The Large Rope, Death Goes to School 53; River Beat, The Sleeping Tiger 54 (not dir. although credited).

209 HAND David (1900–   ) Cartoon director, producer. B: Plainfield N.J. 19: cartoon films Chicago, later dir. Walt Disney. 45: forms G.B.-Animation at Moor Hall Studios, Cookham. Ads. & instructionals, then two series Animaland (A), Musical Paintbox (M). Bound for the Rio Grande, The Lion (A), The Thames (M), The Cuckoo (A), The House Cat (A) 48; Wales (M), The Platypus (A), Somerset (M), The Ostrich (A), A Fantasy on Ireland (M), A Yorkshire Ditty (M), It's a Lovely Day (A), Sketches of Scotland (M), Cornwall (M), Ginger Nutt's Bee Bother (A), Canterbury Road (M), Ginger Nutt's Christmas Circus (A) 49; Devon Whey (M), A Fantasy on London Life (M), Ginger Nutt's Forest Dragon (A) 50.

210 HANLEY Jimmy (1918–   ) Actor. B: Norwich. Stage: 30. M: (42–53) Dinah SHERIDAN. Curly kid who grew into Rank's 'Boy Next Door'. Red Wagon, Those Were the Days, Little Friend 34; Royal Cavalcade, Forever England, Boys Will Be Boys 35; The Tunnel 36; Landslide, Cotton Queen, Night Ride 37; Housemaster, Coming of Age 38; Beyond Our Horizon (short), There Ain't No Justice 39; Gaslight 40; Salute John Citizen 42; The Gentle Sex 43; The Way Ahead, Kiss the Bride Goodbye 44; For You Alone, 29 Acacia Avenue, Henry V, Murder in Reverse 45; The Captive Heart 46; Holiday Camp, Master of Bankdam, It Always Rains on Sunday 47; Here Come the Huggetts, It's Hard to Be Good 48; The Huggetts Abroad, Don't Ever Leave Me, Boys in Brown, The Blue Lamp 49; Room to Let 50; The Galloping Major 51; Radio Cab Murder, The Black Rider 54; The Deep Blue Sea 55; Satellite in the Sky, Look This Way (short) 56; The Lost Continent 68.

211 HARDWICKE Sir Cedric (1893–1964) Actor. B: Stourbridge. Stage: 12. Distinguished character star; lesser work in Hollywood. Riches and Rogues (short) 13; Nelson 26. Sound: Dreyfus 31; Rome Express 32; Orders is Orders, The Ghoul 33; The Lady is Willing, Bella Donna, Nell Gwyn, Jew Suss, King of Paris 34; Peg of Old Drury 35; Things to Come, Tudor Rose, Laburnum Grove, Calling the Tune 36; King Solomon's Mines 37; Nicholas Nickleby 47; The Winslow Boy 48; Now Barabbas 49; Richard III 56; The Pumpkin Eater 64.

212 HARE Robertson (1891–   ) Actor. B: Barnesbury. Stage: 11. Small bald comic of WALLS/LYNN farces, later starred with Alfred Drayton. Rookery Nook, On Approval 30; Tons of Money, Plunder 31; A Night Like This, Thark 32; Just My Luck, It's a Boy, A Cuckoo in the Nest, Friday the 13th, Turkey Time 33; A Cup of Kindness, Are You a Mason, Dirty Work 34; Oh Daddy, Fighting Stock, Stormy

Weather, Car of Dreams, Foreign Affairs 35; Jack of All Trades, Pot Luck, You Must Get Married 36; Aren't Men Beasts 37; A Spot of Bother 38; So This Is London 39; Yesterday Is Over Your Shoulder 40; Banana Ridge 41; Women Aren't Angels 42; He Snoops to Conquer 44; Things Happen at Night 48; One Wild Oat, The Magic Box 51; Our Girl Friday 53; Three Men in a Boat, My Wife's Family 56; The Night We Got The Bird 60; The Young Ones, Out of the Shadow 61; Seven Keys, Crooks Anonymous 62; Hotel Paradiso 66.

213 HARKER Gordon (1885–1967) Actor. B: London. Stage: 03. Comical cockney cove, crook or cop. The Ring 27; The Farmer's Wife, Champagne, The Wrecker 28; Return of the Rat, The Crooked Billet, Taxi for Two 29. Sound: The Cockney Spirit in War series, Elstree Calling, The W Plan, The Squeaker, Escape 30; Third Time Lucky, The Stronger Sex, The Sport of Kings, Shadows, The Ringer, The Man They Could Not Arrest, The Calendar, The Professional Guest 31; Condemned to Death, The Frightened Lady, Whiteface, Love on Wheels, Rome Express 32; Lucky Number, Britannia of Billingsgate, This is the Life, Friday the Thirteenth 33; My Old Dutch, Road House, Dirty Work 34; The Phantom Light, The Lad, Admirals All, Squibs, Boys Will Be Boys, Hyde Park Corner 35; The Amateur Gentleman, Wolf's Clothing, Two's Company, Millions, The Story of Papworth (short) 36; Beauty and the Barge, The Frog 37; Blondes for Danger, No Parking, Lightning Conductor, Return of the Frog 38; Inspector Hornleigh, Inspector Hornleigh on Holiday 39; Saloon Bar, Channel Incident (short) 40; Inspector Hornleigh Goes to It, Once a Crook 41; Warn That Man 42; 29 Acacia Avenue 45; Things Happen at Night 48; Her Favourite Husband 50; The Second Mate 51; Derby Day 52; Bang You're Dead 54; Out of the Clouds 55; A Touch of the Sun 56; Small Hotel 57; Left Right and Centre 59.

214 HARLOW John (1896–) Director. B: Ross-on-Wye. Concert party; actor. 27: asst. dir. B.I.P. Some fair 40s thrillers. My Lucky Star, Songbirds 33; Master and Man, Bagged 34; Spellbound 41; Headline, This Was Paris 42; The Dark Tower, One Company (short) 43; Candles at Nine, Meet Sexton Blake 44; The Echo Murders, The Agitator 45; Appointment with Crime, Green Fingers 46; While I Live 47; Old Mother Riley's New Venture 49; Old Mother Riley Headmistress 50; Those People Next Door 52; The Blue Parrot 53; Dangerous Cargo, Delayed Action 54.

215 HARRIS Richard (1932–) Actor. Tough masculine star of the modern school. Also Hollywood. Alive and Kicking 58; Shake Hands with the Devil 59; A Terrible Beauty 60; The Long and the Short and the Tall, The Guns of Navarone 61; This Sporting Life 63; Heroes of Telemark 65.

216 HARRISON Rex (1908–) Actor. B: Huyton. RN: Reginald. Stage: 24. M: (1) Lilli PALMER, (2) Kay KENDALL. Charming leading gentleman with a light touch. The Great Game 30; Get Your Man, Leave It To Blanche 34; All at Sea 35; Men Are Not Gods 36; Storm in a Teacup, School for Husbands, Over the Moon 37; St. Martin's Lane, The Citadel 38; The Silent Battle 39; Ten Days in Paris, Night Train to Munich 40; Major Barbara 41; Blithe Spirit, I Live in Grosvenor Square, The Rake's Progress 45; Escape 48; The Long Dark Hall 50; King Richard and the Crusaders 54; The Constant Husband 55; The Yellow Rolls Royce 64.

217 HARTFORD - DAVIS Robert (1923–) Director (also producer).

Films: 39. Contemporary quickies: sex, pops, etc. *Dollars for Sale* (prod. & sc. only) 53; *The Man on the Cliff* (short) 55; *A Christmas Carol* (short) (also prod.) 60; *Crosstrap* 62; *That Kind of Girl* (prod. only), *Yellow Teddy Bears* (also prod.) 63; *Saturday Night Out*, *The Black Torment* (also prod.) 64; *Gonks Go Beat* (also prod.) 65; *The Sandwich Man* (also prod. & sc.), *Press for Time* (prod. only) 66; *Corruption*, *The Smashing Bird I Used to Know* 68.

218 HARTNELL Billy / William

(1908–) Actor. B: Devon. 24: stage. Light leads, tough heroes, tougher sergeants. *I'm an Explosive, Follow the Lady, The Lure* 33; *Seeing Is Believing, The Perfect Flaw* 34; *Swinging the Lead, While Parents Sleep* 35; *Nothing Like Publicity, Midnight at Madame Tussauds* 36; *Farewell Again* 37; *Murder Will Out, They Drive By Night, Flying Fortress, Sabotage at Sea, Too Dangerous to Live* 39; *They Came By Night* 40; *Suspected Person, The Peterville Diamond* 42; *The Bells Go Down, The Dark Tower, Headline* 43; *The Way Ahead* 44; *The Agitator, Murder in Reverse* 45; *Strawberry Roan, Appointment with Crime* 46; *Odd Man Out, Temptation Harbour, Brighton Rock* 47; *Escape* 48; *Now Barabbas, The Lost People* 49; *Double Confession, The Dark Man* 50; *The Magic Box* 51; *The Holly and the Ivy, The Ringer, The Pickwick Papers* 52; *Will Any Gentleman* 53; *Footsteps in the Fog* 54; *Josephine and Men, Private's Progress, Doublecross* 55; *Tons of Trouble* 56; *The Hypnotist, Hell Drivers, Yangtse Incident* 57; *On the Run, Carry On Sergeant* 58; *Shake Hands With the Devil, The Mouse That Roared, The Night We Dropped a Clanger, The Desperate Man* 59; *And the Same to You, The Jackpot, Piccadilly Third Stop* 60; *Tomorrow at Ten* 62; *This Sporting Life, Heaven's Above, The World Ten Times Over, To Have and to Hold* 63.

219 HARVEY Laurence (1927–)

Actor. B: Yonishkis. RN: Larry Skikne. Stage: 47. M: Margaret LEIGHTON. Star who worked his way to the top; also Hollywood. *House of Darkness* 48; *Man on the Run, Landfall, Man From Yesterday* 49; *Cairo Road, The Black Rose* 50; *There Is Another Sun, Scarlet Thread, I Believe In You* 51; *A Killer Walks, Women of Twilight* 52; *Innocents in Paris* 53; *The Good Die Young, Romeo and Juliet* 54; *I Am a Camera, Storm Over the Nile* 55; *Three Men in a Boat* 56; *After the Ball, The Truth About Women, The Silent Enemy* 57; *Room at the Top* 58; *Expresso Bongo* 59; *The Long and the Short and the Tall* 61; *The Running Man* 63; *Of Human Bondage* 64; *Darling, Life at the Top* 65; *The Spy With a Cold Nose* 66; *A Dandy in Aspic, The Winter's Tale* 68.

220 HAWKINS Jack, C.B.E. (1910–)

Actor. B: London. Stage: 23. Gruff, tough hero of war and peace. *Birds of Prey* 30; *The Lodger* 32; *The Good Companions, The Lost Chord, I Lived With You, The Jewel, A Shot in the Dark* 33; *Autumn Crocus, Death at Broadcasting House* 34; *Peg of Old Drury* 35; *Beauty and the Barge, The Frog* 37; *Who Goes Next, A Royal Divorce* 38; *Murder Will Out* 39; *The Flying Squad* 40; *Next of Kin* 42; *The Fallen Idol, Bonnie Prince Charlie, The Small Back Room* 48; *State Secret, The Black Rose, The Elusive Pimpernel* 50; *The Adventurers, No Highway, Home at Seven* 51; *Angels One Five, Mandy, The Planter's Wife, The Cruel Sea* 52; *Twice Upon a Time, Malta Story, The Intruder, Front Page Story* 53; *The Seekers* 54; *The Prisoner, Touch and Go* 55; *The Long Arm, Man in the Sky* 56; *Fortune is a Woman, The Bridge on the River Kwai, Battle for Britain* (short) (voice) 57; *Gideon's Day*, *The Two-headed Spy* 58; *League of Gentlemen* 59; *Lawrence of Arabia* 62; *Zulu* 63; *The Third Secret*, *Guns at Batasi*, *Masquerade* 64; *Lord Jim* 65; *Great Catherine*, *Shalako*, *Oh! What a Lovely War* 68.

221 HAY Will (1888–1949) Actor. B: Stockton-on-Tees. 09: Music Halls. Became a top box-office star with screen version of his seedy schoolmaster act for Gainsborough & Ealing. *Know Your Apples* (short) 33; *Those Were the Days*, *Radio Parade of 1935* 34; *Dandy Dick*, *Boys Will Be Boys* 35; *Where There's a Will*, *Windbag the Sailor* 36; *Good Morning Boys* 37; *Convict 99*, *Old Bones of the River* 38; *Ask a Policeman*, *Where's That Fire* 39; *The Ghost of St. Michaels*, *The Black Sheep of Whitehall* (also co-dir.) 41; *The Big Blockade*, *Go to Blazes* (short), *The Goose Steps Out* (also co-dir.) 42; *My Learned Friend* (also co-dir.) 44.

222 HAYERS Sidney (1921–) Director. B: Edinburgh. 41: films; 48: ed. *Warning to Wantons*. Some fine work among his seven pictures for Independent Artists. *Violent Moment*, *The White Trap* 59; *Circus of Horrors*, *The Malpas Mystery* 60; *Echo of Barbara*, *Payroll* 61; *Night of the Eagle* 62; *This Is My Street* 63; *Three Hats for Lisa* 65; *The Trap*, *Finders Keepers* 66.

223 HAYNES H. Manning (18 – 1957) Director. B: Lyminster. Stage: 04. Film actor: 14. W. W. Jacobs stories silent, quota quickies sound. *Monty Works the Wires* 21; *Sam's Boy*, *A Will and a Way*, *Head of the Family*, *The Skipper's Wooing* 22; *The Monkey's Paw*, *The Constable's Move* (short), *The Odd Freak* (short), *The Convert* (short) 23; *Lawyer Quince* (short), *Dixon's Return* (short), *The Boatswain's Mate* (short) 24; *London Love* 26; *Passion*

Island 27; *The Ware Case* 28; *Those Who Love* 29; sound: *Should a Doctor Tell* 30; *To Oblige a Lady*, *The Old Man*, *The Officer's Mess* 31; *Love's Old Sweet Song* 33; *The Perfect Flaw* 34; *Smith's Wives* 35; *Highland Fling*, *Tomorrow We Live* 36; *East of Ludgate Hill*, *Pearls Bring Tears* 37; *The Claydon Treasure Mystery*, *Coming of Age* 38; *The Man at the Gate* (sc. only) 41.

224 HEARNE Richard (1908–) Actor. Boy clown in father's acrobatic act; musical comedy. Slapstick star, usually as 'Mr. Pastry'. *Give Her a Ring* 34; *Dance Band*, *No Monkey Business* 35; *Millions* 36; *Splinters in the Air* 37; *Miss London Ltd.*, *The Butler's Dilemma* 43; *One Night With You*, *Woman Hater* 48; *Helter Skelter* 49; *Something in the City*, *Mr. Pastry Does the Laundry* (short) 50; *Captain Horatio Hornblower R.N.*, *Madame Louise* 51; *What a Husband* (short) 52; *The Time of his Life* 55; *Tons of Trouble* 56.

225 HENDRY Ian (1931–) Actor. B: Ipswich. Stage, TV. Virile star of the neo-naturalism school. M: Janet MUNRO. *In the Nick* 60; *Live Now Pay Later* 62; *Girl in the Headlines*, *Children of the Damned*, *This Is My Street* 63; *The Beauty Jungle* 64; *Repulsion*, *The Hill* 65; *The Sandwich Man*, *Casino Royale* 66.

226 HENSON Leslie (1891–1958) B: London. Stage: 10. Fish-eyed, gravel-voiced comic in filmed farces. *Wanted a Widow* (short), *The Real Thing at Last* (short), *The Lifeguardsman* 16; *Broken Bottles* (short), *Alf's Button* 20; *Tons of Money* 24; *On With the Dance* (short) 27. Sound: *A Warm Corner* 30; *The Sport of Kings* 31; *It's a Boy*, *The Girl from Maxims* 33; *Oh Daddy* 35; *The Demi-Paradise* 43; *Home and Away* 56.

227 HEPWORTH Cecil M. (1874– 1953) Director, producer. B: London.

Father: T. C. Hepworth magic lanternist. 95: patented hand feed arc lamp for lantern, sold to R. W. PAUL. 96: assisted Birt ACRES at Royal film show. Toured own show. 97: wrote book *Animated Photography*. Improved American Bioscope apparatus and thus joined Charles Urban's Warwick Trading Co. 98: ph.: Boat Race, etc. 99: set up film printing lab at Walton on Thames, then as Hepwix Films in backyard studio. Dir. and acted at first; 04: supervised 100s of films until returning to dir. in 14. Major prod. of typically British features 15–23 when his co. collapsed. Small film printing business, later joined N.S.S. making trailers. 40: *Food Facts* series. Main shorts: *The Quarrelsome Anglers, Two Fools in a Canoe* 98; *The Stolen Drink, Two Cockneys in a Canoe* 99; *Wiping Something off the Slate, The Conjurer and the Boer, The Explosion of a Motor Car, How It Feels to Be Run Over* 00; *How the Burglar Tricked the Bobby, The Glutton's Nightmare* 01; *The Call to Arms, That Eternal Ping Pong, Peace With Honour* 02; *Alice in Wonderland, The Unclean World, Firemen to the Rescue* 03; *Blind Fate, Unfit, The Hills Are Calling, His Country's Bidding, The Quarry Mystery* 14; *The Refugee, Tares, Broken in the Wars* 18. Features: *The Basilisk, Time the Great Healer, The Deadly Drug, The Canker of Jealousy, Courtmartialled, The Bottle, The Man Who Stayed at Home, The Outrage, Sweet Lavender, Iris, The Baby on the Barge* 15; *Trelawney of the Wells, Annie Laurie, Sowing the Wind, Comin' Thro' the Rye, The Marriage of William Ashe, Molly Bawn, The Cobweb* 16; *The American Heiress, Nearer My God to Thee* 17; *The Blindness of Fortune, The Touch of a Child, Boundary House* 18; *The Nature of the Beast, Sunken Rocks, Sheba, The Forest on the Hill* 19; *Anna the Adventuress, Alf's Button, Helen of Four Gates, Mrs. Erricker's Reputation* 20;

Tinted Venus, Narrow Valley, Wild Heather, Tansy 21; *The Pipes of Pan, Mist in the Valley, Strangling Threads, Comin' Thro' the Rye* 22; *The House of Marney* 27.

228 HEYWOOD Anne (1932–   ) Actress. B: Handsworth. RN: Violet Pretty. Beauty queen. M: Raymond Stross. Also acted abroad (Czechoslovakia, Canada etc.). *Find the Lady, Checkpoint, Doctor at Large* 56; *Dangerous Exile, The Depraved* 57; *Violent Playground, Floods of Fear* 58; *Heart of a Man, Upstairs and Downstairs* 59; *A Terrible Beauty* 60; *Petticoat Pirates* 61; *Stork Talk, Vengeance* 62; *The Very Edge* 63.

229 HICKS Sir Seymour (1871–1949) Actor, also writer. B: St. Helier. Stage: 87. M: Ellaline Terriss. Farceur who turned into fine character star. Acted: *Seymour Hicks and Ellaline Terriss* (short), *David Garrick, Scrooge* (also sc.) 13; *Always Tell Your Wife* (short) (also sc.) 14; *A Prehistoric Love Story* (short) (also sc.) 15; *Always Tell Your Wife* (short) (also sc.) 23; sound: *Telltales* (short) (also sc.), *Sleeping Partners* (also sc. & dir.) 30; *The Love Habit* (also sc.), *Glamour* (also sc. & co-dir.) 31; *Money for Nothing* (also sc.) 32; *Secret of the Loch* 34; *Royal Cavalcade, Mr. What's-his-name* (also sc.), *Vintage Wine* (also sc.), *Scrooge* (also sc.) 35; *Eliza Comes to Stay, It's You I Want* 36; *Change for a Sovereign* (also sc.) 37; *The Lambeth Walk, Young Man's Fancy* 39; *Pastor Hall, Busman's Honeymoon* 40; *Fame is the Spur* 47; *Silent Dust* 48.

230 HILL James, D.F.C. (1919–   ) Director. 37: asst. G.P.O. Film Unit. 39: ph. R.A.F. Film Unit. Stylish comedies and thrillers. Shorts: *Science Joins an Industry* 46; *Journey for Jeremy, Friend of the Family* 49; *Britain's Comet* 52; *Cold Comfort* 57; *Giuseppina* 60; *David and Golightly* 61; *The Home-made Car* 64; *The*

Specialist 66. Features: *The Stolen Plans* 52; *The Clue of the Missing Ape* 53; *Peril for the Guy* 56; *Mystery in the Mine* 59; *The Kitchen* 61; *The Dock Brief, Lunch Hour* 62; *Every Day's a Holiday* 64; *A Study in Terror, Born Free* 65.

231 HILL Sinclair, O.B.E. (1894–1945) Director (also writer). B: Surbiton. 12: office boy Tyler Films. 13: Savoia Films, Turin. Directed many medium-class silents for Stoll and talkies. Scriptwriting: *At the Villa Rose, The Hundreth Chance, A Question of Trust, The Tavern Knight* 20. Directed: *The Tidal Wave* 20; *One Week to Live* (short), *Place of Honour, The Mystery of Mr. Bernard Brown* 21; *Open Country, Truants, The Experiment, Half a Truth, The Lonely Lady of Grosvenor Square, Expiation, The Nonentity, Petticoat Loose* 22; *The Indian Love Lyrics, One Arabian Night* 23; *The Conspirators, White Slippers, The Acid Test* (short), *The Drum* (short), *The Honourable Member for Outside Left* (short), *The Prehistoric Man* (sc. only) 24; *The Presumption of Stanley Hay M.P., The Squire of Long Hadley, The Qualified Adventurer, The Secret Kingdom* 25; *Sahara Love, The Chinese Bungalow* 26; *A Woman Redeemed, The King's Highway* 27; *The Guns of Loos, The Price of Divorce, Boadicea* 28. Sound: *Mr. Smith Wakes Up* (short), *Peace and Quiet* (short), *The Unwritten Law, Dark Red Roses* 29; *Such is the Law, Greek Street* 30; *A Gentleman of Paris, Other People's Sins, The Great Gay Road* 31; *The First Mrs. Fraser, The Man From Toronto* 32; *Britannia of Billingsgate* 33; *My Old Dutch* 34; *Hyde Park Corner* 35; *The Cardinal, The Gay Adventure* 36; *Take a Chance, Command Performance, Midnight Menace* 37; *Follow Your Star* 38.

232 HILLER Wendy (1912–   ) Actress. B: Bramhall. Stage: 22. M: Ronald Gow. Few films but each one good. Also

Hollywood. *Lancashire Luck* 37; *Pygmalion* 38; *Major Barbara* 41; *I Know Where I'm Going* 45; *An Outcast of the Islands* 51; *Singlehanded* 53; *How to Murder a Rich Uncle* 57; *Sons and Lovers* 60; *A Man For All Seasons* 66.

233 HISCOTT Leslie (1894–1968) Director. B: London. 19: Italian films; 29: asst. dir. Famous Players-Lasky British. The man who put the quickie into quotas, mostly comedies for Julius Hagen and British Lion. Also novelist. *Mrs. May* series 25; *This Marriage Business* 27; *The Passing of Mr. Quin, S.O.S.* 28; *Ringing the Changes, The Feather* 29. Sound: *At the Villa Rose, The House of the Arrow, The Call of the Sea* 30; *The Sleeping Cardinal, Brown Sugar, Alibi, Black Coffee, A Night in Montmartre* 31; *The Missing Rembrandt, Murder at Covent Garden, Once Bitten, The Crooked Lady, Double Dealing, A Safe Proposition, When London Sleeps, A Tight Corner, The Face at the Window* 32; *The Iron Stair, The Stolen Necklace, Out of the Past, The Melody Maker, Yes Madam, That's My Wife, Cleaning Up, Stickpin, I'll Stick to You, Great Stuff, Strike It Rich, Marooned* 33; *Flat No. 3, The Man I Want, Keep It Quiet, Passing Shadows, Gay Love, Crazy People, The Big Splash* 34; *The Triumph of Sherlock Holmes, Annie Leave the Room, Death on the Set, Three Witnesses, Inside the Room, Department Store, A Fire Has Been Arranged, She Shall Have Music* 35; *Fame, Millions, The Interrupted Honeymoon* 36; *Fine Feathers, Ship's Concert* 37; *Take Cover* (short) 38; *Tilly of Bloomsbury* 40; *The Seventh Survivor* 41; *Sabotage at Sea, The Lady from Lisbon* 42; *The Butler's Dilemma* 43; *Welcome Mr. Washington* 44; *The Time of his Life* 55; *Tons of Trouble* 56.

234 HITCHCOCK Alfred (1899–   ) Director, also writer. B: London. 29:

title design Famous Players-Lasky British; asst. dir. to Graham CUTTS. Dir. first two features in Germany for Michael Balcon. Swiftly became household name, especially with thrillers. Hollywood from 40. M: his asst. and writer, Alma Reville. Scriptwriting: *Woman to Woman* 23; *The White Shadow, The Prude's Fall, The Passionate Adventure* 24; *The Blackguard* 25. Directed: *Always Tell Your Wife* (short) (co-dir.) 23; *The Pleasure Garden, The Mountain Eagle, The Lodger* 26; *Downhill, Easy Virtue* 27; *The Ring, The Farmer's Wife, Champagne* 28; *The Manxman* 29. Sound: *Blackmail* 29; *Juno and the Paycock, Elstree Calling* (co-dir.), *Murder, An Elastic Affair* (short) 30; *The Skin Game* 31; *Rich and Strange, Number Seventeen* 32; *Waltzes from Vienna* 33; *The Man Who Knew Too Much* 34; *The 39 Steps* 35; *Secret Agent, Sabotage* 36; *Young and Innocent* 37; *The Lady Vanishes* 38; *Jamaica Inn* 39; *Bon Voyage* (short), *Aventure Malgache* (short) 44; *Under Capricorn* 49; *Stage Fright* 50.

235 HOBBS Jack (1893–   ) Actor. B: London. Stage: 06. Light leading man for more than two decades. *Love's Legacy* 15; *Tom Brown's Schooldays* 16; *The Lady Clare* 19; *The Face at the Window, Inheritance, The Shuttle of Life, The Call of Youth* 20; *The Skin Game* 21; *The Lonely Lady of Grosvenor Square, The Naval Treaty* (short), *The Crimson Circle* 22; *The Crooked Man* (short) 23; *The Eleventh Commandment* 24; *The Happy Ending* 25. Sound: *Never Trouble Trouble, Love Lies, Dr. Josser K.C., Mischief, The Love Race* 31; *Josser Joins the Navy, The Last Coupon, His Wife's Mother, Josser in the Army* 32; *Double Wedding, Too Many Wives, Beware of Women* 33; *Trouble in Store, Oh No Doctor* 34; *Handle with Care, Car of Dreams, No Limit* 35; *The Interrupted Honeymoon, Millions, All That Glitters* 36;

When the Devil Was Well, The Show Goes On, Fine Feathers, Why Pick On Me, Leave It to Me, Intimate Relations 37; *It's In the Air* 38; *Miracles Do Happen* 39.

236 HOBSON Valerie (1917–   ) Actress. B: Larne. Stage: 32. Ladylike leading lady, also Hollywood. M: producer Anthony Havelock-Allan (39–52). *Eyes of Fate* 33; *Path of Glory, Two Hearts in Waltztime, Badger's Green* 34; *Oh What a Night* 35; *Secret of Stamboul, No Escape* 36; *Jump for Glory* 37; *The Drum, This Man is News* 38; *Q Planes, The Spy in Black, The Silent Battle, This Man in Paris* 39; *Contraband* 40; *Atlantic Ferry* 41; *Unpublished Story* 42; *Adventures of Tartu* 43; *The Years Between, Great Expectations* 46; *Blanche Fury* 47; *The Small Voice* 48; *Kind Hearts and Coronets, Train of Events, The Interrupted Journey, The Rocking Horse Winner* 49; *The Card* 51; *Who Goes There, Meet Me Tonight, The Voice of Merrill* 52; *Background* 53; *Knave of Hearts* 54.

237 HOLLOWAY Stanley, O.B.E. (1890–   ) B: London. Stage: 19, singer. From comedian to rich, human characters. Also Hollywood. *The Rotters* 21. Sound: *The Co-optimists* 30; *Sleeping Car, The Girl from Maxim's* 33; *Lily of Killarney, Love at Second Sight, Sing as We Go, Road House* 34; *D'Ye Ken John Peel, In Town Tonight, Squibs, Play Up the Band* 35; *Song of the Forge, The Vicar of Bray, Cotton Queen, Sam Small Leaves Town, Our Island Nation* 37; *Co-operette* (short) 39; *Major Barbara* 41; *Salute John Citizen* 42; *The Way Ahead, This Happy Breed, Champagne Charlie* 44; *The Way to the Stars, Brief Encounter* 45; *Wanted for Murder, Caesar and Cleopatra, Carnival, Meet Me at Dawn* 46; *Nicholas Nickleby* 47; *Saraband for Dead Lovers, One Night With You, Noose, The Winslow Boy, Another Shore* 48; *Passport to Pimlico, The Perfect*

Woman, Hamlet 49; Midnight Episode, One Wild Oat 50; The Lavender Hill Mob, The Magic Box, Lady Godiva Rides Again, Sailor's Consolation (short) (voice) 51; The Happy Family, Meet Me Tonight, The Titfield Thunderbolt 52; The Beggar's Opera, A Day to Remember, Meet Mr. Lucifer, Fast and Loose 53; An Alligator Named Daisy, Jumping for Joy 55; Alive and Kicking 58; No Trees in the Street, Hello London 59; No Love for Johnny, On the Fiddle 61; Ten Little Indians 65; The Sandwich Man 66; Mrs. Brown You've Got A Lovely Daughter 68.

238 HOLT Seth (1923–   ) Director. B: Palestine. 42: asst. ed. Strand Films. 51: ed. Lavender Hill Mob. 55: assoc. prod. Touch and Go. Makes sharp little thrillers. Nowhere to Go 58; Jessy (doc.) (sc. only) 59; Taste of Fear 61; Station Six Sahara 62; The Nanny 65; Danger Route 67; Monsieur Lecoq 68.

239 HOPPER Victoria (1909–   ) Actress. B: Vancouver. Brief reign as a screen queen, when she wed her prod. Basil DEAN. The Constant Nymph 33; Lorna Doone 34; Whom the Gods Love, Laburnum Grove, The Lonely Road 36; The Mill on the Floss 37; Escape From Broadmoor 48.

240 HOPSON Violet Actress. B: San Francisco. HEPWORTH's 'Dear Delightful Villainess', subsequently heroine in Broadwest sporting dramas usually opposite Stewart ROME. M: (1) co-star Alec Worcester (2) director Walter WEST. Main shorts: The Umbrella They Could Not Lose, Love in a Laundry 12; The Jewel Thieves Outwitted, Drake's Love Story 13; The Girl Who Played The Game, Stress of Circumstances, Unfit, The Quarry Mystery, Time the Great Healer, The Man From India, Life's Dark Road, The Shepherd of Souls 14. Features: The Vicar of Wakefield 13; The Heart of Midlothian, The Tragedy of Basil Grieve, The Cry of the Captive, The Terror of the Air, The Schemers, The Chimes 14; The Canker of Jealousy, Barnaby Rudge, The Curtain's Secret, The Baby on the Barge, The Second String, The Man Who Stayed At Home, The White Hope, The Outrage, The Nightbirds of London, The Recalling of John Grey, Trelawney of the Wells 15; A Bunch of Violets, The White Boys, Sowing the Wind, The Marriage of William Ashe, Grand Babylon Hotel, Exploits of Tubby series, Comin' Thro' The Rye, The House of Fortescue, Molly Bawn 16; Her Marriage Lines, The Cobweb, The American Heiress, The Blindness of Fortune, The Eternal Triangle, The Ware Case, The House Opposite, A Munition Girl's Romance, A Gamble For Love, The Ragged Messenger, The Adventures of Dick Dolan 17; Missing the Tide, The Snare, A Fortune at Stake, A Turf Conspiracy, The Woman Wins, Sisters in Arms (short) 18; A Soul's Crucifixion, The Irresistible Flapper, In The Gloaming, A Daughter of Eve, The Gentleman Rider (also prod.), Snow in the Desert 19; Her Son, The Romance of a Movie Star, The Case of Lady Camber, Kissing Cup's Race (also prod.) 20; A Sportsman's Wife, Vi of Smith's Alley, The Imperfect Lover 21; Scarlet Lady (also prod.), When Greek Meets Greek, Son of Kissing Cup, The White Hope 22; The Lady Owner, Beautiful Kitty, What Price Loving Cup 23; The Great Turf Mystery, The Stirrup Cup Sensation 24; Daughter of Love 25; Beating the Book (short) 26; Remembrance 27; Widecombe Fair 28; sound: His Apologies (short) 35.

241 HOUSTON Donald (1924–   ) Actor. B: Tonypandy. Stage: 42. Heavily handsome Welsh star. The Blue Lagoon 48; A Run for Your Money 49; Dance Hall 50; My Death Is a Mockery, Crow Hollow

52; *The Red Beret, Small Town Story, The Large Rope, Point of No Return* (short) 53; *Doctor in the House, The Devil's Pass, The Happiness of Three Women* 54; *The Flaw, Doublecross* 55; *Find the Lady* 56; *Yangtse Incident, The Surgeon's Knife, Every Valley* (short) (voice) 57; *A Question of Adultery, The Man Upstairs, Danger Within, Room at the Top* 58; *Jessy* (doc.) 59; *The Mark* 61; *Twice Round the Daffodils, The Prince and the Pauper, Maniac* 62; *Doctor in Distress, Carry On Jack* 63; *A Study in Terror* 65; *The Viking Queen* 66.

242 HOWARD Joyce (1922–)
Actress. B: London. M: Basil Sydney. Blonde wartime star. *Freedom Radio* 40; *Love on the Dole, The Common Touch, Back Room Boy* 41; *The Night Has Eyes, Talk About Jacqueline* 42; *The Gentle Sex, They Met in the Dark* 43; *They Knew Mr. Knight* 45; *Appointment With Crime, Woman to Woman* 46; *Mrs. Fitzherbert* 47; *Shadow of the Past* 50.

243 HOWARD Leslie (1893–1943)
Actor. B: London. RN: Stainer. Uncle: Wilfred NOY; son: Ronald HOWARD Clerk; stage: 17. Romantic Hollywood star, returned home during the war to produce & direct. *The Happy Warrior* 17; *The Lackey and the Lady* 19; *£5 Reward* (short), *Bookworms* (short) 20. Sound: *Service for Ladies* 32; *The Lady is Willing* 34; *The Scarlet Pimpernel* 35; *Pygmalion* (also co-dir.) 38; *Pimpernel Smith* (also prod. & dir.), *49th Parallel, From the Four Corners* (short) 41; *The First of the Few* (also dir.) 42; *The Gentle Sex* (co-dir. only) 43.

244 HOWARD Ronald (1918–)
Actor. B: Anerley. Father: Leslie HOWARD. Journalist, sailor. Followed in his father's film footsteps. *Pimpernel Smith* 41; *While the Sun Shines* 46; *My Brother Jonathan* 47; *Night Beat, Bond Street, Queen of Spades* 48; *Now Barabbas* 49; *Double Confession, Portrait of Clare, Flesh and Blood, The Browning Version* 50; *Assassin for Hire, Night Was Our Friend* 51; *Wide Boy, Street Corner, Black Orchid* 52; *Noose for a Lady, Glad Tidings, Flannelfoot* 53; *The World's a Stage* series (voice) 54; *Hideout* 56; *Gideon's Day, The House in the Woods* 57; *Moment of Indiscretion, I Accuse, No Trees in the Street* 58; *Man Accused* 59; *The Spider's Web, The Malpas Mystery, Compelled* 60; *The Monster of Highgate Ponds, The Naked Edge, Murder She Said, Bomb in the High Street* 61; *The Spanish Sword, Fate Takes a Hand, Kill, Live Now Pay Later* 62; *Nurse on Wheels, The Bay of Saint Michel, The Siege of the Saxons* 63; *The Curse of the Mummy's Tomb* 64; *Africa Texas Style* 67.

245 HOWARD Sydney (1884–1946)
Actor. B: Yeadon. 12: concert party, pierrot, revue. Unique comic with stately style and strange gestures. *Splinters* 29; *French Leave* 30; *Tilly of Bloomsbury, Almost a Divorce, Up for the Cup, Splinters in the Navy* 31; *The Mayor's Nest, It's a King* 32; *Up for the Derby, Night of the Garter, Trouble* 33; *It's a Cop* 34; *Where's George* 35; *Fame, Chick* 36; *Splinters in the Air, What a Man* 37; *Shipyard Sally* 39; *Tilly of Bloomsbury* 40; *Once a Crook, Mr. Proudfoot Shows a Light* (short) 41; *When We Are Married* 43; *Flight From Folly* 45.

246 HOWARD Trevor (1916–)
Actor. B: Cliftonville. Stage: 33. M: Helen Cherry. Romantic gentleman to hardbitten hero. Also Hollywood. *The Way Ahead* 44; *The Way to the Stars, Brief Encounter* 45; *I See a Dark Stranger, Green for Danger* 46; *They Made Me a Fugitive, So Well Remembered* 47; *The Passionate Friends* 48; *The Third Man, The Golden*

Salamander 49; Odette, The Clouded Yellow 50; Outcast of the Islands 51; The Gift Horse 52; The Heart of the Matter 53; The Stranger's Hand 54; Cockleshell Heroes, April in Portugal (short) (voice) 55; Interpol, Manuela 57; The Key 58; Moment of Danger 59; Sons and Lovers 60; The Lion 62; Man in the Middle 63; Operation Crossbow, The Liquidator 65; Triple Cross 66; The Long Duel, Pretty Polly 67; The Charge of the Light Brigade 68.

247 HOWES Bobby (1895–)
Actor. B: Chelsea. 09: acrobat, singer. Daughter: Sally Ann HOWES. Bright and bouncy star of 30s musicals. On With the Dance (short) 27; Guns of Loos 28. Sound: Third Time Lucky 31; Lord Babs, For the Love of Mike 32; Over the Garden Wall 34; Please Teacher 37; Sweet Devil, Yes Madam 38; The Trojan Brothers 45; Happy Go Lovely 51; The Good Companions 57; Watch It Sailor! 61.

248 HOWES Sally Ann (1930–)
Actress. B: London. Father: Bobby HOWES. Her best work as a child star. Thursday's Child 43; Halfway House 44; Dead of Night, Pink String and Sealing Wax 45; Nicholas Nickleby 47; My Sister and I, Anna Karenina, The History of Mr. Polly 48; Fools Rush In 49; Stop Press Girl 50; Honeymoon Deferred 51; The Admirable Crichton 57; Chitty Chitty Bang Bang 68.

249 HUGHES Harry Director, also writer. B: Leyton. 07: Pathe salesman; publicist; ed. Brisk comedies. Shadow of Evil (sc. only) 21; A Rogue in Love (sc. only) 22; Unnatural Life Studies (short), Adam's Film Review (short) 24; House of Marney (sc.) 26; A Daughter in Revolt 27; Hellcat, Virginia's Husband, Troublesome Wives 28; Little Miss London 29; sound: A Wet Night (short) 26; We Take Off Our Hats (short), Star Impersonations (short) 30; Glamour (co-dir.), The Man at Six 31; Bachelor's Baby, His Wife's Mother 32; Their Night Out, Facing the Music, A Southern Maid 33; Song at Eventide, The Broken Rosary, Womanhood 34; Barnacle Bill, Joy Ride, Play Up The Band 35; The Improper Duchess, Tropical Trouble 36; The Last Chance (sc. only) 37; The Gables Mystery, The Mountains o' Mourne 38; Dead Men Are Dangerous (sc. only) 39; In the Drink (short) 43; Stage Frights 47; The Voyage of Peter Joe 48.

250 HUGHES Ken (1922–)
Director. B: Liverpool. 36: Won amateur film contest. 37: projectionist. 44: music arranger docs. Radio/TV playright, novelist. Crime films, short, medium, major, plus one (The Trials of Oscar Wilde) for posterity. Shorts: The Burning Question 45; Beach Recovery, Those Nuisances 46; The Drayton Case, The Missing Man, Candlelight Murder 53; The Blazing Caravan, The Dark Stairway, The Strange Case of Blondie, The Silent Witness, Passenger to Tokio 54; Night Plane to Amsterdam, Murder Anonymous 55. Features: Wide Boy 52; The Brain Machine, Little Red Monkey, Confession, Timeslip, Black Thirteen 53; The House Across the Lake 54; Joe Macbeth 55; Wicked as They Come 56; The Long Haul 57; Jazzboat, In the Nick, The Trials of Oscar Wilde 60; The Small World of Sammy Lee 63; Of Human Bondage 64; Drop Dead Darling 66; Casino Royale (co-dir.) 67; Chitty Chitty Bang Bang 68.

251 HULBERT Claude (1900–1963)
Actor. B: London. Stage: 20. Brother: Jack HULBERT. Star of the Silly Ass school of comedy. Champagne 28; Naughty Husbands 30. Sound: A Night Like This, The Mayor's Nest, Thark, The Face at the Window 32; Let Me Explain Dear, Their

Night Out, Radio Parade, Heads We Go, The Song You Gave Me 33; The Girl in Possession, A Cup of Kindness, Lilies of the Field, Big Business 34; Bulldog Jack, Hello Sweetheart, Man of the Moment 35; Wolf's Clothing, Where's Sally, The Interrupted Honeymoon, Hail and Farewell, Honeymoon Merry-go-round 36; Take a Chance, The Vulture, It's Not Cricket, Ship's Concert, You Live and Learn 37; Simply Terrific, The Viper, It's in the Blood, His Lordship Regrets, Many Tanks Mr. Atkins 38; Sailors Three 40; The Ghost of St. Michaels 41; The Dummy Talks 43; My Learned Friend 44; London Town 46; Ghosts of Berkeley Square 47; Under the Frozen Falls 48; Cardboard Cavalier 49; Fun at St. Fanny's 56; Not a Hope in Hell 60.

252 HULBERT Jack (1892–) Actor. B: Ely. Stage: 11. Brother: Claude HULBERT; M: Cicely COURTNEIDGE. Long chin, big smile; polished comedy actor. Elstree Calling 30; The Ghost Train, Sunshine Susie 31; Jack's the Boy, Love on Wheels, Happy Ever After 32; Falling for You 33; Jack Ahoy, The Camels are Coming 34; Bulldog Jack 35; Jack of All Trades 36; Take My Tip, Paradise for Two 37; Kate Plus Ten 38; Under Your Hat 40; Into the Blue, The Magic Box 51; The Spider's Web 60.

253 HUME Benita (1906–1967) Actress. B: London. Stage: 23. Polite attractive star; to Hollywood. The Happy Ending, Her Golden Hair Was Hanging Down Her Back (short), They Wouldn't Believe Me (short) 25; Second to None 26; Easy Virtue 27; The Constant Nymph, The South Sea Bubble, The Wrecker, A Light Woman, The Lady of the Lake, Balaclava 28; The Clue of the New Pin 29. Sound: High Treason 29; The House of the Arrow, Symphony in Two Flats 30; The Flying Fool, A Honeymoon Adventure, The Happy Ending 31; Service for Ladies, Women Who Play, Help Yourself, Men of Steel, Diamond Cut Diamond, Sally Bishop, Lord Camber's Ladies 32; Discord, The Little Damozel 33; The Private Life of Don Juan, Jew Suss 34; The Divine Spark, 18 Minutes 35.

254 HUNTER Ian (1900–) Actor. B: Cape Town. Stage: 19. Staunch star, dependably 'dependable'. Also Hollywood. Not for Sale 24; Confessions, A Girl of London 25; Downhill, Easy Virtue, The Ring 27; His House in Order, The Physician, Throughbred, Valley of the Ghosts 28. Sound: Escape 30; Cape Forlorn, Sally in our Alley 31; The Water Gipsies, The Sign of Four, Marry Me 32; The Man From Toronto, Orders is Orders, Skipper of the Osprey (short) 33; Silver Spoon, Night of the Party, The Church Mouse, No Escape, Death at Broadcasting House 34; The Phantom Light, Lazybones, The Morals of Marcus 35; Bedelia 46; White Cradle Inn, The White Unicorn 47; Edward My Son 48; Hunted 51; It Started in Paradise, Appointment in London 52; Don't Blame the Stork, Eight O'Clock Walk 53; The Battle of the River Plate, Fortune is a Woman, Door in the Wall (short) 56; Rockets Galore 58; North West Frontier 59; The Bulldog Breed 60; Dr. Blood's Coffin, The Queen's Guards 61; Guns of Darkness 62.

255 HUNTER T. Hayes (18 –1944) Director. B: Philadelphia. Stage: 14: U.S. films. Lively thrillers. One of the Best 27; A South Sea Bubble, The Triumph of the Scarlet Pimpernel 28; The Silver King 29; sound: The Man They Couldn't Arrest, The Calendar 31; The Frightened Lady, Whiteface, Sally Bishop 32; The Ghoul 33; Warn London, The Green Pack, Josser on the Farm 34.

256 HUNTINGTON Lawrence (1900–) Director (also writer). B:

63

London. Mainly thrillers; at his peak in the late 40s. *After Many Years* 29; sound: *Romance in Rhythm* 34; *Strange Cargo, Full Speed Ahead, Café Mascot, Two on a Doorstep, Bad Boy* (also sc.) 36; *Screentruck, Passage to London, The Bank Messenger Mystery* 37; *Dial 999, Twin Faces* 38; *I Killed the Count* (sc. only) 39; *Flickers* 40; *This Man Is Dangerous, Tower of Terror* 41; *Suspected Person* (also sc.), *Women Aren't Angels* 42; *Warn That Man* 43; *Night Boat to Dublin, Wanted For Murder* 46; *When the Bough Breaks, The Upturned Glass* 47; *Mr. Perrin and Mr. Traill* 48; *Man on the Run* (also sc.) 49; *The Franchise Affair* (also sc.) 51; *There Was a Young Lady* (also sc.), *Deadly Nightshade* (sc. only) 53; *Contraband Spain* (also sc.), *Impulse* (sc. only) 55; *Deadly Record* 59; *A Question of Suspense* (sc. only), *The Trunk* (prod. only) 61; *Stranglehold* (also sc.), *The Fur Collar* (also sc.) 62; *Death Drums Along the River* 64; *The Vulture* 66.

257 HURST Brian Desmond (1902–) Director. B: Castle Reagh. Art student. 25: asst. John Ford, U.S.A. Varied output, in subject and quality. *The Tell Tale Heart, Irish Hearts* 34; *Riders to the Sea* 35; *Ourselves Alone* (co-dir.), *The Tenth Man* 36; *Sensation, Glamorous Night* 37; *Prison Without Bars* 38; *The Lion Has Wings* (co-dir.), *On the Night of the Fire* 39; *A Call for Arms* short), *Miss Grant Goes to the Door* (short) 40; *Dangerous Moonlight* 41; *Alibi* 42; *Men of Arnhem* (doc.) (co-dir.), *Caesar and Cleopatra* (co-dir.) 44; *The Hundred Pound Window* 43; *Hungry Hill* 46; *Mark of Cain* 48; *Trottie True* 49; *Tom Brown's Schooldays* (prod. only) 50; *Scrooge* 51; *Malta Story* 53; *Simba* 55; *The Black Tent* 56; *Dangerous Exile* 57; *Behind the Mask* 58; *His and Hers* 61; *Playboy of the Western World* 62.

258 HUTH Harold (1892–1967) Actor, director, producer. B: Huddersfield. Car salesman. From bits to suave continental crooks and romantics. Acted: *One of the Best* 27; *A South Sea Bubble, Sir or Madam, The Triumph of the Scarlet Pimpernel, Balaclava* 28; *City of Play, The Silver King, Downstream* 29; sound: *Hours of Loneliness, Leave it to Me* 30; *Guilt, Bracelets, The Outsider, Down River, Honeymoon Adventure, Madame Guillotine* (sc. only) 31; *Women Who Play, The First Mrs. Fraser, Flying Squad, Sally Bishop, The World the Flesh and the Devil, Rome Express* 32; *Discord, My Lucky Star, The Ghoul* 33; *The Camels are Coming* 34; *Take My Tip* 37; *This Was Paris* 42; *Blackmailed* 51. Directed: *Hell's Cargo* 39; *Bulldog Sees It Through* 40; *East of Piccadilly* 41; *Breach of Promise* 42; *Night Beat* (also prod.) 47; *My Sister and I* (also prod.), *Look Before You Love* (also prod.) 48; *The Hostage* 56. Produced: *Busman's Honeymoon* 40; *Love Story, Adventures of Tartu* 44; *They Were Sisters* 45; *The Root of all Evil, Caravan* 46; *The White Unicorn* 48; *Blackmailed, One Wild Oat, Sing Along With Me* 51; *Police Dog* 55; *Idle on Parade, Bandit of Zhobe* 59; *The Trials of Oscar Wilde, In the Nick* 60; *The Hellions* (also sc.) 61.

259 HYLAND Peggy Actress. B: Harbourne. RN: Gladys Hutchinson. Pretty blonde star, mainly in Hollywood. *In the Ranks* 14; *John Halifax Gentleman, Lochinvar, Angels of Mons* (short), *Infelice, Caste, Fetters of Fear* (short), *Twixt Cup and Lip* (short) 15; *Sally Bishop, Sir James Mortimer's Wager* (short), *A Pair of Spectacles* 16; *At the Mercy of Tiberius, The Honeypot* 20; *Love Maggy, Mr. Pim Passes By, With Father's Help* (short) (also prod., dir. & sc.), *Shifting Sands* 21; *Forbidden Cargoes* 25.

Top: Gordon Harker, Richard Harris, Rex Harrison
Centre: Laurence Harvey, Jack Hawkins, Will Hay, Richard Hearne
Bottom: Ian Hendry, Cecil Hepworth, Anne Heywood, Stanley Holloway

Top: Violet Hopson, Donald Houston, Sydney Howard
Centre: Trevor Howard, Ian Hunter, Isabel Jeans
Bottom: Glynis Johns, Richard Johnson, Kay Kendall

I

260 INCE Ralph (1887–) Director. B: Boston. 06: film actor, director from 12. Lively quota pictures for Warners. *No Escape, A Glimpse of Paradise, What's In a Name* 34; *Murder at Monte Carlo, Mr. What's His Name, Crime Unlimited, Black Mask, Blue Smoke, Rolling Home* 35; *Jury's Evidence, It's You I Want, Jail Break, Twelve Good Men, Fair Exchange, Hail and Farewell* 36; *The Vulture, Side Street Angel, It's Not Cricket, The Perfect Crime, The Man Who Made Diamonds* 37.

J

261 JACKSON Pat (1916–) Director. B: London. 34: G.P.O. Film Unit. His doc. grounding shows surprisingly little in his fiction features. Also Hollywood. Shorts & docs.: *Book Bargain* 35; *Big Money* (co-dir.) 36; *Men in Danger, Happy in the Morning* 38; *The First Days* (co-dir.) 39; *Health in War* 40; *Ferry Pilot* 41; *Builders* 42; *Western Approaches* 44. Features: *Encore* (co-dir.), *White Corridors* 51; *Something Money Can't Buy* 52; *The Feminine Touch* 56; *Virgin Island* 58; *Snowball* 60; *What a Carveup* 61; *Seven Keys, Don't Talk to Strange Men* 62; *Seventy Deadly Pills, Dead End Creek* 64.

262 JEANS Isabel (1891–) Actress. B: London. Stage: 09. Late silents, some sound, then Hollywood. *The Profligate* 17; *Tilly of Bloomsbury* 21; *The Rat* 25; *Windsor Castle* (short), *The Triumph of the Rat* 26; *Downhill, Easy Virtue, The Further Adventures of the Flag Lieutenant* 27; *Power Over Men, The Return of the Rat* 29; sound: *Sally Bishop* 32; *Rolling in Money* 34; *The Love Affair of the Dictator, The Crouching Beast* 35; *Banana Ridge* 41; *Great Day* 45; *Heaven's Above* 63.

263 JEANS Ursula (1906–) Actress. B: Simla. RN: McMinn. M: (1) Robin Irvine, (2) Roger LIVESEY. Her best parts came late. *The Gypsy Cavalier* 22; *The Virgin Queen* 23; *Silence* (short) 26; *False Colours* (short), *The Fake, Quinneys* 27; *The Passing of Mr. Quin, S.O.S.* 28; sound: *The Love Habit, The Flying Fool* 31; *The Crooked Lady, Once Bitten, The Barton Mystery* 32; *I Lived With You, Friday the 13th* 33; *The Man in the Mirror* 36; *Dark Journey, Storm in a Teacup, Over the Moon* 37; *The Life and Death of Colonel Blimp* 43; *Mr. Emmanuel* 44; *Gaiety George* 46; *The Woman in the Hall* 47; *The Weaker Sex, Elizabeth of Ladymead* 48; *The Night My Number Came Up,*

The Dambusters 55; North West Frontier 59; The Green Helmet, The Queen's Guards 61; Boy With a Flute (short) 64; Battle of the Villa Fiorita 65.

264 JENNINGS Gladys (1902–)
Actress. B: Oxford. Stage 08. Silent star. The Lady Clare, The Face at the Window 19; The Shuttle of Life, In the Night 20; Prey of the Dragon, Gwynneth of the Welsh Hills 21; The Lamp in the Desert, Man and his Kingdom, Rob Roy 22; The Crooked Man (short), Little Miss Nobody, Young Lochinvar, Constant Hot Water (short), Becket 23; The Colleen Bawn, Henry King of Navarre, The Prude's Fall 24; The Happy Ending, The Painted Lady (short) 25; The Mistletoe Bough (short), Kenilworth Castle (short), Bodiam Castle (short), Escape short), Back to the Trees (short), The Woman Juror (short) 26; Hindle Wakes, Woman in Pawn, Whispering Gables (short), Fangs of Death (short) 27; Lady Godiva (short) 28; sound: Should a Doctor Tell 30; To Oblige a Lady 31; I'm an Explosive 33; Sometimes Good, Lilies of the Field 34; Alibi Inn 35.

265 JENNINGS Humphrey (1907–1950) Director. B: Suffolk. Surrealist painter. 34: G.P.O. Film Unit. Sensitive, poetic docs. matching the intellectual mood of their time. Pett and Pott (sc.) 34; Birth of a Robot (co-dir.) 36; The First Days (co-dir.), Spare Time, An Unrecorded Victory, Speaking From America, Her Last Trip 39; London Can Take It (co-dir.), Welfare of the Workers 40; Words for Battle, Heart of Britain, Listen to Britain 41; The Silent Village, Fires Were Started (I Was a Fireman) 43; The True Story of Lilli Marlene, V.1 44; A Diary for Timothy, The Eighty Days 45; A Defeated People 46; The Cumberland Story 47; Dim Little Island 49; Family Portrait 50.

266 JOHN Rosamund (1913–)
Actress. B: Tottenham. RN: Nora Jones. Soft, gentle redhead. Secret of the Loch 34; The First of the Few 42; The Gentle Sex, The Lamp Still Burns 43; Tawny Pipit 44; The Way to the Stars 45; Green for Danger 46; The Upturned Glass, Fame is the Spur, When the Bough Breaks 47; No Place for Jennifer 49; She Shall Have Murder 50; Never Look Back 52; Street Corner 53; Operation Murder 56.

267 JOHNS Glynis (1923–) Actress. B: Pretoria. Father: Mervyn Johns. Stage: 35. From husky teenager to husky heroine. Also Hollywood. South Riding, Murder in the Family, Prison Without Bars 38; On the Night of the Fire 39; The Briggs Family, Under Your Hat 40; The Prime Minister, 49th Parallel 41; Adventures of Tartu 43; Halfway House 44; Perfect Strangers 45; This Man is Mine 46; Frieda, An Ideal Husband 47; Miranda, Third Time Lucky 48; Dear Mr. Prohack, Helter Skelter 49; State Secret, Flesh and Blood 50; No Highway, Appointment With Venus, Encore, The Magic Box 51; The Card 52; The Sword and the Rose, Personal Affair, Rob Roy the Highland Rogue, The Weak and the Wicked 53; The Seekers, The Beachcomber, Mad About Men 54; Josephine and Men 55; Loser Takes All 56; Another Time Another Place 58; Shake Hands With the Devil 59; The Spider's Web 60; The Sundowners 61; Lock Up Your Daughters 68.

268 JOHNSON Celia (1908–)
Actress. B: Richmond. Stage: 28. Several perfect if gentlewomanly performances. A Letter From Home (short) 41; In Which We Serve 42; Dear Octopus 43; This Happy Breed 44; Brief Encounter 45; The Astonished Heart 49; I Believe In You 51; The Holly and the Ivy 52; The Captain's Paradise 53; A Kid for Two Farthings 55;

The Good Companions 57; The Prime of Miss Jean Brodie 68.

269 JOHNSON Richard (1929–   ) Actor. B: Upminster. Stage: 57. Highly regarded stage actor; also Hollywood. Cairo, The Haunting, 80,000 Suspects 63; The Pumpkin Eater 64; The Amorous Adventures of Moll Flanders, Operation Crossbow 65; Khartoum, Deadlier Than the Male 66; Danger Route 67; Oedipus the King, Twist of Sand 68.

270 JUDD Edward (1932–   ) Actor. B: Shanghai. Manly and forthright in a crisis. X the Unknown 56; The Man Upstairs, Carry On Sergeant, I Was Monty's Double, Subway in the Sky 58; No Safety Ahead, Shakedown 59; The Challenge 60; The Day the Earth Caught Fire 61; Mystery Submarine 62; Stolen Hours, The World Ten Times Over 63; The Long Ships, The First Men in the Moon 64; Invasion 65; Island of Terror 66; The Vengeance of She 67.

K

271 KELLINO Roy (1912–1956) Director. B: London. Father W. P. KELLINO. 15: child actor. 26: asst. ph. 29: ph. Gainsborough. Remembered more for his photography than his quota quickies. The Last Adventurers, Concerning Mr. Martin, Catch as Catch Can 37; Father o' Nine 38; I Met a Murderer 39; Guilt Is My Shadow 50; The Silken Affair 56.

272 KELLINO Will P. (1873–1958) Director. B: London. RN: William Philip Gislingham. 78: circus clown; music hall acrobat. 10: films. From slapstick shorts with fellow artists to features for Gaumont & Stoll. Also Hollywood. Son: Roy KELLINO. Main shorts: Pimple Does the Turkey Trot, Grand Harlequinade 12; Bumbles series, Nobby series, Inkey & Co. series 13; Happy Dustmen series, Picture Palace Piecans, Potted Pantomimes 14; Romeo and Juliet by the Mudford Amateur Dramatic Society 15; The Dustman's Wedding, A Wife in a Hurry, Billy's Stormy Courtship, Parker's Weekend, The Dummy, The Dustmen's Outing 16; Billy the Truthful, Economy,

Who's Your Lady Friend, The Missing Link, How's Your Poor Wife, Billy Strikes Oil, Splash Me Nicely 17. Features: Billy's Spanish Love Spasm, The Man in Possession, The Only Man 15; The Terrible Tec, The Tale of a Shirt, The Perils of Pork Pie 16; The Green Terror, Angel Esquire 19; The Fall of a Saint, The Fordington Twins, Saved From the Sea, Will o' the Wisp series 20; The Fortune of Christina McNab, The Autumn of Pride, Class and No Class 21; A Soul's Awakening, Rob Roy 22; Young Lochinvar 23; The Colleen Bawn, His Grace Gives Notice, The Mating of Marcus, Not for Sale 24; We Women, Confessions, The Gold Cure, The Art of Love series 25; The Further Adventures of the Flag Lieutenant 27; Sailors Don't Care, Smashing Through 28; sound: Alf's Carpet 29; Alf's Button, Hot Heir, Bull Rushes, Who Killed Doc Robbin, Aroma of the South Seas 30; Wishes, The Poisoned Diamond, Sometimes Good 34; Lend Me Your Wife 35; Hot News, Paybox Adventure 36.

273 KELLY Judy (1913–   ) Actress. B: Sydney. Dark-eyed lovely of the 30s. Lord Camber's Ladies, Sleepless Nights,

Money Talks 32; Their Night Out, The Love Nest, Crime on the Hill, The Private Life of Henry VIII, Mannequin, Hawleys of High Street 33; The Black Abbot, Four Masked Men, Anything Might Happen 34; Things Are Looking Up, It's a Bet, Royal Cavalcade, Marry the Girl, Charing Cross Road, Captain Bill 35; Under Proof, First Offence, A Star Fell From Heaven, The Limping Man 36; Aren't Men Beasts, The Price of Folly, Ship's Concert, Makeup, Boys Will Be Girls, Over She Goes, The Last Chance 37; Jane Steps Out, Queer Cargo, The Luck of the Navy, Premiere 38; Dead Man's Shoes, The Midas Touch, At the Villa Rose 39; George and Margaret 40; Tomorrow We Live 42; The Butler's Dilemma 43; It Happened One Sunday 44; Dead of Night 45; Dancing With Crime 47; Warning to Wantons 48.

274 KENDALL Henry (1898–1962) Actor. B: London. Stage: 14. Best at comedy yet became a popular all-round hero. Mr. Pim Passes By, Tilly of Bloomsbury 21; sound: French Leave 30; The House Opposite, The Flying Fool, Rich and Strange 31; Innocents of Chicago, Mr. Bill the Conqueror, Watch Beverly 32; The Iron Stair, The Shadow, Counsel's Opinion, King of the Ritz, Timbuctoo, The Man Outside, The Stickpin, Great Stuff, The Ghost Camera, This Week of Grace, The Flaw 33; Without You, The Man I Want, Guest of Honour, The Girl in Possession, Sometimes Good, Leave It To Blanche, Crazy People, Death at Broadcasting House 34; Death on the Set, Three Witnesses, Lend Me Your Wife 35; A Wife or Two, Twelve Good Men, The Amazing Quest of Ernest Bliss, The Mysterious Mr. Davis 36; Take a Chance, Side Street Angel, It's Not Cricket (also sc.), The Compulsory Wife, School for Husbands 37; The Butler's Dilemma 43; 29 Acacia Avenue, Dumb Dora Discovers Tobacco 45; Helter Skelter 49; The Voice of

Merrill 52; An Alligator Named Daisy 55; Shadow of the Cat 61.

275 KENDALL Kay (1927–1959) Actress. B: Withernsea. RN: Justine McCarthy. M: Rex HARRISON. Redhead with delicious sense of comedy. Also Hollywood. Fiddlers Three, Champagne Charlie, Dreaming 44; Waltz Time 45; London Town 46; Dance Hall 50; Happy Go Lovely, Lady Godiva Rides Again 51; Wings of Danger, Curtain Up, It Started in Paradise, Mantrap 52; Street of Shadows, The Square Ring, Genevieve, Meet Mr. Lucifer 53; Fast and Loose, Doctor in the House, The Constant Husband 54; Simon and Laura 55; Adventures of Quentin Durward 56.

276 KENT Jean (1921–   ) Actress. B: Brixton. RN: Joan Summerfield. Stage: 33. Not quite a top rank Gainsborough girl, her best films came later. Rocks of Valpre 35; Hullo Fame 40; It's That Man Again 42; Miss London Ltd., Warn That Man, Bees in Paradise 43; Fanny By Gaslight, 2000 Women, Champagne Charlie, Madonna of the Seven Moons, Waterloo Road 44; The Rake's Progress 45; Caravan, Carnival, The Magic Bow 46; The Man Within, The Loves of Joanna Godden 47; Bond Street, Sleeping Car to Trieste 48; Trottie True 49; The Reluctant Widow, The Woman in Question, Her Favourite Husband 50; The Browning Version 51; Before I Wake 54; The Prince and the Showgirl 57; Bonjour Tristesse, Grip of the Strangler 58; Beyond This Place, Please Turn Over 59; Bluebeard's Ten Honeymoons 60.

277 KERR Deborah (1921–   ) Actress. B: Helensburgh. RN: Kerr-Trimmer. Stage: 39. A star from the start, she tended to lose her 'ladylike' qualities in Hollywood, but all her roles have a certain poise. Major Barbara, Love on the Dole, Penn of Pennsylvania, Hatter's Castle 41; The Day Will Dawn 42; The Life and Death of Colonel Blimp 43; Perfect Strangers 45; I See a Dark Stranger 46; Black Narcissus 47; Edward My Son 49; The End of the Affair 54; Bonjour Tristesse 58; The Sundowners, The Grass is Greener, The Naked Edge, The Innocents 61; The Chalk Garden 63; Eye of the Devil 66; Casino Royale 67; Prudence and the Pill 68.

278 KIMMINS Anthony (1901–1963) Director and writer (also actor and producer). B: Harrow. Navy to 32. Playwright. Started as a star of quota quickies, soon became top comedy writer and director: George FORMBY etc. Acted: The Golden Cage 33; White Ensign 34. Directed: Bypass to Happiness, How's Chances 34; Once in a New Moon, His Majesty and Co., All at Sea 35. Scripting: Designing Women 34; Midshipman Easy, While Parents Sleep 35; Laburnum Grove, The Lonely Road, Keep Your Seats Please, Talk of the Devil 36; Feather Your Nest, The Show Goes On, Who's Your Lady Friend 37' Writer-director: Keep Fit 37; I See Ice, It's in the Air 38; Come On George, Trouble Brewing 39; Under Your Hat (sc. only) 40. Directed: Mine Own Executioner (also prod.) 47; Bonnie Prince Charlie 48; Flesh and Blood 50; Mr. Denning Drives North 51; Who Goes There 52; The Captain's Paradise, Aunt Clara 54; Smiley (also prod.) 56; Smiley Gets a Gun (also prod.), Gateway to Adventure (short) (voice only) 58; The Amorous Prawn (also prod. & sc.) 62.

279 KING George (1899–1966) Director and producer. B: London. Mechanic; exhibitor; agent. Earned his title 'King of the Quickies'. Sc. Remembrance 27. Directed & produced: Too Many Crooks, Leave It to Me 30; Midnight, Number Please, Deadlock (dir. only), The Professional Guest 31; Self Made Lady 32. Directed: Two Way Street, Men of Steel 32; To Brighton With Gladys, Matinee Idol, Too Many Wives, Beware of Women, High Finance, Mayfair Girl, Enemy of the Police, Smithy, Her Imaginary Lover, I Adore You 33; The Silver Spoon, Murder at the Inn, Guest of Honour, Nine Forty Five, The Office Wife, The Blue Squadron, To Be A Lady, Get Your Man, Adventure Limited 34. Directed & produced: Oh No Doctor, Little Stranger 34; Maria Marten (prod. only), Full Circle (dir. only), Windfall, The Man Without a Face, Gay Old Dog 35; Sweeney Todd, The Crimes of Stephen Hawke, Reasonable Doubt (dir. only) 36; Wanted, Merry Comes to Town, Under a Cloud, Ticket of Leave Man, It's Never too Late to Mend (prod. only), House of Silence (prod. only), When the Poppies Bloom Again (prod. only) 37; Silver Top, Sexton Blake and the Hooded Terror, John Halifax Gentleman 38; The Face at the Window 39; The Chinese Bungalow, Crimes at the Dark House, The Case of the Frightened Lady (dir. only), Two for Danger (dir. only), George and Margaret (dir. only) 40; Tomorrow We Live, The First of the Few (prod. only) 42; Candelight in Algeria 43; Gaiety George 45; The Shop at Sly Corner 46; Forbidden 48; Eight O'Clock Walk (prod. only) 53.

280 KNIGHT Castleton, O.B.E. (1894–) Director. Exhibitor; made an experimental short, then some visually good features before producing G.B. News, Universal News, Rank docs. Prelude (short) 27; Plaything 29; sound: The Flying Scotsman, The Lady from the Sea 29; The Cockney Spirit in War series (4), Kissing Cup's Race 30; For Freedom (co-dir.) 40.

281 KNIGHT James (1891–19) Actor. B: Canterbury. Engineer, gymnast. He-man hero whose parts grew leaner as he grew fatter. *The Happy Warrior* 17; *The Splendid Coward, Big Money, The Romany Lass, Deception, Nature's Gentleman* 18; *The Silver Greyhound, The Power of Right, Gates of Duty, The Man Who Forgot* 19; *Brenda of the Barge* 20; *The Education of Nicky, Love in the Welsh Hills* 21; *No. 7 Brick Row,* (shorts:) *Crushing the Drug Traffic, Ticket o' Leave, The Old Actor's Story, The Lights o' London, Rowing to Win, Playing the Game, Pluck v. Plot, The Last Hundred Yards, Rainbow series* 22; *The Hornet's Nest, The Lady Owner, Beautiful Kitty, What Price Loving Cup* 23; *The Great Turf Mystery, Claude Duval, The Happy Prisoner* (short) 24; *Trainer and Temptress, A Dear Liar, The Impatient Patient* (short), *Famous Music Melodies* 25; *Ball of Fortune,* (shorts:) *Legend of Tichborne Dole, Woodcroft Castle, When Giants Fought, The Happy Rascals* 26; *Motherland, Mr. Nobody* 27; *Maria Marten, Bad Sir Brian Botany* (short), *Houpla, Spangles* 28; *Cupid in Clover, Power Over Men, W. W. Jacobs series* 29; sound: *Kissing Cup's Race* 30; *A Safe Affair* 31; *The Third String, That Night in London, When London Sleeps* 32; *Commissionaire* 33; *Lost in the Legion* 34; *Sexton Blake and the Bearded Doctor* 35; *The Life and Death of Colonel Blimp* 43; *San Demetrio London, Medal for the General* 44; *Johnny Frenchman, The Agitator* 45; *Girl in a Million, Loyal Heart, Appointment with Crime* 46; *My Sister and I* 48.

282 KNOWLES Bernard (1900–) Director. B: Manchester. 21: ph. *Detroit News.* 22: asst. ph. Gainsborough. 28: ph. *Dawn.* At his best with a story worth photographing. *A Place of One's Own* 45; *The Magic Bow* 46; *The Man Within, The White Unicorn, Jassy* 47; *Easy Money* 48; *The Lost People, The Perfect Woman* 49;

The Reluctant Widow 50; *Park Plaza 605* 53; *Barbados Quest* 55; *Frozen Alive* 64; *Spaceflight IC-1* 65.

KNOX Teddy see CRAZY GANG.

283 KORDA Sir Alexander (1893–1956). Director, producer. B: Turkeye, Hungary. M: two of his stars, Maria Corda, Merle OBERON. Journalist. 15: films in Hungary; then Austria, Berlin, Paris, Hollywood. To England to make quota films, formed London Films for which he directed, then produced many of the best and most profitable British films. A man of taste, he assembled a team of many talents. Directed: *Service for Ladies, Wedding Rehearsal* 32; *The Private Life of Henry VIII, The Girl from Maxims* 33; *The Private Life of Don Juan* 34; *Rembrandt* 36; *Perfect Strangers* 45; *An Ideal Husband* 48.

284 KORDA Zoltan (1895–) Director. B: Turkeye, Hungary. Brothers: Vincent Korda (art dir., London Films), Alexander KORDA. Made several good adventures for brother Alex; also Hollywood. *Cash* 33; *Sanders of the River* 35; *Forget Me Not, Conquest of the Air* (co-dir.), *Elephant Boy* (co-dir.) 36; *The Drum* 38; *The Four Feathers* 39; *Cry the Beloved Country* 52; *Storm Over the Nile* (co-dir.) 55.

285 KRISH John (1923–) Director. B: London. 40: asst. ed. Crown Film Unit. 42: ed. Army Film Unit. 46: dir. docs. Shorts: *This Year London* 50; *The Elephant Will Never Forget* 53; *Stryker of the Yard series* 54; *Return to Life* 60; *Mr. Marsh Comes to School, Let My People Go* 61; *Our School* 62; *I Think They Call Him John* 64. Features: *The Salvage Gang* 58; *Unearthly Stranger, The Wild Affair* 63; *Decline and Fall* 68.

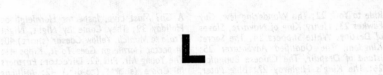

L

286 LACHMAN Harry (1886–   )
Director: B: La Salle. Painter. Films: 22,
Nice. 27: Tech. supervisor B.I.P. Swiftly
became a first-rate director and went to
Hollywood. *Weekend Wives* 28; sound:
Under the Greenwood Tree 29; *Song of
Soho, The Yellow Mask* 30; *The Love Habit,
The Outsider* 31; *Aren't We All, Down Our
Street, Insult* 32; *They Came By Night* 40.

287 LAMONT Molly (1910–   ) Act-
tress. B: Benoni. Built up by B.I.P., she
went to Hollywood. *The Black Hand
Gang* 30; *Uneasy Virtue, Old Soldiers Never
Die, What a Night, Shadows, My Wife's
Family, The House Opposite, Dr. Josser K.C.*
31; *Strictly Business, The Strangler,
Brother Alfred, Lucky Girl, The Last
Coupon, Josser on the River, His Wife's
Mother* 32; *Letting in the Sunshine, Leave It
To Me, Paris Plane* 33; *White Ensign, Irish
Hearts, The Third Clue, Wedding Anni-
versary* (short) 34; *Murder at Monte
Carlo, Oh What a Night, Handle With Care,
Rolling Home, Alibi Inn* 35.

288 LANCHESTER Elsa (1902–   )
Actress. B: Lewisham. RN: Elizabeth
Sullivan. M: Charles LAUGHTON. Stage:
18; cabaret; writer. Character actress at
her best with comedy; also Hollywood.
One of the Best 27; *The Constant Nymph,*
(shorts:) *Bluebottles, The Tonic, Day-
dreams* 28; sound: *Mr. Smith Wakes Up*
(short) 29; *Comets, The Love Habit* 30;
*The Stronger Sex, Potiphar's Wife, The
Officer's Mess* 31; *The Private Life of
Henry VIII* 33; *Miss Bracegirdle Does Her*
Duty (short), *The Ghost Goes West,
Rembrandt* 36; *Vessel of Wrath* 38.

289 LANE Lupino (1892–1959) Actor,
(also director). B: London. RN: Henry
Lane. Cousin: Stanley LUPINO. Stage:
96. Knockabout acrobatic comic. 22:
Hollywood, returned as star and director.
Shorts: *His Cooling Courtship, Nipper's
Busy Holiday, Nipper and the Curate, The
Man in Possession* 15; *Nipper's Busy Bee
Time, A Wife in a Hurry, The Dummy* 16;
*Hello Who's Your Lady Friend, The Missing
Link, Splash Me Nicely* 17; *Unexpected
Treasure, Trips and Tribunals, His Busy
Day, His Salad Days, Love and Lobster* 18;
*A Dreamland Frolic, Clarence Crooks and
Chivalry* 19; *A Lot About a Lottery, A Night
Out and a Day In* 20; sound: *The Yellow
Mask* 30; *Never Trouble Trouble* (also dir.),
No Lady (also dir.) 31. Directed: *Love
Lies, The Love Race* 31; *Innocents of
Chicago, Old Spanish Customers, The Maid
of the Mountains* 32; *Letting in the Sunshine*
33; *Oh What a Duchess!* 34. Acted: *A
Southern Maid* 33; *Who's Your Father?,
The Deputy Drummer, Trust the Navy* 35;
Hot News 36; *The Lambeth Walk* 39.

290 LANG Matheson (1879–1948)
Actor. B: Dundee. Stage: 97. One of the
few great stage players to become a full
film star despite his theatrical style. *The
Merchant of Venice* 16; *Masks and Faces,
The Ware Case, The House Opposite,
Everybody's Business* (short) 17; *Victory
and Peace* 18; *Mr. Wu* 19; *Carnival* 21;
A Romance of Old Bagdad, Dick Turpin's

Ride to York 22; *The Wandering Jew, Guy Fawkes* 23; *Henry King of Navarre, Slaves of Destiny, White Slippers* 24; *The Secret Kingdom, The Qualified Adventurer* 25; *Island of Despair, The Chinese Bungalow* 26; *The King's Highway* 27; *Blue Peter, Triumph of the Scarlet Pimpernel* 28; sound: *The Chinese Bungalow* 30; *Carnival* 31; *Channel Crossing* 33; *Little Friend* 34; *Royal Cavalcade, Drake of England, The Cardinal* 35.

291 LAUGHTON Charles (1899–1962) Actor. B: Scarborough. M: Elsa LANCHESTER. Hotel clerk; stage: 26. Brilliant character star, most of his films in Hollywood but his best in Britain. *Bluebottles* (short), *Daydreams* (short) 28; *Piccadilly* 29; sound: *Comets, Wolves* 30; *Down River* 31; *The Private Life of Henry VIII* (AA) 33; *Rembrandt* 36; *I Claudius* 37; *Vessel of Wrath, St. Martin's Lane* 38; *Jamaica Inn* 39; *Hobson's Choice* 54.

292 LAUNDER Frank (1907–) Director, writer. B: Hitchin. Civil servant, playwright; 28: scenario dept. B.I.P. Writing partnership with Sidney GILLIAT extended to producing as Individual Films. Scriptwriting: *Under the Greenwood Tree* 29; *Song of Soho, The W Plan, The Middle Watch, Children of Chance* 30; *How He Lied To Her Husband, Keepers of Youth, Hobson's Choice* 31; *After Office Hours, The Last Coupon, Josser in the Army, For the Love of Mike* 32; *Hawleys of High Street, Facing the Music, You Made Me Love You, A Southern Maid* 33; *Happy, Those Were the Days* 34; *Emil and the Detectives, So You Won't Talk, Mr. What's His Name, Get Off My Foot, I Give My Heart, The Black Mask* 35; *Twelve Good Men, Where's Sally, Seven Sinners, Educated Evans* 36; *Don't Get Me Wrong, Oh Mr. Porter* 37; *The Lady Vanishes* 38;

A Girl Must Live, Inspector Hornleigh on Holiday 39; *They Came By Night, Night Train to Munich, Yellow Caesar* (short) 40; *Inspector Hornleigh Goes To It, Kipps* 41; *The Young Mr. Pitt* 42. Director: *Partners in Crime* (short) (co-dir.) 42; *Millions Like Us* (co-dir.), *2,000 Women* 43; *I See a Dark Stranger* 46; *Captain Boycott* 47; *The Blue Lagoon* 49; *The Happiest Days of Your Life* 50; *Lady Godiva Rides Again* 51; *Folly to Be Wise* 52; *The Belles of St. Trinian's* 54; *Geordie* 55; *Blue Murder at St. Trinian's* 57; *The Bridal Path* 59; *The Pure Hell of St. Trinian's* 60; *Joey Boy* 65; *The Great St. Trinian's Train Robbery* (co-dir.) 66.

293 LAWRENCE Quentin Director. B: Gravesend. 46: TV engineer. 54: TV producer. Middle-weight thrillers. *The Trollenberg Terror* 58; *Cash on Demand* 61; *Playback, The Man Who Finally Died* 62; *We Shall See, The Secret of Blood Island* 64.

294 LAWSON Wilfrid (1900–1966) Actor. B: Bradford. RN: Worsnop. Stage: 16. Up from characters to 40s stardom, then back to characters. Also Hollywood. *East Lynne on the Western Front* 31; *Strike It Rich* 33; *Turn of the Tide* 35; *The Man Who Made Diamonds* 37; *Bank Holiday, The Terror, Yellow Sands, The Gaunt Stranger, Pygmalion* 38; *Stolen Life, Dead Man's Shoes* 39; *Pastor Hall, Gentleman of Venture* 40; *The Man at the Gate, Danny Boy, Jeannie, The Farmer's Wife, Tower of Terror* 41; *Hard Steel, The Night Has Eyes, The Great Mr. Handel* 42; *Thursday's Child* 43; *Fanny by Gaslight* 44; *Macbeth* (short) 45; *The Turners of Prospect Road* 47; *Make Me an Offer, The Prisoner, An Alligator Named Daisy* 55; *Now and Forever* 56; *The Naked Truth, Hell Drivers* 57; *Room at the Top, Tread Softly Stranger* 58; *Expresso Bongo* 60; *The*

Naked Edge, Nothing Barred, Over the Odds 61; *Go to Blazes, Postman's Knock* 62; *Tom Jones* 63; *Becket* 64; *The Wrong Box, The Viking Queen* 66.

295 LAWTON Frank (1904–) Actor. B: London. Stage 23. M: Evelyn Laye. Young English gentleman; also Hollywood. *Young Woodley, Birds of Prey* 30; *The Skin Game, The Outsider, Michael and Mary* 31; *After Office Hours* 32; *Heads We Go, Friday the 13th* 33; *The Mill on the Floss* 37; *The Four Just Men* 39; *Dangerous Comment* (short) 40; *Went the Day Well* 42; *The Winslow Boy* 48; *Rough Shoot* 52; *Doublecross* 55; *The Rising of the Moon, Gideon's Day* 57; *A Night to Remember* 58.

296 LEACOCK Philip (1917–) Director. B: London. 35: docs. Seeming to specialise in handling young people, but his later Hollywood work belied this. Shorts & docs.: *Island People, The Story of Wool* 40; *Out of True, Life in Her Hands, Festival in London* 51. Features: *Riders of the New Forest* 46; *The Brave Don't Cry* 52; *Appointment in London, The Kidnappers* 53; *Escapade* 55; *The Spanish Gardener* 56; *High Tide at Noon* 57; *Innocent Sinners* 58; *Hand in Hand* 60; *Reach for Glory* 61; *The War Lover* 62; *Tamahine* 63.

297 LEAN David (1908–) Director. B: Croydon. M: (1) Kay WALSH, (2) Ann TODD. 28: clapperboy *Quinneys*. 30: ed. Gaumont Sound News; British Movietonews. 34: ed. Paramount British quota quickies; 35: ed. *Escape Me Never*. One of the world's top directors ranging from intimate miniatures to blockbusters. *In Which We Serve* (co-dir.) 42; *This Happy Breed* 44; *Blithe Spirit, Brief Encounter* 45; *Great Expectations* 46; *Oliver Twist* 48; *The Passionate Friends* 49; *Madeleine* 50; *The Sound Barrier* 52; *Hobson's Choice* 54;

Summer Madness 55; *The Bridge on the River Kwai* (AA) 57; *Lawrence of Arabia* (AA) 62.

298 Le BRETON Flora (1898–) Actress. B: Croydon. Stage: 17. Pretty star who did better in Hollywood. *La Poupée* 20; *The Glorious Adventure* 21; *House of Peril, Ta-ra-ra-boom-de-re* (short), *While London Sleeps, A Soul's Awakening, Gipsy Cavalier, The Crimson Circle, Love's Influence* 22; *Through Fire and Water, The Mistletoe Bough* (short), *The Cause of All the Trouble* (short), *God's Prodigal, Little Miss Nobody, I Will Repay* 23; *Tons of Money* 24; *The Rolling Road* 27; sound: *Flora Le Breton* (short) 29; *Comets* 30.

299 LEE Anna (1913–) Actress. B: Ightham. RN: Joanna Winnifrith. Stage: 31. M: (1) Robert STEVENSON. Little blonde star; also Hollywood. *Ebb Tide, Yes Mr. Brown, Say It With Music* 32; *King's Cup, Mayfair Girl, The Bermondsey Kid, Mannequin, Chelsea Life* 33; *Faces, Lucky Loser, Rolling in Money, The Camels Are Coming* 34; *Heat Wave, The Passing of the Third Floor Back, First a Girl* 35; *The Man Who Changed His Mind* 36; *O.H.M.S., King Solomon's Mines, Non Stop New York* 37; *The Four Just Men* 39; *Young Man's Fancy, Return to Yesterday* 40; *Gideon's Day* 57.

300 LEE Belinda (1935–1961) Actress. B: Budleigh Salterton. Blonde beauty; also continental sex/spectaculars. *The Runaway Bus* 53; *Life With the Lyons, Meet Mr. Callaghan, The Belles of St. Trinians, Murder by Proxy* 54; *Footsteps in the Fog, Man of the Moment, No Smoking, Who Done It* 55; *The Feminine Touch, Eyewitness, The Secret Place, The Big Money* 56; *Miracle in Soho, Dangerous Exile* 57; *Nor the Moon by Night* 58.

301 LEE Christopher (1922–)
Actor. B: London. Many small parts until
Hammer saw the horror potential of his
tall gauntness. Also continental films.
Corridor of Mirrors 47; *Hamlet, One Night
With You, Penny and the Pownall Case,
Scott of the Antarctic, A Song for Tomorrow,
Saraband for Dead Lovers, My Brother's
Keeper* 48; *Trottie True, They Were Not
Divided* 49; *Prelude to Fame* 50; *Captain
Horatio Hornblower R.N., Valley of the
Eagles* 51; *Paul Temple Returns, The
Crimson Pirate* 52; *Innocents in Paris,
Moulin Rouge* 53; *That Lady, The Dark
Avenger* 54; *Storm Over the Nile, The
Cockleshell Heroes, Private's Progress,
Crossroads* (short) 55; *Port Afrique, Alias
John Preston, Beyond Mombasa, Battle of
the River Plate, Moby Dick* 56; *Ill Met By
Moonlight, Fortune Is a Woman, Curse of
Frankenstein, The Traitor, The Truth About
Women, A Tale of Two Cities* 57; *Dracula,
Battle of the VI, Corridors of Blood* 58;
*The Hound of the Baskervilles, The Man
Who Could Cheat Death, The Mummy, The
Treasure of San Teresa* 59; *The Two Faces
of Dr. Jekyll, Beat Girl, Too Hot to Handle,
City of the Dead, The Hands of Orlac* 60;
Taste of Fear, Terror of the Tongs 61; *The
Devil's Daffodil, Pirates of Blood River, The
Devil's Agent* 62; *Devil Ship Pirates, The
Gorgon, Dr. Terror's House of Horrors* 63;
*She, The Face of Fu Manchu, The Skull,
Dracula Prince of Darkness, Rasputin the
Mad Monk* 63; *Brides of Fu Manchu,
Theatre of Death, Circus of Fear* 66; *Night
of the Big Heat, Vengeance of Fu Manchu,
Five Golden Dragons* 67; *The Devil Rides
Out, The Face of Eve, Crimson Altar,
Dracula Has Risen from the Grave* 68.

302 LEE Jack (1913–) Director. B:
Stroud. 38: assoc. prod. G.P.O. Film Unit.
40: Ed. *London Can Take It.* His doc.
background emerges in his location
features. To Australia. Docs.: *The Pilot Is
Safe* 41; *Ordinary People* 42; *Close
Quarters* 43; *By Sea and Land* 44; *The
Eighth Plague* 45; *Children on Trial* 46.
Features: *The Woman in the Hall* 47;
Once a Jolly Swagman 48; *The Wooden
Horse* 50; *South of Algiers* 52; *Turn the Key
Softly* 53; *A Town Like Alice* 56; *Robbery
Under Arms* 57; *The Captain's Table* 58;
Circle of Deception 60.

303 LEE Norman (1898–)
Director (also writer). B: Sutton.
Cartoonist. 15: stage as actor, then writer
producer. 17: Films in Africa as prod. dir.
& sc. Fast B-pictures a cut above quickies.
Sacred Dramas series (sc.), *The Streets of
London, Lure of the Atlantic* 28; *Scrags*
(sc.), *City of Shadows* 30. Sound: *Dr.
Josser K.C.* 31; *The Strangler, Josser Joins
the Navy, Strip Strip Hooray, Josser on the
River, Josser in the Army, Money Talks* 32;
The Pride of the Forces 33; *A Political
Party, The Outcast, Doctor's Orders* 34;
Happy Days Are Here Again, Forgotten Men
(doc.) 35; *Don't Rush Me, No Escape* 36;
*Kathleen Mavourneen, Knights For a Day,
Bulldog Drummond at Bay, French Leave,
Saturday Night Revue, Dangerous Fingers*
37; *Almost a Honeymoon, Save a Little
Sunshine, Luck of the Navy, Yes Madam,
Mr. Reeder in Room 13* 38; *Murder in Soho*
39; *Mein Kampf My Crimes, The Door With
Seven Locks* 40; *The Farmer's Wife* (co-
dir.), *Spring Meeting* (sc. only), *My Wife's
Family* (sc. only), *South American George*
(sc. only), *The Team* (short) (co-dir.) 41;
This Man Is Mine (sc. only) 46; *The
Phantom Shot* (sc. only), *The Idol of Paris*
(sc. only) 47; *The Monkey's Paw* 48; *The
Case of Charles Peace* 49; *The Girl Who
Couldn't Quite* 50.

304 LEE THOMPSON J. (John)
(1914–) Director, formerly writer.
B: Bristol. 31: stage actor, playwright.
34: scenario dept. B.I.P. Keeps his

pictures moving in visual if clichéd style. Also Hollywood. Scriptwriting: *The Price of Folly, Glamorous Night* 37; *The Middle Watch* 39; *East of Piccadilly* 41; *For Them That Trespass, No Place for Jennifer* 49. Dir. & sc.: *Murder Without Crime* 50; *The Yellow Balloon* 52; *The Weak and the Wicked, For Better For Worse* 54. Director: *As Long as They're Happy, An Alligator Named Daisy* 55; *Yield to the Night* 56; *The Good Companions, Woman in a Dressing Gown* 57; *Ice Cold in Alex* 58; *No Trees in the Street, Tiger Bay, Northwest Frontier* 59; *The Guns of Navarone* 61; *Return from the Ashes* 65; *Eye of the Devil* 66; *Before Winter Comes* 68.

305 LEIGH Vivien (1913–1967) Actress. B: Darjeeling. RN: Vivian Hartley. M: (2) Laurence OLIVIER. Pretty, petite; world fame in Hollywood. *Things Are Looking Up* 34; *The Village Squire, Gentleman's Agreement, Look Up and Laugh* 35; *Fire Over England, Dark Journey, Storm in a Teacup, 21 Days* 37; *A Yank at Oxford, Saint Martin's Lane* 38; *Guide Dogs for the Blind* (short) 39; *Caesar and Cleopatra* 46; *Anna Karenina* 48; *The Deep Blue Sea* 55; *The Roman Spring of Mrs. Stone* 61.

306 LEIGHTON Margaret (1922–) B: Barnt Green. M: (2) Laurence HARVEY. Stage: 38. Elegant leading lady. *Bonnie Prince Charlie* 47; *The Winslow Boy* 48; *Under Capricorn, The Astonished Heart* 49; *The Elusive Pimpernel* 50; *Calling Bulldog Drummond, Home at Seven* 51; *The Holly and the Ivy* 52; *The Good Die Young* 53; *The Teckman Mystery, Carrington V.C.* 54; *The Constant Husband* 55; *Passionate Summer* 56; *The Waltz of the Toreadors* 61; *The Third Secret* 63.

307 LESTER Richard (1932–) Director. B: U.S.A. 50: TV. In England

his TV work with 'The Goons' (SELLERS, Spike Milligan, etc.) developed his fast, crazy, visual movie style. *The Running Jumping and Standing Still Film* (short) 60; *It's Trad Dad* 62; *Mouse on the Moon* 63; *A Hard Day's Night* 64; *The Knack, Help* 65; *A Funny Thing Happened on the Way to the Forum* 66; *How I Won the War* 67; *The Bed Sitting Room* 68.

308 LEWIS Jay (1914–) Director, also producer. B: Warwickshire. 31: stage actor. 33: asst. Elstree. 35: asst. dir. *Dandy Dick*. 38: ed. docs. 40: formed Verity Films with Sydney Box. He has directed mainly comedies. Shorts directed: *Cooking Hints* series 40; *Ah Tishoo* (prod.), *Canteen on Wheels, Queen's Messenger, Sea Cadets* 41; *Knights of St. John* 42; *The House on the Hill* 48. Features produced: *A Man's Affair* (also dir.) 49; *Morning Departure* 50; *The Gift Horse* 51; *Front Page Story* 53. Directed: *The Baby and the Battleship* 56; *Invasion Quartet* 61; *Live Now Pay Later* 62; *A Home of Your Own* 64.

309 LISTER Moira (1923–) Actress. B: Cape Town. Attractive blonde star. *The Shipbuilders* 43; *Love Story, My Ain Folk* 44; *Don Chicago, The Agitator* 45; *Wanted for Murder* 46; *Uneasy Terms, Mrs. Fitzherbert* 47; *So Evil My Love, Another Shore, Once a Jolly Swagman* 48; *A Run for your Money* 49; *Pool of London, Files from Scotland Yard* 50; *White Corridors* 51; *Something Money Can't Buy, The Cruel Sea* 52; *Grand National Night, Trouble in Store, The Limping Man* 53; *John and Julie, The Deep Blue Sea* 55; *Seven Waves Away* 57; *The Yellow Rolls Royce* 64; *The Double Man, Stranger in the House* 67.

310 LIVESEY Roger (1906–) Actor. B: Barry. Stage: 17. M: Ursula JEANS. Throaty character star. *Where* the Rainbow Ends, The Four Feathers 21; Married Love 23; sound: East Lynne on the Western Front 31; A Veteran of Waterloo, Cuckoo in the Nest 33; Blind Justice 34; Lorna Doone, The Price of Wisdom, Midshipman Easy 35; Rembrandt 36; The Drum, Keep Smiling 38; Spies of the Air, Rebel Son 39; The Girl in the News 40; The Life and Death of Colonel Blimp 43; I Know Where I'm Going 45; A Matter of Life and Death 46; Vice Versa 47; That Dangerous Age 49; Green Grow the Rushes 50; Master of Ballantrae 53; The Intimate Stranger 56; The League of Gentlemen 59; The Entertainer 60; No My Darling Daughter 61; Of Human Bondage 64; The Amorous Adventures of Moll Flanders 65; Oedipus the King 68.

311 LOCKWOOD Margaret (1916–) Actress. B: Karachi. RN: Margaret Day. Stage: 32. From stardom as typical healthy English girl to wickedest of the Gainsborough ladies. Daughter: Julia Lockwood. Lorna Doone 34; The Case of Gabriel Perry, Some Day, Honours Easy, Man of the Moment, Midshipman Easy 35; Jury's Evidence, The Amateur Gentleman, Beloved Vagabond, Irish for Luck 36; The Street Singer, Who's Your Lady Friend, Dr. Syn, Melody and Romance 37; Owd Bob, Bank Holiday, The Lady Vanishes 38; A Girl Must Live 39; The Stars Look Down, Night Train to Munich, Girl in the News 40; Quiet Wedding 41; Alibi 42; The Man in Grey, Dear Octopus 43; Give Us the Moon, Love Story 44; A Place of One's Own, I'll Be Your Sweetheart, The Wicked Lady 45; Bedelia, Hungry Hill 46; Jassy, The White Unicorn 47; Look Before You Love 48; Cardboard Cavalier, Madness of the Heart 49; Highly Dangerous 50; Trent's Last Case 52; Laughing Anne 53; Trouble in the Glen 54; Cast a Dark Shadow 55.

312 LODER John (1898–) Actor. B: London. 26: German films under RN

John Lowe. Tall handsome hero, later in Hollywood. The Firstborn 28. Sound: Wedding Rehearsal, Money Means Nothing 32; Money for Speed, The Private Life of Henry VIII, Paris Plane, You Made Me Love You, Love Life and Laughter 33; The Battle, Rolling in Money, Warn London, Java Head, Sing as We Go, My Song Goes Round the World 34; Lorna Doone, The Silent Passenger, It Happened in Paris, 18 Minutes 35; Queen of Hearts, Whom the Gods Love, Ourselves Alone, Guilty Melody, The Man Who Changed His Mind, Sabotage 36; King Solomon's Mines, Dr. Syn, Non Stop New York, Mademoiselle Docteur 37; Owd Bob, Anything to Declare 38; The Silent Battle, Murder Will Out, Meet Maxwell Archer 39; Dead on Time (short) 55; The Story of Esther Costello, Small Hotel, Gideon's Day 57; The Secret Man 58.

313 LOM Herbert (1917–) Actor. B: Prague. RN: Schluderpacheru. 36: actor Czech films. 39: England, B.B.C. European service. Suave, romantic heroes and villains. Also Hollywood. Mein Kampf My Crimes 40; The Young Mr. Pitt, Tomorrow We Live, Secret Mission 42; The Dark Tower 43; Hotel Reserve 44; The Seventh Veil, Night Boat to Dublin 45; Appointment With Crime 46; Dual Alibi, Snowbound 47; Good Time Girl, Portrait from Life, Lucky Mascot 48; Golden Salamander 49; Night and the City, State Secret, The Black Rose, Cage of Gold 50; Hell is Sold Out, Two on the Tiles, Mr. Denning Drives North, Whispering Smith Hits London 51; The Ringer, The Man Who Watched Trains Go By, The Net, Rough Shoot 52; The Love Lottery, Star of India 53; Beautiful Stranger 54; The Ladykillers 55; Fire Down Below, Hell Drivers, Action of the Tiger, Chase a Crooked Shadow 57; Intent to Kill, I Accuse 58; No Trees in the Street, Passport to Shame, North West Frontier, Third Man on the Mountain 59; Mr.

Topaze, The Frightened City 61; Phantom of the Opera, Tiara Tahiti, Mysterious Island 62; The Horse Without a Head 63; Shot in the Dark 64; Return from the Ashes 65; Our Man in Marrakesh 66; The Face of Eve 68.

314 LONGDEN John (1900–) Actor. B: West Indies. Mining engineer; stage 23. Tall star of silents and early talkies. The Ball of Fortune, House of Marney 26; The Glad Eye, The Flight Commander, The Arcadians, Quinneys, Bright Young Things (short) 27; Mademoiselle Parley Voo, What Money Can Buy, Palais de Danse 28; The Last Post, The Flying Squad 29. Sound: Blackmail, Memories (short), Atlantic, Juno and the Paycock 29; Elstree Calling, Flame of Love, Two Worlds, Children of Chance 30; The Skin Game, The Ringer, Two Crowded Hours, The Wickham Mystery, Rynox 31; Murder on the Second Floor, Come Into My Parlour (dir. only), Lucky Sweep, Born Lucky 32; Jennifer Hale 36; French Leave, Little Miss Somebody, Young and Innocent 37; Dial 999, Bad Boy, The Gaunt Stranger 38; Q Planes, Jamaica Inn, The Lion Has Wings 39; Contraband 40; The Common Touch, Tower of Terror, Old Mother Riley's Circus, Post 23 (short) 41; Rose of Tralee, The Silver Fleet 42; Death by Design (short) 44; Ghosts of Berkeley Square, Dusty Bates 47; Anna Karenina, The Last Load, Bonnie Prince Charlie 48; Trapped by the Terror 49; The Lady Craved Excitement, The Elusive Pimpernel, Pool of London, The Dark Light 50; Black Widow, The Man with the Twisted Lip (short), The Magic Box, Trek to Mashomba 51; The Wallet 52; Dangerous Cargo, Meet Mr. Callaghan 54; The Ship That Died of Shame 55; Alias John Preston, Raiders of the River 56; Quatermass II, Three Sundays to Live 57; Broad Waterways (short) (voice) 59; An Honourable Murder 60; So Evil So Young 61;

Lancelot and Guinevere 63; Frozen Alive 64.

315 LONGFELLOW Malvina Actress. B: Virginia. Model, stage. Silent star. Holy Orders, The Will of the People, For All Eternity 17; Thelma, Adam Bede, Nelson, Betta the Gipsy 18; The Romance of Lady Hamilton 19; Grip of Iron, The Story of the Rosary, Calvary, Mary Latimer Nun, Unmarried, A Gamble in Lives 20; The Night Hawk, Moth and Rust 21; (shorts:) The Great Terror, The Last Crusade, The Last King of Wales, Madame Recamier 22; The Wandering Jew, Indian Love Lyrics 23; The Celestial City 29.

316 LORRAINE Harry (1886–19) Actor (also director). B: Brighton. RN: Henry Herd. Stunt expert. In the Days of Robin Hood, Stock is as Good as Money (short), Signals in the Night (short), The Favourite for the Jamaica Cup (short), Tom Cringle in Jamaica (short), Through the Clouds, A Tragedy in the Alps, Lieut. Daring and the Mystery of Room 41, In Fate's Grip, The Little Snow Waif (short), The Master Crook 13; Lieut. Daring Aerial Scout, Detective Daring and the Thames Coiners (dir.), The Belle of Crystal Palace, Mary the Fishergirl (short), The Great Spy Raid, Huns of the North Sea, The World at War, Queenie of the Circus, London's Underworld (also dir.) 14; The Stolen Heirlooms, The Great Cheque Fraud, The Counterfeiters, The Thornton Jewel Mystery, Wireless (also dir) 15; The Happy Warrior, If Thou Wert Blind 17; The Great Impostor, Big Money (dir.) 18; The Lads of the Village (dir.), The Further Exploits of Sexton Blake (also dir.) 19; Sweeney Todd 28; Stranger than Fiction (short), Unto Each Other 29.

317 LOSEY Joseph (1909–) Director. B: Wisconsin. 32: stage prod. 38: films. In England since McCarthy, making intriguing films. First two films under aliases. *The Sleeping Tiger* 54; *The Intimate Stranger, The Man on the Beach* (short) 56; *Time Without Pity* 57; *The Gypsy and the Gentleman* 58; *Blind Date* 59; *The Criminal* 60; *The Damned* 61; *The Servant* 63; *King and Country* 64; *Modesty Blaise* 66; *Accident* 67; *Boom, Secret Ceremony* 68.

318 LOTINGA Ernie (1876–1951) Actor. B: Sunderland. Baker, concert party, music halls. Fred Karno knockabout comic in popular coarse comedies of the 30s. Shorts: *The Raw Recruit, Nap, The Orderly Room, Joining Up* 28; *Josser K.C., Doing His Duty, Spirits, Acci-dental Treatment* 29. Features: *P.C. Josser, Dr. Josser K.C.* 31; *Josser Joins the Navy, Josser on the River, Josser in the Army* 32; *Josser on the Farm* 34; *Smith's Wives* 35; *Love Up the Pole* 36.

319 LUCAN Arthur (Old Mother Riley) (1887–1954) RN: Arthur Towle. B: Boston. Music halls with partner/wife **Kitty McShane** (1898–1964), who co-starred in all his films except the last. Comic 'Irish washerwoman' who cleaned up at the provincial box-offices. *Stars on Parade, Kathleen Mavourneen* 36; *Old Mother Riley* 37; *Old Mother Riley in Paris* 38; *Old Mother Riley M.P., Old Mother Riley Joins Up* 39; *Old Mother Riley in Business* 40; *Old Mother Riley's Ghosts, Old Mother Riley's Circus* 41; *Old Mother Riley Detective* 43; *Old Mother Riley Overseas* 44; *Old Mother Riley at Home* 45; *Old Mother Riley's New Venture* 49; *Old Mother Riley Headmistress* 50; *Old Mother Riley's*

Jungle Treasure 51; *Mother Riley Meets the Vampire* 52.

320 LUPINO Stanley (1893–1942) Actor. B: London. Stage: 1900. Daughter: Ida; brother: Barry; cousins: Wallace, Lupino LANE. Bright, breezy comedian in musical comedies which he wrote himself. *Love Lies, The Love Race* 31; *Sleepless Nights* 32; *King of the Ritz, Facing the Music, You Made Me Love You* 33; *Happy* 34; *Honeymoon for Three* (also prod.) 35; *Cheer Up* (also prod.), *Sporting Love* 36; *Over She Goes* 37; *Hold My Hand* 38; *Lucky To Me* 39.

321 LYNN Ralph (1882–1962) Actor. B: Manchester. Stage: 00. Prototype 'Silly Ass', all teeth and monocle, in films of his stage successes, usually with Tom WALLS. Son: Robert LYNN. *Peace and Quiet* (short) 29; *Rookery Nook* 30; *Tons of Money, Plunder, Chance of a Night Time* (also co-dir.), *Mischief* 31; *A Night Like This, Thark* 32; *Just My Luck, Summer Lightning, Up to the Neck, Turkey Time* 33; *A Cup of Kindness, Dirty Work* 34; *Fighting Stock, Stormy Weather, Foreign Affairs* 35; *In the Soup, Pot Luck, All In* 36; *For Valour* 37.

322 LYNN Robert (1918–   ) Director. B: London. Father: Ralph LYNN. 36: asst. Twickenham. Lowercase thrillers. *Information Received* 61; *Postman's Knock, Two Letter Alibi, Dr. Crippen* 62; *Blaze of Glory, Take Me Over* 63; *Table Bay, Coast of Skeletons, Mozambique, Victim Five* 64; *Change Partners* 65.

M

323 MacDONALD David (1904–)
Director. B: Helensburgh. Rubber
planter; 29: asst. dir. Paramount. Some
good middle-bracket crimes and adven-
tures. *Double Alibi, The Last Curtain, It's
Never Too Late To Mend, When the
Poppies Bloom Again, Riding High, Death
Croons the Blues* 37; *Make It Three, Dead
Men Tell No Tales, Meet Mr. Penny, A Spot
of Bother, This Man is News* 38; *This Man in
Paris, Spies of the Air, The Midas Touch* 39;
Law and Disorder, Men of the Lightship
(doc.) 40; *This England, Lofoten* (short)
41; *The Brothers* 47; *Good Time Girl,
Snowbound* 48; *Christopher Columbus,
Diamond City, The Bad Lord Byron* 49;
Cairo Road 50; *The Adventurers* 51; *The
Lost Hours* 52; *Tread Softly, Operation
Malaya* (doc.) 53; *Devil Girl from Mars* 54;
Alias John Preston 56; *Small Hotel* 57; *The
Moonraker, A Lady Mislaid* 58; *Petticoat
Pirates* 61; *The Golden Rabbit* 62.

324 MACKENDRICK Alexander
(1912–) Director, formerly writer.
B: Boston, U.S.A. Advertising; 37:
scenarist. Having made some of the best
Ealing comedies, he switched style in
Hollywood. Scriptwriting, shorts: *The
Pocket Cartoon* 41; *Carnival in the Clothes
Cupboard* 42; *Fable of the Fabrics, Abu
series* (4) 43; features: *Midnight Menace*
37; *Saraband for Dead Lovers* 48; *Whisky
Galore* (also dir.) 49; *The Blue Lamp,
Dance Hall* 50; *The Man in the White Suit*
(also dir.) 51. Directed: *Mandy* 52; *The
Maggie* 54; *The Ladykillers* 55; *Sammy
Going South* 63; *A High Wind in Jamaica*
65.

325 MALINS Geoffrey H., O.B.E.
(1887–) Director. B: Boston. 11:
ph. Clarendon Films. His features usually
starred Ena Beaumont. Shorts: *Hearts of
Gold, The Castaways, Abide With Me* 15;
The Rainbow Chasers 19; *Watch Your
Step, Our Girls and Their Physique series*
(12) 20; *Watching Eyes series* (6), *Ally
Sloper series* (6) 21; *Romances of the Prize
Ring series* (7) 26; *W. W. Jacobs series*
(6) 28. Features: *On the Banks of Allan
Water, The Battle of the Somme* (doc.),
With the French Army in the Vosges (doc.)
16; *A Peep Behind the Scenes, The Girl from
Downing Street* 18; *The Golden Web, All the
Winners* 20; *Bluff* 21; *Recoil* 22; *Fortune's
Fool, The Wonderful Wooing* 25; *East of
Singapore* (doc.) 27; sound: *London
Melody* 30.

326 MALO Gina (1909–) Actress.
B: Cincinatti. RN: Janet Flynn. Stage
dancer. M: Romney Brent. Pretty star of
the 30s. *In a Monastery Garden, Goodnight
Vienna, Tight Corner* 32; *King of the Ritz,
Strike It Rich, Waltz Time* 33; *Lily of
Killarney, My Song for You* 34; *The Private
Life of Don Juan* 35; *Jack of All Trades,
Where There's a Will, Southern Roses, All
In* 36; *It's a Grand Old World, The Gang
Show, Over She Goes* 37; *His Lordship
Regrets* 38; *The Door With Seven Locks* 40.

327 MANDER Miles (1888–1946)
Actor (also director and writer). B:
Wolverhampton. RN: Lionel Mander.
Acted at first as Luther Miles. 08:
farmer; 10: aviator; novelist, play-
wright; 13: exhibitor, renter. Starred **as**

a moustachioed cad; later Hollywood.
Once Upon a Time 18; *The Children of Gibeon, Testimony, The Old Arm Chair, A Rank Outsider* 20; *The Road to London, Place of Honour*, then as Miles Mander *A Temporary Lady* 21; *Half a Truth, Open Country* 22; *Lovers in Araby* (also sc.), *The Prude's Fall* 24; *The Painted Lady* (short), *The Lady in Furs* (short) 25; *Riding for a King* (short), *The Pleasure Garden, London Love* 26; *Tiptoes, The Fake* 27; *The Physician, The First Born* (also prod., dir. & sc.), *Balaclava* 28; *The Crooked Billet* 29; sound: *Phonofilms* (also dir. & sc.) 26–7; *Loose Ends, Murder* 30; *The Woman Between* (dir. & sc. only), *Fascination* (dir. only) 31; *Frail Woman, The Missing Rembrandt, Lily Christine, The Lodger*, (sc. only), *That Night in London* 32; *Matinee Idol, Loyalties, Don Quixote, Bitter Sweet, The Private Life of Henry VIII* 33; *Four Masked Men, The Battle, The Case for the Crown, Youthful Folly* (dir. only) 34; *The Morals of Marcus* (dir. & sc. only), *Death Drives Through* 35; *The Flying Doctor* (dir. only) 36.

328 MARMONT Percy (1883–   ) Actor. B: Gunnersbury. Stage: 1900. U.S. films: 13. Top romantic silent star retired into perfect 'English gentleman'. *Yellow Stockings, Sir or Madam, The Warning* (short), *Lady of the Lake* 28; *The Silver King* 29. Sound: *The Squeaker, Cross Roads* 30; *The Loves of Ariane, The Written Law, Rich and Strange* 31; *The Silver Greyhound, Blind Spot, Say It With Music* 32; *Her Imaginary Lover* 33; *White Lilac, Vanity* 35; *Secret Agent, David Livingstone, The Captain's Table* (dir.), *Conquest of the Air* 36; *Action for Slander, Young and Innocent* 37; *Bringing It Home* (short) 40; *Penn of Pennsylvania* 41; *Those Kids from Town* 42; *I'll Walk Beside You* 43; *Loyal Heart* 46; *Swiss Honeymoon* 47; *No Orchids for Miss Blandish* 48; *Dark Secret*

49; *The Gambler and the Lady* 52; *Four Sided Triangle* 53; *Knave of Hearts* 54; *Footsteps in the Fog* 55.

329 MARSH Carol (1929–   ) Actress. B: Southgate. Stage: 46. RN: Norma Simpson. Tapered off after brilliant début as an 'ordinary' heroine. *Brighton Rock* 47; *Marry Me, Helter Skelter, The Romantic Age* 49; *Scrooge, Salute the Toff* 51; *Private Information* 52; *Mysterious Bullet* (short) 55; *Dracula* 58; *Man Accused* 59.

330 MARTIN Millicent (1934–   ) Actress. B: London. Singer, stage: 54. Tiny, attractive star. *The Girl on the Boat, The Horsemasters, Invasion Quartet* 61; *Nothing But the Best* 63; *Those Magnificent Men in Their Flying Machines* 65; *Stop the World I Want to Get Off, Alfie* 66.

331 MARTINEK H. Oceano Director. Painter, sculptor, author; films from 1898. Many lively films for B. & C. and Big Ben, often starring himself and his ex-equestrienne sister Ivy (*The Sleuth Hounds*). Main shorts: *Her Lover's Honour, Exploits of Three Fingered Kate* series 09; *The Fireman's Wedding, When Women Join the Force* 10; *Weary Willie and Tired Tim* series (4), *The Puritan Maid* 11; *Robin Hood Outlawed, The Mountaineer's Romance, Don Q* series (4), *Lieut. Daring and the Plans of the Minefield* 12; *Reub's Little Girl, The Nest on the Black Cliff* 13; *Black Roderick the Poacher* 14; Features: *The Hidden Witness, The Friend in Blue, The Mystery of the Old Mill, Power to Kill, The Corner House Burglary, The Rajah's Tiara, A Desperate Stratagem, The False Wireless, In the Grip of Spies* 14; *Harry the Swell, The Clue of the Cigar Band, The Deadly Model, The Stolen Masterpiece, At the Torrent's Mercy* 15; *Answer the Call, The Way of the World*,

Top: Jean Kent, Deborah Kerr, Matheson Lang, Charles Laughton
Centre: Belinda Lee, Vivien Leigh, Margaret Leighton
Bottom: Moira Lister, Herbert Lom, Arthur Lucan, Millicent Martin

Top: Virginia Maskell, Jessie Matthews, Virginia McKenna
Centre: Sarah Miles, Max Miller, Hayley Mills
Bottom: John Mills, Kieron Moore, Kenneth More

The Ingrate, Jim the Scorpion, The Octopus Gang 16; Glastonbury Past and Present (doc.) 22.

332 MASKELL Virginia (1936–1968)
Actress. B: Shepherd's Bush. Attractive, intelligent star. Happy Is the Bride 57; Virgin Island 58; The Man Upstairs, Jet Storm 59; Suspect, Doctor in Love 60; Only Two Can Play, The Wild and the Willing 62; Interlude 68.

333 MASON Herbert, M.C. (1891–) Director. B: Moseley. 08: stage actor. 28: prod. stage shows for Gaumont circuit. 31: asst. dir. Gaumont. Efficient family films. Later a producer. First Offence, East Meets West, His Lordship 36; Take My Tip 37; Strange Boarders 38; A Window in London, The Silent Battle 39; Dr. O'Dowd, The Briggs Family, Fingers 40; Mr. Proudfoot Shows a Light (short), Once a Crook 41; Back Room Boy 42; Night Invader, It's In The Bag 43; Flight From Folly 45.

334 MASON James (1909–) Actor. B: Huddersfield. Architect; 31: stage. Handsome brooding star, in top box-office ten 44–47 thanks to Gainsborough romances. Also Hollywood. Late Extra 35; Twice Branded, Troubled Waters, Prison Breaker, Blind Man's Bluff, Secret of Stamboul 36; The Mill on the Floss, Fire Over England, The High Command, Catch as Catch Can, The Return of the Scarlet Pimpernel 37; I Met a Murderer (also prod. & sc.) 39; This Man Is Dangerous, Hatter's Castle 41; The Night Has Eyes, Alibi, Secret Mission, Thunder Rock 42; The Bells Go Down, The Man in Grey, They Met in the Dark, Candlestick in Algeria 43; Fanny by Gaslight, Hotel Reserve 44; A Place of One's Own, They Were Sisters, The Seventh Veil, The Wicked Lady 45; Odd Man Out 46; The Upturned

Glass 47; Pandora and the Flying Dutchman 50; The Man Between 53; Island in the Sun 57; A Touch of Larceny 59; The Trials of Oscar Wilde 60; Tiara Tahiti, Lolita 62; The Pumpkin Eater 64; Lord Jim 65; The Blue Max, Georgy Girl, The Deadly Affair 66; Stranger In The House 67; Duffy, Subterfuge 68.

335 MASSEY Raymond (1896–) Actor. B: Toronto. Stage: 22. M: (2) Adrianne Allen; children: Daniel & Anna. Character star; also Hollywood. The Speckled Band 31; The Face at the Window 32; The Scarlet Pimpernel 35; Things to Come 36; Fire Over England, Dreaming Lips, Under the Red Robe 37; The Drum, Black Limelight 38; 49th Parallel 41; A Matter of Life and Death 46; The Queen's Guards 61.

336 MASSINGHAM Richard (1898–1953) Director; writer, actor, producer. Doctor; 33: Amateur films. 37: G.P.O. Film Unit. Arguably the brightest and most individual talent ever lost to British features: he made only shorts. Tell Me If It Hurts 35; And So to Work 36; The Daily Round 37; At the Third Stroke, Come for a Stroll 39; Fear and Peter Brown 40; Dangers in the Dark 41; The Five Inch Bather, Young and Healthy, We Speak to India, Who'll Buy a Warship, Believe It or Not, Salvage 42; Post Haste, In Which We Live, Piccadilly Roundabout, Random Harvest 43; Some Like It Rough, Cambridge, First Aid in Action 44; Family Doctor, Down at the Local, Coughs and Sneezes 45; Pool of Contentment, Influenza 46; Harvest Camp, Pedal Cyclists, Women Must Work 47; Flight of Fancy, The Greedy Boy's Dream, Jet-propelled Germs 48; Moving House, Handkerchief Drill 49; The Cure 50; He Won't Bite You, Introducing the New Worker 51; To the Rescue 52; The Blakes Slept Here (co-dir.) 53.

337 MATTHEWS Jessie (1907–   )
Actress. B: Soho. Stage: 19, singer, dancer. Leading lady of 30s musicals, once wed to her co-star/director Sonnie HALE. *Beloved Vagabond* 23; *Straws in the Wind* 24; sound: *Out of the Blue* 31; *There Goes the Bride, The Midshipmaid* 32; *The Man From Toronto, The Good Companions, Friday the 13th* 33; *Waltzes From Vienna, Evergreen* 34; *First a Girl* 35; *It's Love Again, Head Over Heels* 36; *Gangway* 37; *Sailing Along* 38; *Climbing High* 39; *Victory Wedding* (short) (dir.), *Candles at Nine* 40; *Life Is Nothing Without Music* (short) 47; *Tom Thumb* 58.

338 MATTHEWS Lester (1900–   )
Actor. B: Nottingham. Stage: 16. M: Anne GREY. Leading gent, later in Hollywood. *The Lame Duck* (short), *Creeping Shadows, The Man at Six, The Wickham Mystery, Gypsy Blood, The Old Man* 31; *The Indiscretions of Eve, Fires of Fate, Their Night Out* 32; *Stolen Necklace, Out of the Past, Called Back, She Was Only a Village Maiden, Melody Maker, Facing the Music, The Song You Gave Me, On Secret Service* 33; *Borrowed Clothes, Boomerang, Song at Eventide, Blossom Time, Irish Hearts, The Poisoned Diamond* 34.

339 McCARTHY Michael (1917–1959)
Director. B: Birmingham. 34: asst. dir. Twickenham. 46: Docs. *Town Patrol* (short) 49; *Assassin For Hire, Mystery Junction* 51; *John of the Fair, Crow Hollow* 52; *Shadow of a Man* 55; *It's Never Too Late* 56; *The Traitor* 57; *Operation Amsterdam* 59.

340 McGOOHAN Patrick (1928–   ) Actor. B: New York. 53: London stage. Tough hero. *Passage Home, I Am a Camera* 55; *Zarak, High Tide at Noon* 56; *Hell Drivers, The Gypsy and the Gentleman* 57; *Nor the Moon By Night* 58; *All Night Long, The Quare Fellow, Life For Ruth* 62; *Dr. Syn Alias The Scarecrow* 63; *Three Lives of Thomasina* 64.

341 McKENNA Virginia (1931–   )
Actress. B: London. M: (1) Denholm ELLIOTT, (2) Bill TRAVERS. Stage: 51. Slim, blonde English beauty, and a fine actress. *Father's Doing Fine, The Cruel Sea* 52; *The Oracle* 53; *The Second Mrs. Tanqueray, Simba* 54; *The Ship That Died of Shame, A Town Like Alice* 55; *The Barretts of Wimpole Street* 56; *The Smallest Show on Earth, Carve Her Name With Pride* 57; *Passionate Summer* 58; *Born Free* 65.

342 McLAGLEN Victor (1886–1959)
Actor. B: Tunbridge Wells. Boy soldier, miner, boxer: Army heavyweight champion. Grinning tough guy hero, main work in Hollywood. Brothers in films (Leopold, Arthur, Clifford, Kenneth and Cyril) failed to match him. *The Call of the Road* 20; *Carnival, Corinthian Jack, Prey of the Dragon, The Sport of Kings* 21; *The Glorious Adventure, A Romance of Old Baghdad, Little Brother of God, A Sailor Tramp, The Crimson Circle* 22; *The Romany, Heartstrings, M'Lord of the White Road, In the Blood* 23; *The Boatswain's Mate* (short), *Women and Diamonds, The Gay Corinthian, Passionate Adventure* 24. Sound: *Dick Turpin* 33; *We're Going to be Rich* 38; *Trouble in the Glen* 54; *Sea Fury* 58.

McSHANE Kitty see Arthur LUCAN.

343 MEDINA Patricia (1921–   )
Actress. B: Liverpool. M: (1) Richard Greene. Dark, bright-eyed star, latterly in Hollywood. *Simply Terrific, Double or Quits* 38; *Secret Journey* 39; *The Day Will Dawn* 42; *They Met in the Dark* 43; *Hotel Reserve, Don't Take It to Heart, Kiss the Bride Goodbye* 44; *Waltz Time* 45; *Children*

of Chance 51; The Black Knight 54; Battle of the VI 58.

344 MERSON Billy (1881–1947) Actor. B: Nottingham. RN: William Thompson. 01: music hall comic. Leading British silent comedy star of his period. *Billy's Spanish Love Spasm, The Man in Possession, The Only Man* 15; *The Terrible Tec, The Tale of a Shirt, The Perils of Pork Pie, Billy's Stormy Courtship* (short) 16; *Billy the Truthful* (short), *Billy Strikes Oil* (short) 17; sound: *Phonofilm* 26; *Comets* 30; *Bill and Coo* 31; *The Show Goes On, Riding High* 37; *Chips, Scruffy* 38.

345 MILES Bernard (1907–   ) Actor (also director). B: Hillingdon. Teacher; stage: 30; scenic painter, actor. Specialist in country characters and real human beings. *Channel Crossing* 33; *The Love Test* 35; *Twelve Good Men, Midnight at Madame Tussauds* 36; *The Challenge, Thirteen Men and a Gun* 38; *Rebel Son, The Lion Has Wings* 39; *Pastor Hall* 40; *Dawn Guard* (short), *Freedom Radio, Quiet Wedding, Home Guard* (short), *The Common Touch, The Big Blockade* 41; *This Was Paris, One of Our Aircraft Is Missing, The Day Will Dawn, In Which We Serve, The First of the Few* 42; *Two Fathers* (short), *Tawny Pipit* (prod., dir. & sc.), *Tunisian Victory* (doc.) (voice) 44; *Carnival, Great Expectations* 46; *Nicholas Nickleby, Fame is the Spur* 47; *The Guinea Pig* 48; *Chance of a Lifetime* (dir.) 50; *The Magic Box* 51; *Never Let Me Go* 53; *Tiger in the Smoke, Moby Dick, Zarak* 56; *Fortune is a Woman, The Smallest Show on Earth, Saint Joan* 57; *Tom Thumb, The Vision of William Blake* (short) (voice) 58; *Sapphire* 59; *Heavens Above* 63; *The Specialist* (short) 66.

346 MILES Sarah (1941–   ) Actress. B: London. Attractive new star. *Term of*

Trial 62; *The Servant, The Six Sided Triangle* (short) 63; *Those Magnificent Men in Their Flying Machines, I Was Happy Here* 65; *Blow-Up* 66.

347 MILLAND Ray (1905–   ) Actor. B: Neath. RN: Reginald Truscott-Jones. Seaman, soldier; stage. Handsome patent-haired hero soon snapped up for Hollywood stardom. *The Flying Scotsman, Lady From the Sea, Plaything* 29; *Orders is Orders, This is the Life* 33; *French Without Tears* 39; *Circle of Danger* 51; *High Flight, The Safecracker* (also dir.) 57; *Hostile Witness* (also dir.) 67.

348 MILLER Frank (1891–195) Director and writer. B: London. 06: actor, *Oh That Doctor's Boy*. Series for PARKINSON in 20s, B.I.P. comedies in 30s. Writer-director: *Odd Charges* (short), *Skipper of the Osprey* (short), *Persecution of Bob Pretty* (short), *A Marked Man* (short) 16; *Till Our Man Comes In* series (6) (dir. only), *The March Hare* 19; *Stop Press* series, *The Joyous Adventures of Aristide Pujol* 20. Scripting: *Let's Pretend* (short), *The Law Divine* 20; *Leaves from My Life* series (12), *Daniel Deronda, Knave of Diamonds, A Dear Fool, Love at the Wheel* 21; *Trapped by the Mormons, Married to a Mormon, False Evidence, While London Sleeps, Crushing the Drug Traffic* (short), *Tense Moments from Great Plays* series (8), *Tense Moments from Operas* series (12), *Famous Poems by G. R. Sims* series (12), *The Sporting Twelve* series (12), *Wheels of Chance, Treasure Trove* (short) (also dir.) 22; *Syncopated Picture Plays* (6), *The School for Scandal, Beloved Vagabond* 23; *Alley of Golden Hearts, Her Redemption* 24. Writer-director: *The Happy Rascals* series (5) 26; *When We Were Very Young* series (6), *Houpla* (dir. only) 28; *Cupid in Clover, Mr. Nobody* 29. Sound, scripting:

Shadows, Love Lies, Out of the Blue 31; Lucky Girl (also co-dir.), Let Me Explain Dear (also co-dir.), Maid of the Mountains, Verdict of the Sea (also dir.), Money Talks 32; Letting in the Sunshine, A Southern Maid 33; The Scotland Yard Mystery, Love at Second Sight, Those Were the Days, Mr. Cinders 34; Dandy Dick, It's a Bet, A Honeymoon for Three 35; She Knew What She Wanted, Annie Laurie, Bed and Breakfast (also acted) 36; The Landlady (short), Consider Your Verdict (short) 38; Inquest, Trunk Crime 39.

349 MILLER Max (1895–1963) Actor. B: London. RN: Thomas Sargent. 03: circus; later music halls. 'The Cheeky Chappie' did characteristic cameos, then starred in 8 comedies for Warners. The Good Companions, Channel Crossing, Friday the 13th 33; Princess Charming 34; Things Are Looking Up 35; Educated Evans, Get Off My Foot 36; Take It From Me, Don't Get Me Wrong 37; Thank Evans, Everything Happens to Me 38; The Good Old Days, Hoots Mon 39; Asking For Trouble 43.

350 MILLS Hayley (1946–   ) Actress. B: London. Father: John MILLS. Child/teenage star; also Hollywood. Tiger Bay 59; Whistle Down the Wind 61; In Search of the Castaways 62; The Chalk Garden 63; The Moon Spinners, The Truth About Spring 64; Sky West and Crooked 65; The Family Way 66; Pretty Polly 67; Twisted Nerve 68.

351 MILLS John (1908–   ) Actor. B: North Elmham. 28: chorus boy. Daughters: Juliet Mills, Hayley MILLS. One of the most consistently popular stars; has a common touch. The Midshipmaid 32; Britannia of Billingsgate, The Ghost Camera 33; River Wolves, A Political Party, Those Were the Days, The Lash, Blind Justice, Doctor's Orders 34; Royal Cavalcade, Forever England, Charing Cross Road, Car of Dreams 35; First Offence, Tudor Rose 36; O.H.M.S., The Green Cockatoo 37; Goodbye Mr. Chips 39; All Hands (short), Old Bill and Son 40; Cottage to Let, The Black Sheep of Whitehall 41; The Big Blockade, The Young Mr. Pitt, In Which We Serve 42; We Dive at Dawn 43; This Happy Breed, Victory Wedding (short), Waterloo Road 44; The Way to the Stars, Land of Promise (short) 45; Great Expectations 46; So Well Remembered, The October Man 47; Scott of the Antarctic 48; The History of Mr. Polly, The Rocking Horse Winner, Friend of the Family (short) (voice) 49; Morning Departure 50; Mr. Denning Drives North 51; The Gentle Gunman, The Long Memory 52; Hobson's Choice 53; The Colditz Story, The End of the Affair 54; Above Us the Waves, Escapade 55; It's Great to be Young, The Baby and the Battleship 56; Town on Trial, Vicious Circle 57; Dunkirk, Ice Cold in Alex, I Was Monty's Double 58; Tiger Bay 59; Summer of the Seventeenth Doll, Tunes of Glory 60; The Singer Not The Song, The Swiss Family Robinson, Flame in the Streets 61; The Valiant, Tiara Tahiti 62; The Chalk Garden 63; The Truth About Spring 64; Operation Crossbow, Sky West and Crooked (also dir.) 65; The Wrong Box, The Family Way 66; Africa Texas Style 67; Oh! What a Lovely War 68.

352 MITCHELL Oswald (18 –1949) Director (also writer and producer). 19: Stoll cinema mgr. 27: Stoll prod. mgr. Low budget comedies, 19 of them for Butchers. Danny Boy (prod., sc. only) 34; Cock o' the North (also sc. & prod.), Stars on Parade 35; Shipmates o' Mine (also sc.), Variety Parade, King of Hearts 36; Rose of Tralee (also sc.), Old Mother Riley 37; Lily of Laguna, Almost a Gentleman, Little Dolly

Daydream, Old Mother Riley in Paris 38; Music Hall Parade, Old Mother Riley M.P. (also sc.), Jailbirds, Night Journey 39; Pack Up Your Troubles, Sailors Don't Care 40; Danny Boy (also sc.), Bob's Your Uncle (also sc.) 41; Asking for Trouble (also sc.) 42; The Dummy Talks 43; Old Mother Riley Overseas (also prod.) 44; Old Mother Riley at Home (also sc.) 45; Loyal Heart (also sc.) 46; The Mysterious Mr. Nicholson (also prod.), Black Memory (also prod.) 47; The Greed of William Hart (also prod.), House of Darkness 48; Man from Yesterday, The Temptress (also prod.) 49.

353 MITCHELL Yvonne (1925–   )
Actress. B: Cricklewood. Stage: 39. Playwright and novelist. Dark, attractive, intelligent. Queen of Spades 48; Children of Chance 51; Turn the Key Softly 53; The Divided Heart 54; Escapade 55; Yield to the Night 56; Woman in a Dressing Gown 57; Passionate Summer 58; Tiger Bay, Sapphire 59; Conspiracy of Hearts, The Trials of Oscar Wilde 60; Johnny Nobody 61; The Main Attraction 63.

354 MOORE Kieron (1925–   )
Actor. B: Skibbereen. RN: O'Hanrahan. Stage: 42. Handsome, hefty Irish hero. The Voice Within 45; A Man About the House, Mine Own Executioner 47; Anna Karenina 48; Saints and Sinners 49; The Naked Heart 50; Honeymoon Deferred 51; Mantrap 52; Recoil 53; Conflict of Wings, The Green Scarf 54; Blue Peter 55; Satellite in the Sky 56; The Steel Bayonet, Three Sundays to Live 57; The Key, The Angry Hills 58; League of Gentlemen 59; The Day They Robbed the Bank of England, The Siege of Sidney Street 60; Dr. Blood's Coffin 61; The Day of the Triffids, I Thank a Fool, The Main Attraction 62; Hide and Seek, Girl in the Headlines 63; Arabesque 66.

355 MORAN Percy (18 –1958) Actor (also director). B: Ireland. Boy boxer, circus, music halls, stuntman. Probably the best of the Lieut. Darings. Main shorts: Gaumont chase comedies 04; Lieut. Daring and the Secret Service Agents 11; Dick Turpin series (4), The Belle of Bettys-y-Coed, Lieut. Daring and the Plans of the Minefield, The Great Anarchist Mystery, The Mountaineer's Romance 12; The Favourite for the Jamaica Cup, Tom Cringle in Jamaica, Lieut. Daring and the Dancing Girl 13; The Chase of Death 14. Features: Heroes of the Mine 13; The Live Wire, The Houseboat Mystery 14. Actor-director: O.H.M.S. Our Helpless Millions Saved 14; Britain's Naval Secret, Slavers of the Thames, London Nighthawks, At the Torrent's Mercy (acted only), How Men Love Women, Parted by the Sword, Nurse and Martyr 15; London's Enemies, It Is for England (acted only) 16; The Redemption of his Name 18; Jack Sam and Pete 19; The Field of Honour 22; Lieut. Daring R.N. and the Water Rats (acted only).

356 MORE Kenneth (1914–   )
Actor. B: Gerrards Cross. Stage: 36. Likeable leading man with a light touch. Windmill Revels, Carry On London 38; Scott of the Antarctic 48; Man on the Run, Now Barabbas, Stop Press Girl 49; Morning Departure, Chance of a Lifetime, The Clouded Yellow, The Franchise Affair 50; No Highway, Appointment with Venus 51; Brandy for the Parson, The Yellow Balloon 52; Never Let Me Go, Genevieve, Our Girl Friday 53; Doctor in the House, Raising a Riot 54; The Deep Blue Sea 55; Reach for the Sky 56; The Admirable Crichton 57; A Night to Remember, Next to No Time, The Sheriff of Fractured Jaw, The 39 Steps 58; North West Frontier 59; Sink the Bismarck, Man in the Moon 60; The Greengage Summer 61; Some People, We Joined the Navy 62; The Comedy Man 63; The

Mercenaries 67; *Oh! What a Lovely War* 68.

357 MORE O'FERRALL George (1906–) Director. 35: asst. dir. *Midshipman Easy.* 36: TV producer. His first few features were his best. *Angels One Five, The Holly and the Ivy* 52; *The Heart of the Matter* 53; *The Green Scarf* 54; *Three Cases of Murder* (co-dir.), *The Woman for Joe* 55; *The March Hare* 56.

358 MORGAN Joan (1905–) Actress, writer. B: Kent. Child actress who grew into a pretty teenage star and later turned scenarist (as Joan Wentworth Wood and Iris North), novelist and playwright. Father: Sidney MORGAN. Actress: *The Cup Final Mystery, The Great Spy Raid, Queenie of the Circus* 14; *The World's Desire, Iron Justice, The Woman Who Did, Light* 15; *Frailty, Her Greatest Performance* 16; *Drink, Because* 18; *Lady Noggs, The Scarlet Wooing, Little Dorrit, Two Little Wooden Shoes, The Children of Gibeon* 20; *The Road to London, A Lowland Cinderella* 21; *Dicky Monteith, The Lilac Sunbonnet, Truants, Fires of Innocence, The Crimson Circle* 22; *Curfew Must Not Ring Tonight* (short) 23; *The Great Well, Shadow of Egypt* 24; *The Woman Tempted* 26; *A Window in Piccadilly* 28; *Three Men in a Cart* 29; sound: *Her Reputation* 31. Scripted: *The Alley Cat* 29; sound: *Contraband Love* 31; *The Callbox Mystery* 32; *Mixed Doubles, Chelsea Life* 33; *Honeymoon Merry-go-Round* 36; *The Minstrel Boy* 37; *Lily of Laguna* 38; *This Was a Woman* 48.

359 MORGAN Sidney (1873–1946) Director, writer. Daughter: Joan MORGAN. Adapted most of his features from novels, 19 for Progress. B: London. *The Brass Bottle, The Great Spy Raid, Huns of the North Sea, Dr. Paxton's Last Crime* 14; *Our Boys, The World's Desire, Iron Justice, Esther Redeemed, Light* 15; *Temptation's Hour, The Charlatan, The Stolen Sacrifice* 16; *Auld Lang Syne, Derelicts, A Bid for Fortune* 17; *Drink, Because, Democracy* 18; *After Many Days, All Men Are Liars, Sweet and Twenty* 19; *Lady Noggs, The Black Sheep, The Scarlet Wooing, Little Dorrit, The Woman of the Iron Bracelets, Two Little Wooden Shoes, The Children of Gibeon, By Berwen Banks, A Man's Shadow* 20; *Moth and Rust, The Mayor of Casterbridge, A Lowland Cinderella* 21; *The Lilac Sunbonnet, Fires of Innocence* 22; *The Woman Who Obeyed* 23; *Miriam Rozella, The Shadow of Egypt* 24; *Bulldog Drummond's Third Round, Somebody's Darling* (sc. only) 25; *A Window in Piccadilly, Thoroughbred* 28; sound: *Mixed Doubles, Chelsea Life, Faces, Honeymoon Merry-go-Round* (prod. only) 36; *The Minstrel Boy* 37; *Lily of Laguna* (prod. only), *Almost a Gentleman* (prod. only) 38.

360 MORGAN Terence (1921–) Actor. B: London. Stage: 43. Handsome star of the 50s with a 30s look. *Hamlet* 48; *Shadow of the Past* 50; *Captain Horatio Hornblower R.N., Encore* 51; *Mandy, It Started in Paradise* 52; *Street Corner, Turn the Key Softly, The Steel Key, Always a Bride* 53; *Forbidden Cargo, Dance Little Lady, Svengali* 54; *They Can't Hang Me* 55; *The March Hare, It's a Wonderful World* 56; *The Scamp* 57; *Tread Softly Stranger* 58; *Shakedown* 59; *Piccadilly Third Stop* 60; *The Curse of the Mummy's Tomb* 64; *The Penthouse* 67.

361 MORLEY Robert, O.B.E. (1908–) Actor. B: Semley. Salesman, author, playwright. 28: stage. Films: 37 (U.S.A.). Rotund character star at his best in comedy. *You Will Remember* 40; *Major Barbara* 41; *This Was Paris, The Big Blockade, The Foreman Went to France, The*

Young Mr. Pitt 42; I Live in Grosvenor Square 45; Ghosts of Berkeley Square 48; The Small Back Room 49; Outcast of the Islands, The African Queen 51; Curtain Up 52; The Final Test, The Story of Gilbert and Sullivan, Beat the Devil 53; The Good Die Young, The Rainbow Jacket, Beau Brummell 54; The Adventures of Quentin Durward 55; Loser Takes All 56; Law and Disorder, The Sheriff of Fractured Jaw 58; The Doctor's Dilemma, Libel 59; The Battle of the Sexes, Oscar Wilde 60; The Young Ones 61; Go to Blazes, The Road to Hong Kong, The Boys 62; Nine Hours to Rama, Murder at the Gallop, The Old Dark House, Ladies Who Do, Hot Enough For June 63; Of Human Bondage, Rhythm 'n' Greens (short) (voice) 64; Those Magnificent Men in Their Flying Machines, The Alphabet Murders, A Study in Terror, Life at the Top 65; Finder's Keepers, Hotel Paradiso 66; The Trygon Factor 67; Sinful Davey, Hot Millions 68.

362 MORRIS Ernest (1915–   ) Director. B: London. 32: asst. dir. Brisk little B thrillers, 18 of them for the Danzigers. Operation Murder, Three Sundays to Live, Son of a Stranger 57; Betrayal, Woman of Mystery, On the Run, Three Wanted Men 58; Night Train to Inverness, The Telltale Heart 60; Highway to Battle, The Strip Tease Murder, Tarnished Heroes, Transatlantic, The Court Martial of Major Keller 61; What Every Woman Wants, The Spanish Sword, Three Spare Wives, Operation Stogie, Night Cargoes, Masters of Venus 62; Echo of Diana, Shadow of Fear 63; The Sicilians, Five Have a Mystery to Solve 64; The Return of Mr. Moto 65.

363 MOXEY John (1920–   ) Director. B: Hurlingham. Films: 46, asst.; 50: TV producer. Thrillers. City of the Dead, Foxhole in Cairo 60; Death Trap, The £20,000 Kiss 62; Ricochet 63; Downfall,

Face of a Stranger 64; Strangler's Web 65; Circus of Fear 66.

364 MUNRO Janet (1934–   ) Actress. B: Blackpool. Stage: 49. M: (1) Tony WRIGHT (57–60), (2) Ian HENDRY. A Disney family favourite. Small Hotel 57; The Trollenberg Terror 58; The Young and the Guilty, Tommy the Toreador, Third Man on the Mountain 59; Swiss Family Robinson 60; The Horsemasters, The Day the Earth Caught Fire 61; Life for Ruth 62; Bitter Harvest, Hide and Seek, A Jolly Bad Fellow 63; Daylight Robbery 64; Sebastian 67.

365 MURRAY Stephen (1912–   ) Actor. B: Partney. Stage: 33. Character star. Pygmalion 39; The Prime Minister 41; Next of Kin 42; Undercover 43; Master of Bankdam, My Brother Jonathan 47; London Belongs to Me, Silent Dust 48; For Them That Trespass, Now Barabbas 49; The Magnet 50; 24 Hours of a Woman's Life 52; Four Sided Triangle 53; The Stranger's Hand 54; The End of the Affair 55; Guilty, The Door in the Wall (short) 56; At the Stroke of Nine 57; A Tale of Two Cities 58; Master Spy 63.

366 MYCROFT Walter Charles (1891–1959) Director, writer; producer. B: London. Journalist. 22: film critic Evening Standard. 28: scenario chief B.I.P. 32: Director of productions B.I.P. (over 200 features). Main man behind the scenes of British production in the 30s. Scriptwriting: Champagne, Tesha 28; Elstree Calling, The Yellow Mask, Murder, Almost a Honeymoon, The Man from Chicago 30; Dreyfus, Let's Love and Laugh, Keepers of Youth, Gypsy Blood, Men Like These 31; Money for Nothing 32; The Phantom Shot 47; Girls at Sea 58. Directed: Spring Meeting, My Wife's Family, Banana Ridge 41; Coming Thro' the Rye 47. Produced: The Woman's Angle 52.

N

367 NARES Owen (1888–1943) Actor. RN: Ramsay. B: Maiden Erleigh. Stage: 08. The longest-lasting matinee idol in the movies. *Dandy Donovan* 14; *The Real Thing at Last* (short), *Just a Girl, Milestones* 16; *One Summer's Day, The Labour Leader, Flames* 17; *Tinker Tailor Soldier Sailor, The Elder Miss Blossom, God Bless Our Red White and Blue, Onward Christian Soldiers, The Man Who Won* 18; *Edge o' Beyond, Gamblers All* 19; *The Last Rose of Summer, A Temporary Gentleman, All the Winners* 20; *For Her Father's Sake* 21; *Brown Sugar, The Faithful Heart* 22; *The Indian Love Lyrics, Young Lochinvar* 23; *Miriam Rozella* 24; *This Marriage Business* 27; sound: *Sentence of Death* (short) 27; *Loose Ends, The Middle Watch* 30; *The Woman Between, Sunshine Susie* 31; *Frail Women, Women Who Play, The Impassive Footman, The Love Contract, There Goes the Bride, Where Is This Lady* 32; *Discord, One Precious Year* 33; *The Private Life of Don Juan, After Eight* (short) 34; *Royal Cavalcade, I Give My Heart* 35; *Head Office, The Story of Papworth* (short) 36; *The Show Goes On* 37; *A Peep in the Dark* (short) 38; *The Prime Minister* 41.

368 NASH Percy Director. Boy actor; minstrel manager; Selfridge's publicist. 12: started London Film Co. at St. Margarets. 14: started Neptune Films at Elstree. 27: Prod. mgr. British Lion. *David Garrick, Jack Sheppard* 12; *In the Shadow of the Rope, The Golden Chance, Monty's Proposal* (short), *Black Eyed Susan* (short), *The Burglar's Child* (short) 13; *Harbour Lights, Enoch Arden, In the Ranks* 14; *The Little Minister, The Romany Rye, The Trumpet Call, Master and Man, The Coal King, A Rogue's Wife, Flying From Justice, A Royal Love, The Devil's Bondman* 15; *Disraeli* (co-dir.) 16; *Motherhood, Boy Scouts Be Prepared* 17; *Herself* (short), *Boys of the Otter Patrol, The Elder Miss Blossom* 18; *Women Who Win, Her Lonely Soldier, The Flag Lieutenant, Westward Ho, Darby and Joan* 19; *The Story of the Rosary, Hobson's Choice, Won By a Head, Rodney Stone, The Old Armchair* 20; *The Likeness of the Night, The Croxley Master, His Other Wife, Ships That Pass In The Night, How Kitchener Was Betrayed* 21.

NAUGHTON Charlie see CRAZY GANG.

369 NEAGLE Anna, C.B.E. (1904–) Actress, later producer. B: Forest Gate. RN: Marjorie Robertson. Stage: 26, dancer. The First Lady of British Films. M: her prod.-dir. Herbert WILCOX. Also Hollywood. *Should a Doctor Tell, The Chinese Bungalow* 30; *Goodnight Vienna, The Flag Lieutenant* 32; *The Little Damozel, Bitter Sweet* 33; *The Queen's Affair, Nell Gwyn* 34; *Peg of Old Drury* 35; *Limelight, The Three Maxims* 36; *London Melody, Victoria the Great* 37; *Sixty Glorious Years* 38; *They Flew Alone* 42; *The Yellow Canary* 43; *I Live in Grosvenor Square* 45; *Piccadilly Incident* 46; *The Courtneys of Curzon Street, Royal Wedding* (voice) 47; *Spring in Park Lane,*

Elizabeth of Ladymead 48; Maytime in Mayfair 49; Odette 50; Lady With the Lamp 51; Derby Day 52; Lilacs in the Spring 54; King's Rhapsody 55; My Teenage Daughter 56; These Dangerous Years (prod.), No Time for Tears, The Man Who Wouldn't Talk 57; Wonderful Things (prod.), The Lady Is a Square 58; The Heart of a Man (prod.) 59.

NEAME Elwin see Ivy CLOSE.

370 **NEAME Ronald** (1911–   ) Director and producer. B: London. Parents: Elwin Neame, Ivy CLOSE. 28: asst. ph. Blackmail. 34: lighting camera-man, Drake of England. Well-made box-office successes. Also U.S.A. Produced: Brief Encounter 45; Great Expectations 46; Oliver Twist 48; The Passionate Friends 49; The Magic Box 51. Directed: Take My Life 47; The Golden Salamander 50; The Card (also prod.) 52; The Million Pound Note 53; The Man Who Never Was 56; Windom's Way 58; The Horse's Mouth 59; Tunes of Glory 60; I Could Go On Singing 62; The Chalk Garden 63; Mister Moses 64; The Prime of Miss Jean Brodie 68.

NERVO Jimmy see CRAZY GANG.

371 **NEWALL Guy** (1885–1937) Actor, director, writer. B: Isle of Wight. 11: stage. M: (2) his co-star Ivy DUKE; (3) ex-child star Dorothy BATLEY. Roman-tic gentleman of the 20s, Quota Quickster of the 30s. Acted: The Heart of Sister Anne 15; Esther, Driven, Money for Nothing (short) (also sc.), Vice Versa, Motherlove, Trouble for Nothing (short) (also sc.), The Manxman 16; Smith 17; Comradeship, I Will, The March Hare (also sc.), Fancy Dress, The Garden of Resurrection (also sc.) 19; The Lure of Crooning Water (also sc.), Duke's Son (also sc.), The Mirage (also sc.) 20. Acted, scripted, directed: Testimony

20; The Bigamist 21; Beauty and the Beast (short), The Persistent Lovers, Boy Wood-burn, Fox Farm, Maid of the Silver Sea 22; The Starlit Garden 23. Acted: What the Butler Saw 24; The Ghost Train 27; Number 17 28; sound: The Road to Fortune 30; The Eternal Feminine, Poti-phar's Wife 31; The Marriage Bond 32; Grand Finale 36; Merry Comes to Town 37. Directed: The Rosary, Rodney Steps In, Chin Chin Chinaman, The Other Mrs. Phipps 31; The Chinese Puzzle 32; The Admiral's Secret 34.

372 **NEWLAND Mary** (1905–   ) Actress. B: Gloucester. Stage: 24. M: Reginald DENHAM. All silent films under RN: Lillian Oldland. The Secret Kingdom 25; Bindle series; The Flag Lieutenant 26; A Daughter in Revolt, Passion Island, The Further Adventures of the Flag Lieutenant 27; City of Youth (short), Virginia's Husband, Troublesome Wives 28; sound: To Oblige a Lady, The Officers Mess, Jealousy 31; The Jewel, Ask Beccles 32; Easy Money 33; Death at Broadcasting House 34; The Price of Wisdom, The Small Man, The Silent Passenger 35.

373 **NEWLEY Anthony** (1931–   ) Actor. B: Clapton. Child star, composer, comedian. M: Joan COLLINS. Dusty Bates, The Little Ballerina, Vice Versa 47; Oliver Twist, The Guinea Pig, Vote for Huggett 48; A Boy a Girl and a Bike, Don't Ever Leave Me 49; Highly Dangerous 50; Those People Next Door 51; Top of the Form 52; Up to His Neck 54; Blue Peter, Cockleshell Heroes, Above Us the Waves 55; Port Afrique, Last Man to Hang, Battle of the River Plate, X the Unknown, The Good Companions 56; How to Murder a Rich Uncle, Fire Down Below, High Flight 57; No Time to Die, The Man Inside, The Lady is a Square 58; Idle on Parade, Bandit of Zhobe, Heart of a Man, Killers of Kilimanjaro,

Jazzboat 59; Let's Get Married, In the Nick 60; The Small World of Sammy Lee 63; Stop the World I Want to Get Off 66.

374 NEWMAN Widgey R. (1900–1944) Director, producer. B: Bedford. 21: Publicist First National; 23: ed. Made shorts in series and very minor B-pictures. Off the Beaten Track series, The Romance of Broadcasting, Derby Secrets series 25; John Tilley series (6) 26; Daily Jesters series (4) 27; De Forest Phonofilms 28; A Reckless Gamble 29; sound: Castle Sinister, Heroes of the Mine, Little Waitress 32; Lucky Blaze 33; Merry Men of Sherwood 34; What the Parrot Saw, Immortal Gentleman 35; What the Puppy Said, Pal o' Mine, Apron Fools 36; The Inspector; Funeral March of a Marionette, Lullabye (shorts) 37; On Velvet, Horse Sense, Ghost Tales Retold series 38; Men Without Honour, Pandamonium (short) 39; Two Smart Men, Henry Steps Out 40; Strange to Relate 43.

375 NEWTON Robert (1905–1956) Actor. B: Shaftesbury. Stage: 20. Character star of the first water. Also Hollywood. Reunion 32; Dark Journey, Fire Over England, Farewell Again, The Squeaker, 21 Days, The Green Cockatoo, I Claudius 37; Vessel of Wrath, Yellow Sands 38; Dead Men Are Dangerous, Jamaica Inn, Poison Pen, Hell's Cargo 39; Bulldog Sees It Through, Gaslight, Busman's Honeymoon, Channel Incident (short) 40; Major Barbara, Hatter's Castle 41; They Flew Alone 42; This Happy Breed 44; Henry V 45; Night Boat to Dublin, Odd Man Out 46; Temptation Harbour 47; Snowbound, Oliver Twist 48; Obsession 49; Treasure Island, Waterfront 50; Tom Brown's Schooldays 51; The Beachcomber 54.

376 NIVEN David (1909–   ) Actor. B: Kirriemuir. Soldier, athlete, novelist.

35: films in Hollywood. Charming gentleman with a moustache. Dinner at the Ritz 37; The First of the Few 42; The Way Ahead 44; A Matter of Life and Death 46; Bonnie Prince Charlie 48; The Elusive Pimpernel 50; Happy Go Lovely, Appointment With Venus 51; The Love Lottery 53; Happy Ever After, Carrington V.C. 54; The Silken Affair 57; Bonjour Tristesse 58; The Guns of Navarone 60; The Road to Hong Kong, Guns of Darkness 62; Where the Spies Are 65; Eye of the Devil 66; Casino Royale 67; Prudence and the Pill, Before Winter Comes 68.

377 NORDEN Christine (1924–   ) Actress. B: Sunderland. RN: Mary Thornton. 42: singer. Blonde star of the late 40s. M: (I) Jack CLAYTON. Night Beat, Mine Own Executioner 47; An Ideal Husband, Idol of Paris 48; Saints and Sinners, Interrupted Journey 49; Black Widow, Reluctant Heroes, A Case for P.C. 49 51.

378 NORMAN Leslie (1911–   ) Director, producer. B: London. 27: asst. De Forest Phonofilms. 30: ed. Features good but not outstanding. Too Dangerous to Live (co-dir.) 39; Eureka Stockade (prod.) 48; A Run For Your Money (sc.) 49; Where No Vultures Fly (prod. & sc.) 51; Mandy (prod.) 52; The Cruel Sea (prod.) 53. Directed: The Night My Number Came Up 55; X the Unknown 56; The Shiralee 57; Dunkirk 58; Summer of the Seventeenth Doll 59; The Long and the Short and the Tall 60; Spare the Rod 61; Mix Me a Person 62.

379 NORWOOD Eille (1841–1948) Actor. B: Yorkshire. 84: Stage. Silent screen fame as Sherlock Holmes in 47 films. Princess Clementina 11; The Charlatan, Frailty 16; The Hundreth Chance, The Tavern Knight 20; The Adventures of

Sherlock Holmes series (15), A Gentleman of France, The Hound of the Baskervilles, Gwyneth of the Welsh Hills 21; The Further Adventures of Sherlock Holmes series (15), Recoil, The Crimson Circle 22; The Last Adventures of Sherlock Holmes series (15), The Sign of Four 23.

380 NOVELLO Ivor (1893–1951) Actor. B: Cardiff. RN: Davies. Composer, actor, playwright. 19: Films in France. Romantic hero of the silent screen, more successful with stage musicals in 30s. Also Continent, Hollywood. Carnival 21; The Bohemian Girl 22; Bonnie Prince Charlie, The Man Without Desire 23; The Rat (also sc.) 25; The Triumph of the Rat, The Lodger 26; Downhill, The Vortex 27; The Constant Nymph, The South Sea Bubble 28; The Return of the Rat 29. Sound: Symphony in Two Flats 30; The Lodger 32; Sleeping Car, I Lived With You (also sc.) 33; Autumn Crocus 34. Scriptwriting only: Glamorous Night, The Rat 37; The Dancing Years 50.

381 NOY Wilfred (1882–19) Director. B: Kensington. 98: stage actor/producer. Many shorts and features for Clarendon in 8 years, then Butchers, returning to prod. & dir. for them in sound. Also Hollywood. Main shorts:

Father and Son, The Jealous Cavalier, Daddy's Didums series, Dr. Brian Pellie series 10; Maud, A Miraculous Recovery, Finger of Fate, The Strike Leader 11; At the Hour of Three, Norah's Debt of Honour 12. Features: The Flooded Mine, Lorna Doone 12; A Strong Man's Love, Behind the Scenes, The House of Mystery, Face to Face, The Convent Gate, The Gardener's Daughter, King Charles 13; Old Saint Pauls, Secret Life, Southern Blood, The Love of an Actress, The Family Solicitor, Wreck and Ruin, The Passions of Men, In Peace and War 14; The Great Bank Sensation, When East Meets West, Master of Merripit, Night and Morning, In the Blood, Under the German Yoke, The Seventh Word, The Locket, The Ivory Hand, Under the Red Robe, Verdict of the Heart, When Passions Rise, The Queen Mother, A Princess of the Blood 15; In Search of a Husband, It's Always the Woman, The Little Breadwinner, The Little Damozel, The Lost Chord 16; Home Sweet Home, Asthore, Master of Men 17; What Could a Gentleman Do, Spinner o' Dreams, Ave Maria 18; As He Was Born, Castle of Dreams, The Lady Clare 19; The Face at the Window, Inheritance 20; Her Marriage Lines 21; The Temptation of Carlton Earle, Rogues of the Turf, Little Miss Nobody 23; sound: Father O'Flynn 35; Melody of my Heart, Annie Laurie (prod.) 36; Well Done Henry 37.

O

382 OBERON Merle (1911–) Actress. B: Tasmania. RN: Estelle Thompson. 28: dance hostess. Became Alexander KORDA's leading lady and wife. Also U.S.A. Alf's Button 30; Never

Trouble Trouble, Fascination 31; Service for Ladies, For the Love of Mike, Ebb Tide, Aren't We All, Wedding Rehearsal, Men of Tomorrow 32; The Private Life of Henry VIII 33; The Battle, Broken Melody, The

Private Life of Don Juan 34; *The Scarlet Pimpernel* 35; *I Claudius* (uncompleted), *Over the Moon* 37; *The Divorce of Lady X* 38; *The Lion Has Wings* 39; *24 Hours of a Woman's Life* 52.

383 ODETTE Mary (1901–) Actress. B: Dieppe. Pretty, petite star of silents, first 11 films under RN: Odette Goimbault. *Cynthia in the Wilderness* 16; *Dombey and Son* 17; *The Way of an Eagle, The Greatest Wish in the World, Spinner o' Dreams, Top Dog, The Wages of Sin, Peace Perfect Peace* (short) 18; *As He Was Born, The Lackey and the Lady, Whosoever Shall Offend, Castle of Dreams, The Lady Clare* 19; *With All Her Heart, Mr. Gilfil's Love Story, Enchantment, As God Made Her, John Heriot's Wife, Breed of the Treshams, Inheritance, Torn Sails* 20; *The Double Event, Cherry Ripe, Street of Adventure, The Wonderful Year, Number 5 John Street, All Roads Lead to Calvary* 21; *The Crimson Circle, The Lion's Mouse* 22; *The Hypocrites* 23; *Eugene Aram, The Diamond Man, Not For Sale, Nets of Destiny* 24; *She* 25; *If Youth But Knew* 26; *The Traitor* (short) 27; *Emerald of the East* 28.

384 O'HARA Gerald Director. B: Boston. Journalist. 41: asst. dir. Verity Films (docs.); 45: asst. dir. British National features. X-ploitation specials. *That Kind of Girl, Game for Three Losers* 63; *The Pleasure Girls* (also sc.) 65; *Maroc 7* 66; *Amsterdam Affair* 68.

385 O'HARA Maureen (1920–) Actress. B: Dublin. RN: Fitzsimons. Radio: 32; stage: 34. Beautiful redheaded colleen who swiftly went to Hollywood. *My Irish Molly, Kicking the Moon Around* 38; *Jamaica Inn* 39; *Britannia Mews* 48; *Malaga* 54; *Our Man in Havana* 60; *Battle of the Villa Fiorita* 65.

OLDLAND Lillian see Mary NEWLAND.

386 OLIVIER Sir Laurence (1907–) Actor and director. B: Dorking. Stage: 22. M: (1) Jill Esmond, (2) Vivien LEIGH, (3) Joan Plowright. Distinguished stage actor and director of the best Shakespeare yet filmed. Also Hollywood. *The Temporary Widow, Too Many Crooks* 30; *Potiphar's Wife* 31; *Perfect Understanding, No Funny Business* 33; *Moscow Nights, As You Like It, Conquest of the Air* 36; *Fire Over England, 21 Days* 37; *The Divorce of Lady X* 38; *Q-Planes* 39; *49th Parallel, Words for Battle* (voice) 41; *The Demi-paradise* 43; *Henry V* (also dir.) 45; *Hamlet* (AA) (also dir.) 49; *The Magic Box* 51; *The Beggar's Opera*, (voice) *A Queen Is Crowned* 53; *Richard III* (also dir.) 56; *The Prince and the Showgirl* (also dir.) 57; *The Devil's Disciple* 59; *The Entertainer* 60; *Term of Trial* 62; *Bunny Lake is Missing, Othello* 65; *Khartoum* 66; *Oh! What a Lovely War* 68.

387 O'TOOLE Peter (1934–) Actor. Stage: 58. Virile, blue-eyed world star. *Kidnapped* 59; *The Savage Innocents, The Day They Robbed the Bank of England* 60; *Lawrence of Arabia* 62; *Becket* 64; *Lord Jim* 65; *Night of the Generals* 66; *Casino Royale* 67; *Great Catherine, Goodbye Mr. Chips, The Lion in Winter* 68.

388 OWEN Cliff (1919–) Director. B: London. 37: asst. dir. Crisp crimes & comedies. *Offbeat* 60; *A Prize of Arms* 61; *The Wrong Arm of the Law* 62; *That Riviera Touch* 66; *The Magnificent Two, The Vengeance of She* 67.

P

389 PALMER Lilli (1914–   ) Actress.
B: Posen. RN: Peiser. M: Rex HARRI-
SON (43–57). Stage: 33. Attractive,
intelligent in comedy and romantic
drama. Also Hollywood. *Crime Unlimited*
35; *First Offence, Wolf's Clothing, Secret
Agent* 36; *Good Morning Boys, The Great
Barrier, Sunset in Vienna, Command Per-
formance* 37; *Crackerjack* 38; *A Girl Must
Live, Blind Folly* 39; *The Door With Seven
Locks* 40; *Thunder Rock* 42; *The Gentle Sex*
43; *English Without Tears* 44; *The Rake's
Progress* 45; *Beware of Pity* 46; *The Long
Dark Hall* 50; *Conspiracy of Hearts* 60; *The
Amorous Adventures of Moll Flanders,
Operation Crossbow* 65; *Sebastian* 67;
Nobody Runs Forever, Oedipus the King 68.

390 PARKER Albert (1889–   )
Director. B: New York. 01: Stage actor,
producer. 16: film actor, then director.
To England to make quota pictures for
Fox British. *After Dark* 32; *The Right to
Live* 33; *Rolling in Money, The Third Clue*
34; *Riverside Murder, White Lilac, Late
Extra* 35; *Troubled Waters, Blind Man's
Bluff* 36; *Strange Experiment, The £5 Man*
37; *Murder in the Family, Second Thoughts*
38.

391 PARKINSON H. B. (1884–   )
Director, later producer. B: Blackburn.
01: Exhibitor; renter; 18: prod. for
Screen Plays, Master Films. Produced
mainly series of shorts, some of which he
directed. *The Law Divine, Love at the
Wheel* (sc.) 20; *Leaves From My Life* series,
Film Song Album series 21; *Tense Moments
With Great Authors* series, *Master Song
Scenas* series, *Trapped by the Mormons,
Married to a Mormon, Crushing the Drug
Traffic* (short), *Tense Moments From Great
Plays* series, *Tense Moments From Operas*
series, *Famous Poems of George R. Sims*
series, *The Sporting Twelve* series 22;
Wonderful London series 24; *London's
Famous Cabarets* series, *London After Dark*
series, *The Only Man* (short) 25; *Bindle*
series, *Horsey* series, *Romances of the
Prize Ring* series, *Across the Footlights*
series, *Wonderful Britain* series 26;
Syncopated Melodies series, *Cameo Operas*
series, *On With the Dance* series 27.
Produced: *The Streets of London, The
Second Mate, Human Cargo* 28; *City of
Shadows, A Broken Romance, Lure of the
Atlantic, The Pride of Donegal* 29; *Scrags*
30; sound: *On Top of the World* (sc.) 35.

392 PARRY Gordon (1908–   )
Director. B: Aintree. 33: asst. dir.
Gaumont. 42: second unit dir. *In Which
We Serve.* Family entertainment with one
X-ception. *Bond Street* 47; *Third Time
Lucky* 48; *Now Barabbas, Golden Arrow* 49;
Midnight Episode 50; *Tom Brown's School-
days* 51; *Women of Twilight* 52; *Innocents
in Paris* 53; *Front Page Story, Fast and
Loose* 54; *A Yank in Ermine* 65; *Sailor
Beware, A Touch of the Sun* 56; *The Sur-
geon's Knife* 57; *Tread Softly Stranger* 58;
Friends and Neighbours, The Navy Lark 59.

393 PATERSON Pat (1911–   ) Actress. B: Bradford. Stage: 26. Pretty star
of the early 30s. To Hollywood. *The*

Other Woman, The Professional Guest, Night Shadows, The Great Gay Road 31; Murder on the Second Floor, Lord Babs, Partners Please, Here's George 32; The Medicine Man, Beware of Women, The Love Wager, Bitter Sweet, Head of the Family, The Right to Live, The Laughter of Fools, The Bermondsey Kid 33.

394 PATRICK Nigel (1913–) Actor (also director). B: London. RN: Wemyss. Stage: 32. M: Beatrice Campbell. Popular hero with a touch of the cad. Mrs. Pym of Scotland Yard 39; Uneasy Terms, Spring in Park Lane, Noose, Silent Dust 48; Jack of Diamonds (also sc.), The Perfect Woman, Morning Departure 49; Trio, Pandora and the Flying Dutchman, The Browning Version 50; Young Wives' Tale, Encore 51; Who Goes There, The Sound Barrier, Meet Me Tonight, The Pickwick Papers 52; Grand National Night 53; Forbidden Cargo, The Sea Shall Not Have Them, A Prize of Gold 54; All for Mary 55; How to Murder a Rich Uncle (also dir.), Count Five and Die 57; The Man Inside 58; Sapphire, League of Gentlemen 59; The Trials of Oscar Wilde 60; Johnny Nobody (also dir.) 61; The Informers 63.

395 PATTERSON Lee (1929–) Actor. B: Vancouver. 48: publicist. 50: stage mgr. TV. Tall, handsome hero of B-budget thrillers. The Good Die Young 53; 36 Hours, The Passing Stranger 54; Soho Incident 55; Reach for the Sky, Dry Rot, Checkpoint, The Counterfeit Plan 56; Time Lock, The Key Man, The Story of Esther Costello, The Flying Scot, The Golden Disc 57; The Spaniard's Curse, Man With a Gun, Breakout, Cat and Mouse 58; Deadly Record, Jack the Ripper, The White Trap, Third Man on the Mountain 59; October Moth, Three Worlds of Gulliver 60.

396 PAUL Fred (1880–19) Director. B: Lausanne. Journalist, medical student. 02: Stage. 07: film actor Cricks & Martin. 12–14: lead in 50 Barker films. 15: actor with SAMUELSON, then director. The Angels of Mons (short), The Face at the Telephone (short), Infelice, The Dop Doctor, Deadwood Dick series 15; Whoso Is Without Sin, Still Waters Run Deep, The Second Mrs. Tanqueray, A Pair of Spectacles, The Valley of Fear, Dr. Wake's Patient, Lady Windermere's Fan, The New Clown, Her Greatest Performance, The Vicar of Wakefield 16; Masks and Faces, The Lyons Mail 17; Duchess of Seven Dials, The House on the Marsh 19; The Little Welsh Girl, Lady Tetley's Decree, The English Rose, Uncle Dick's Darling, The Money Moon, The Lights of Home 20; Grand Guignol series 21; The Faithful Heart, Brown Sugar, If Four Walls Told 22; The Hotel Mouse, The Right to Strike, Let's Pretend 23; shorts: Ragan in Ruins, A Madonna of the Cells, Dr. Fu Manchu series 24; The Last Witness 25; Safety First, Thou Fool, Warwick Castle (short) 26; The Luck of the Navy 27; Dr. Sin Fang series, The Broken Melody, Yellow Stockings (sc. only); sound: Romany Love, In a Lotus Garden, Under the Palms 31.

397 PAUL Robert William (1869–1943) Inventor; producer. B: Highbury. 91: Scientific instrument maker. 94: Builds 4 copies of Edison's Kinetoscope. 95: Builds 60 more; Feb with Birt ACRES takes first kinetoscope films; exhibits at Earl's Court; Sep 23 registers Kinetoscopic Apparatus. 96: Feb 20 projects Finsbury Technical College. Mar 2 patents projector; opens at Olympia Mar 24, Alhambra Mar 25. 99: Builds first studio Muswell Hill. First major prod. of short films, specialising in trick subjects mostly dir. Walter BOOTH.

398 PAVLOW Muriel (1921–   ) Actress. B: Lee. Stage: 36. M: Derek FARR. Attractive, petite star. *Romance in Flanders* 37; *Quiet Weekend* 40; *Night Boat to Dublin* 45; *The Shop at Sly Corner* 46; *Out of True* 51; *It Started in Paradise, The Net* 52; *Malta Story, Doctor in the House* 53; *Conflict of Wings* 54; *Simon and Laura* 55; *Eyewitness, Reach for the Sky, Tiger in the Smoke, Doctor at Large* 56; *Rooney* 57; *Whirlpool* 58; *Murder She Said* 61.

399 PEARSON George (1875–   ) Director (also writer, producer). B: London. Teacher. Rated our top dir. of silents 15–25; quickies in sound. Shorts: *Peg Woffington* (sc. only) 12; *Fair Sussex, In Dickens Land, Rambles through Hopland, Lynmouth, Where History Has Been Written, Kentish Industries, Wonderful Nights of Peter Kinema* series, *A Lighter Burden, Mr. Henpeck's Dilemma* 13; *A Fishergirl's Folly, Christmas Day in the Workhouse, A Son of France* 14; *Buttons, For the Empire* 15; *Canadian Officers in the Making* 17; *Hughie at the Victory Derby* 19; sound: *Souvenirs, Old Soldiers, Mother of Men* 38; *An African in London* 41. Features: *The Fool, Sentence of Death, Heroes of the Mine* 13; *The Live Wire, A Study in Scarlet, Incidents of the Great European War, The Life of Lord Roberts V.C.* 14; *A Cinema Girl's Romance, The True Story of the Lyons Mail, John Halifax Gentleman, Ultus the Man from the Dead* 15; *Ultus and the Grey Lady, Ultus and the Secret of the Night, Sally Bishop* 16; *Ultus and the Three Button Mystery* 17; *The Better 'Ole, The Kiddies in the Ruins* 18; *Pallard the Punter* (sc. only), *Angel Esquire* (sc. only) 19; *Garryowen, Nothing Else Matters* 20; *Mary Find the Gold, Squibs* 21; *Mord Emly, The Wee MacGregor's Sweetheart, Squibs Wins the Calcutta Sweep* 22; *Love Life and Laughter, Squibs M.P., Squibs' Honeymoon*

23; *Reveille* 24; *Satan's Sister* 25; *The Little People, Blinkeyes* 26; *Huntingtower* 27; *Love's Option* 28; *Auld Lang Syne* 29; sound: *East Lynne on the Western Front* 31; *The Third String* 32; *A Shot in the Dark, The Pointing Finger* 33; *River Wolves, Four Masked Men, Whispering Tongues, Open All Night* 34; *Ace of Spades, That's My Uncle, Gentleman's Agreement, Once a Thief, Jubilee Window, Checkmate* 35; *The Secret Voice, Wednesday's Luck, Murder by Rope, Shipmates o' Mine* (sc. only) 36; *The Fatal Hour, Midnight at Madame Tussaud's, Command Performance* (sc. only) 37; *Follow Your Star* (sc. only) 38.

400 PELISSIER Anthony (1912–   ) Director. B: London. Mother: Fay COMPTON. Some fair features in the 50s. *The History of Mr. Polly, The Rocking Horse Winner* 49; *Night Without Stars, Encore* (co-dir.) 51; *Meet Mr. Lucifer, Meet Me Tonight* 52; *Personal Affair* 53; *Tiger in the Smoke* (sc. only) 56.

401 PENNINGTON-RICHARDS C. M. (1911–   ) Director. 32: advertising shorts. 43: ph. *Theirs Is the Glory.* He is best with comedies. *The Oracle* 53; *Hour of Decision* 57; *Stormy Crossing* 58; *Inn for Trouble* 60; *Double Bunk, Dentist on the Job* 61; *Mystery Submarine, Ladies Who Do* 63; *Guns at Batasi* (sc. only) 64; *Danny the Dragon* (also sc.) 66; *A Challenge for Robin Hood* 67.

402 PHILLIPS Bertram Director, producer. Made romantic dramas starring Queenie THOMAS. *White Star* 15; *Won by Losing, Frills* (short) 16; *The Chance of a Lifetime, Ye Wooing of Peggy* (short), *A Man the Army Made* 17; *Meg o' the Woods, It's Happiness That Counts* 18; *Rock of Ages, A Little Child Shall Lead Them* 19; *Trousers* 20; *Syncopated Picture Plays* series, *The School for Scandal* 23; *Her*

Redemption, Straws in the Wind, The Gayest of the Gay, The Alley of Golden Hearts 24; sound: *De Forest Phonofilms* 27.

403 PILBEAM Nova (1919–) Actress. B: Wimbledon. RN: Margery. Stage: 31. M: Pen TENNYSON. Talented child star. *Little Friend, The Man Who Knew Too Much* 34; *Tudor Rose* 36; *Young and Innocent* 37; *Cheer Boys Cheer* 39; *Pastor Hall* 40; *Spring Meeting, Banana Ridge* 41; *Next of Kin* 42; *The Yellow Canary* 43; *This Man Is Mine* 46; *Green Fingers* 47; *Counterblast, Three Weird Sisters* 48.

404 PLUMB Hay (1883–1960) Director; actor. RN: Edward Hay-Plumb. Amateur opera. 10: HEP-WORTH stock co. as cheerful hero (*Heart of Oak*), also writing (11: *Twin Roses*), and as series character *Hawkeye*, before dir. shorts, then features. Small parts in G.B. films in 30s. Main shorts: *P.C. Hawkeye Falls in Love, The Traitress of Parton's Court, Curfew Must Not Ring Tonight, The Emperor's Messenger, The Bishop's Bathe, King Robert of Sicily, Plot and Pash* 12; *Blood and Bosh, Lieut. Lilly and the Splodge of Opium* 13. Features: *George Barnwell the London Apprentice, Drake's Love Story, As the Sparks Fly Upward, Captain Jack V.C., Hamlet, The Cloister and the Hearth, David Garrick* 13; *The Dead Heart* 14; *A Son of David* 19.

405 POLANSKI Roman (1933–) Director, writer. B: Poland. 48: Film school. 54: actor. 57: director. Achieved world reputation, now writing and directing very individual films in Britain and Hollywood. *Repulsion* 65; *Cul-de-Sac* 66; *Dance of the Vampires* 67.

406 POLLOCK George (1907–) Director. B: Leicester. Films 33; asst.

dir. *Contraband* (1940). His features seem to be either Irish or Miss Marple. *Stranger in Town* 56; *Rooney* 57; *Sally's Irish Rogue, And the Same to You* 58; *A Broth of a Boy, Don't Panic Chaps* 59; *Murder She Said* 61; *Village of Daughters, Kill or Cure* 62; *Murder at the Gallop* 63; *Murder Most Foul, Murder Ahoy* 64; *Ten Little Indians* 65.

407 PORTMAN Eric (1903–) Actor. B: Halifax. Salesman; stage: 24. Stardom in the 40s due to Yorkshire humanity, later turned to villainous roles. *Maria Marten, Abdul the Damned, Old Roses, Hyde Park Corner* 35; *The Cardinal, The Crimes of Stephen Hawke, Hearts of Humanity* 36; *Moonlight Sonata* 37; *49th Parallel* 41; *One of Our Aircraft is Missing, Uncensored, Squadron Leader X* 42; *We Dive at Dawn, Escape to Danger, Millions Like Us* 43; *A Canterbury Tale* 44; *Great Day* 45; *Wanted For Murder, Men of Two Worlds* 46; *Dear Murderer, The Mark of Cain, Corridor of Mirrors* 47; *Daybreak, The Blind Goddess* 48; *The Spider and the Fly* 49; *Cairo Road* 50; *The Magic Box, His Excellency* 51; *South of Algiers* 52; *The Colditz Story* 54; *The Deep Blue Sea* 55; *Child in the House* 56; *The Good Companions* 57; *The Naked Edge* 61; *The Man Who Finally Died* 62; *West 11* 63; *The Bedford Incident* 65; *The Spy With a Cold Nose* 66; *The Whisperers* 67; *Deadfall* 68.

408 POULTON Mabel (1903–) Actress. B: London. Became a top silent star and a vocal victim of the talkies. Also Continental films. *Nothing Else Matters* 20; *The Old Curiosity Shop, The God in the Garden* 21; *Moonbeam Magic* (short) 24; *Oscillation* (short), *The Ball of Fortune* 26; *A Daughter in Revolt, The Glad Eye* 27; *The Constant Nymph, The Hellcat, Virginia's Husband, Knights and Ladies*

Top: Joan Morgan, Terence Morgan, Robert Morley, Janet Munro
Centre: Stephen Murray, Owen Nares, Anna Neagle, Ronald Neame
Bottom: Guy Newall, Anthony Newley, David Niven

Top: Christine Norden, Mary Odette, Laurence Olivier, Peter O'Toole
Centre: Lilli Palmer, Nigel Patrick, Muriel Pavlow
Bottom: Nova Pilbeam, Roman Polanski, Eric Portman

Top: Dennis Price, Anthony Quayle, Rene Ray
Centre: Michael Redgrave, Vanessa Redgrave, Oliver Reed, Joan Rice
Bottom: Cliff Richard, Ralph Richardson, Patricia Roc, Guy Rolfe

Top: Stewart Rome, George Sanders, Janette Scott
Centre: Peter Sellers, Susan Shaw, Barbara Shelley, Dinah Sheridan
Bottom: Ronald Shiner, Jean Simmons, Donald Sinden

(short), *Palais de Danse, Not Quite a Lady, Troublesome Wives* 28; *The Silent House, The Alley Cat, Return of the Rat, Taxi for Two* 29. Sound: *Escape, Star Impersonations* (short), *Children of Chance* 30; *Number Please* 31; *Crown v. Stevens, Terror on Tiptoe, Bed and Breakfast* 36; *Pandamonium* (short) 43.

409 POWELL Michael (1905–   ) Director (also producer and writer). B: Canterbury. 25: asst. Rex Ingram in Nice. Ph., ed., asst. dir.; 30–31: sc. *Caste, 77 Park Lane.* From Quota Quickies in partnership with Jerome Jackson to sumptuous, self-indulgent but highly personal pictures in partnership with **Emeric Pressburger** as The Archers (42 –57). Scripted: *Caste* 30; *77 Park Lane* 31. Directed: *Two Crowded Hours, My Friend the King, Rynox, The Rasp, The Star Reporter* 31; *Hotel Splendide, Born Lucky, C.O.D., His Lordship* 32; *Perfect Understanding* (sc. only), *The Fire Raisers* 33; *Night of the Party, Red Ensign, Something Always Happens, The Girl in the Crowd* 34; *Some Day, Lazybones, Her Last Affaire, The Love Test, The Price of a Song, The Phantom Light* 35; *The Brown Wallet, Crown v. Stevens, The Man Behind the Mask* 36; *Edge of the World* 37; *The Spy in Black* (co-dir.), *The Lion Has Wings* (co-dir.) 39; *The Thief of Bagdad* (co-dir.), *Contraband* 40; *An Airman's Letter to his Mother* (short), *49th Parallel* 41; *One of Our Aircraft Is Missing* 42; *The Volunteer, The Life and Death of Colonel Blimp, The Silver Fleet* (co-prod. only) 43; *A Canterbury Tale* 44; *I Know Where I'm Going* 45; *A Matter of Life and Death* 46; *Black Narcissus, End of the River* (co-prod. only) 47; *The Red Shoes, The Small Back Room* 48; *Gone to Earth, The Elusive Pimpernel* 50; *The Tales of Hoffman* 51; *Oh Rosalinda!* 55; *The Battle of the River Plate* 56; *Ill Met By Moonlight* 57; *Peeping Tom* 60; *The Queen's Guards* 61; *They're a Weird Mob* (in Australia) 66; *Sebastian* (co-prod. only) 67.

410 POWELL Sandy (1900–   ) Actor. B: Yorkshire. Music hall comic starred in family comedies. Shorts: *Sandy the Fireman, Sandy the Lost Policeman* 30. Features: *The Third String* 32; *Pathetone Parade* 34; *Can You Hear Me Mother* 35; *It's a Grand Old World, Leave It to Me* 37; *I've Got a Horse* 38; *Home From Home, All At Sea* 39; *Cuptie Honeymoon* 48.

PRESSBURGER Emeric see Michael POWELL.

411 PRICE Dennis (1915–   ) Actor. B: Twyford. RN: Dennistoun Rose-Price. Stage: 37. Top romantic star of the late 40s; survived personal tragedy to become a top character and comedy actor. *A Canterbury Tale* 44; *A Place of One's Own, The Echo Murders* 45; *Caravan, The Magic Bow, Hungry Hill* 46; *Dear Murderer, Jassy, Holiday Camp, Master of Bankdam, The White Unicorn, Easy Money* 47; *Snowbound, Good Time Girl, The Bad Lord Byron* 48; *Kind Hearts and Coronets, The Lost People, Helter Skelter* 49; *The Dancing Years, Murder Without Crime, The Adventurers* 50; *The Magic Box, Lady Godiva Rides Again, The House in the Square* 51; *Song of Paris, The Tall Headlines* 52; *Noose for a Lady, Murder at 3 a.m., The Intruder* 53; *Time Is My Enemy, For Better For Worse* 54; *That Lady, Oh Rosalinda, Private's Progress* 55; *Charley Moon, Port Afrique, A Touch of the Sun* 56; *Fortune Is a Woman, The Naked Truth* 57; *Danger Within, Hello London* 58; *I'm All Right Jack, Don't Panic Chaps* 59; *School for Scoundrels, Oscar Wilde, Piccadilly Third Stop, The Millionairess, Tunes of Glory, The Pure Hell of St. Trinians* 60; *No Love for Johnnie, The Rebel, Five Golden*

Hours, Double Bunk, Watch It Sailor, Victim, What a Carveup 61; Go To Blazes, Play It Cool, Behave Yourself (short), The Pot Carriers, The Amorous Prawn, Kill or Cure, The Wrong Arm of the Law 62; The Cool Mikado, The V.I.P.s, The Cracksman, Doctor in Distress, Tamahine, The Comedy Man, A Jolly Bad Fellow 63; The Horror of it All, Murder Most Foul, The Earth Dies Screaming 64; The Curse of Simba, Ten Little Indians 65; Just Like a Woman 66; Jules Verne's Rocket to the Moon 67.

Q

412 QUAYLE Anthony (1913–)
Actor. B: Ainsdale. 31: stage. Forceful character star. Also Hollywood. *Saraband for Dead Lovers* 48; *Hamlet* 49; *Oh Rosalinda* 55; *The Battle of the River Plate* 56; *No Time for Tears, Woman in a Dressing Gown, The Man Who Wouldn't Talk* 57; *Ice Cold in Alex* 58; *Serious Charge, Tarzan's Greatest Adventure* 59; *The Challenge* 60; *The Guns of Navarone, Drums for a Queen* (short) (voice) 61; *H.M.S. Defiant, Lawrence of Arabia* 62; *East of Sudan* 64; *Operation Crossbow, A Study in Terror* 65.

R

413 RANDLE Frank (1901–1957)
Actor. B: Wigan. RN: Arthur McEvoy. Circus: 16. Music Hall comic who broke box-office records in the provinces with his low budget slapsticks for John E. BLAKELEY. *Somewhere in England* 40; *Somewhere in Camp, Somewhere on Leave* 42; *Somewhere in Civvies* 43; *Home Sweet Home* 45; *When You Come Home, Holidays With Pay* 47; *Somewhere in Politics* 48; *School for Randle* 49; *It's a Grand Life* 53.

414 RAY Rene (1912–) Actress. B: London. RN: Irene Creese. Dancer; novelist. Wide-eyed 30s star. *Palais de Danse* 28; sound: *High Treason* 29; *Young Woodley, Varsity* (short) 30; *Peace and Quiet, Keepers of Youth* 31; *Tonight's the Night, Dance Pretty Lady, Two White Arms, When London Sleeps, Here's George, Born Lucky, Smiling Along, The Changing Year* (short) 32; *King's Cup, Excess Baggage, Tiger Bay* 33; *Rolling in Money, Nine Forty-five, Easy Money* 34; *Once in a New Moon, Street Song, Royal Cavalcade, Full Circle, The Passing of the Third Floor Back* 35; *Beloved Impostor, Crime Over London, His Lordship* 36; *Please Teacher, Farewell Again, Jenifer Hale, The Rat, The Green Cockatoo* 37; *Bank Holiday, Housemaster, The Mountains o' Mourne, Weddings Are Wonderful, The Return of the Frog* 38; *Home From Home* 39; *Old Bill and Son, A Call for Arms* (short) 40; *They*

Made Me a Fugitive 47; The Galloping Major 51; Women of Twilight 52; The Good Die Young 53; Vicious Circle 57. Sc.: The Strange World of Planet X 58.

415 RAYMOND Charles Director (also actor). Stage actor/producer. Main shorts: The Kidnapped Child, Tramps in Clover 04; Dick Turpin's Ride to York 06; A Bird of Freedom 08; Warwick Cinephone Films 09; Every Wrong Shall Be Righted 10; Hamlet, The Great Anarchist Mystery, Dick Turpin series 12; The Favourite for the Jamaica Cup, Tom Cringle in Jamaica, A Creole's Love Story, Lieut. Daring and the Dancing Girl 13. Features: Ju Jitsu to the Rescue, Spiritualism Exposed 13; The Finger of Destiny, The Life of a London Shopgirl, The Mystery of the Diamond Belt, Britain's Secret Treaty, The Kaiser's Spies, Queenie of the Circus 14; The Stolen Heirlooms, The Great Cheque Fraud, The Thornton Jewel Mystery, The Counterfeiters, Traffic 15; Betta the Gypsy 18; The Great London Mystery (serial) 20.

416 RAYMOND Jack (1886–1953) Director. B: Wimborne. RN: John Caines. Engineer; music halls. Film actor: 08, HEPWORTH stock co.: 10–14. 20: asst. dir. Grand Guignol series. Became a top comedy director. The Greater War (short), Second to None 26; Somehow Good 27; Zero 28; A Peep Behind the Scenes 29. Sound: Splinters 29; French Leave, The Great Game 30; Tilly of Bloomsbury, The Speckled Band, Up for the Cup, Mischief 31; Say It With Music, It's a King, Life Goes On 32; Just My Luck, Night of the Garter, Up to the Neck, Sorrell and Son 33; Girls Please, King of Paris 34; Where's George, Come Out of the Pantry 35; When Knights Were Bold 36; The Frog, The Rat 37; Blondes for Danger, No Parking, A Royal Divorce 38; The Mind of Mr. Reeder, The Missing People 39; You Will Remember 40;

Up for the Cup 50; Take Me to Paris, Worm's Eye View, Reluctant Heroes 51; Little Big Shot 52.

417 REDGRAVE Sir Michael, C.B.E. (1908–   ) Actor. B: Bristol. Mother: Margaret Scudamore, M: Rachel Kempson, children: Vanessa, Corin, Lynn. Journalist, teacher, playwright. Stage 34. Soon became one of our best character stars. Also Hollywood. The Lady Vanishes 37; Climbing High 38; Stolen Life, A Window in London 39; The Stars Look Down 40; Kipps, Atlantic Ferry, Jeannie 41; The Big Blockade, Thunder Rock 42; The Way to the Stars, Dead of Night 45; The Captive Heart, The Years Between 46; The Man Within, Fame Is the Spur 47; The Browning Version 50; The Magic Box, Winter Garden (short) (voice) 51; The Importance of Being Earnest 52; The Green Scarf, The Sea Shall Not Have Them 54; The Night My Number Came Up, The Dambusters, Oh Rosalinda 55; 1948, Kings and Queens (short) (voice) 56; Time Without Pity 57; Law and Disorder, Behind the Mask, The Immortal Land (short) (voice) 58; Shake Hands With the Devil 59; No My Darling Daughter, May Wedding (voice) 60; The Innocents 61; The Loneliness of the Long Distance Runner 62; Young Cassidy, The Hill, The Heroes of Telemark 65; Assignment K 67; Goodbye Mr. Chips, Oh! What a Lovely War 68.

418 REDGRAVE Vanessa (1939–   ) Actress. B: London. Stage: 57. Combines her father's talent with her mother's beauty. M: (1) Tony RICHARDSON. Behind the Mask 58; Circus at Clopton Hall (short) (voice) 61; Morgan a Suitable Case for Treatment 65; A Man for All Seasons, Blow-Up 66; The Sailor from Gibraltar, Tonite Let's All Make Love in London (doc.), Red and Blue 67; The Charge of the Light

Brigade, Isadora, Oh! What a Lovely War 68.

419 REED Sir Carol (1906–   ) Director. B: Putney. 27: actor, stage mgr. 32: asst. dir., Basil DEAN. Has made some of our very best films. Also U.S.A. Midshipman Easy, It Happened in Paris, (co-dir.) 35; Talk of the Devil, Laburnum Grove 36; Who's Your Lady Friend 37; No Parking (sc. only), Bank Holiday, Penny Paradise, Climbing High 38; A Girl Must Live, The Stars Look Down 39; Night Train to Munich, The Girl in the News 40; Kipps, A Letter from Home (short) 41; The Young Mr. Pitt 42; The New Lot (doc.) 43; The Way Ahead 44; The True Glory (co-dir.) (doc.) 45; Odd Man Out 47; The Fallen Idol 48; The Third Man 49; Outcast of the Islands 51; The Man Between 53; A Kid For Two Farthings 55; The Key 58; Our Man in Havana 59; The Running Man 63; Oliver 68.

420 REED Maxwell (1919–   ) Actor. B: Larne. M: Joan COLLINS (52–57). Seaman; stage 43. Tall, dark, handsome. Also Hollywood. The Years Between, Gaiety George 46; Daybreak, The Brothers, Dear Murderer, Daughter of Darkness 47; Night Beat 48; Madness of the Heart, The Lost People 49; Blackout, The Clouded Yellow, The Dark Man 50; There Is Another Sun 51; Sea Devils, The Square Ring, Marilyn 53; The Brain Machine, Before I Wake 54.

421 REED Oliver (1938–   ) Actor. B: Wimbledon. Burly, surly hero. League of Gentlemen 59; The Rebel, Beat Girl, The Angry Silence, Sword of Sherwood Forest, The Two Faces of Dr. Jekyll, The Bulldog Breed 60; His and Hers, No Love for Johnnie, The Curse of the Werewolf 61; Pirates of Blood River, Captain Clegg, The Damned 62; Paranoiac, The Scarlet Blade, The Party's Over 63; The System 64; Brigand of Kandahar 65; The Trap 66; The Jokers, The Shuttered Room, I'll Never Forget What's 'isname 67; Oliver, The Assassination Bureau, Hannibal Brooks 68.

422 REISZ Karel (1926–   ) Director, also producer. B: Czechoslovakia. Film critic and theorist. Key figure in Free Cinema movement, making shorts and docs. in touch with reality, but only one feature in this vein. Momma Don't Allow (short) (co-dir.) 55; Every Day Except Christmas (short) (prod.) 57; We Are the Lambeth Boys (doc.) (dir.) 58; March to Aldermaston (short) (assoc. prod.) 59; Saturday Night and Sunday Morning (dir.) 60; This Sporting Life (prod.) 63; Night Must Fall (dir.) 64; Morgan a Suitable Case for Treatment (dir.) 66; Isadora (dir.) 67.

423 RENNIE Michael (1909–   ) Actor. B: Bradford. Salesman; extra from 36. Tall, handsome hero; to Hollywood. Secret Agent 36; Gangway 37; Bank Holiday, The Divorce of Lady X 38; This Man in Paris 39; Dangerous Moonlight, Turned Out Nice Again, Ships With Wings, Pimpernel Smith, Tower of Terror 41; The Big Blockade 42; I'll Be Your Sweetheart, The Wicked Lady 45; Caesar and Cleopatra 46; The Root of All Evil, White Cradle Inn, Idol of Paris 47; Uneasy Terms 48; Golden Madonna, Miss Pilgrim's Progress 49; The Body Said No, Trio, The Black Rose 50; The House in the Square 51; Singlehanded 53; Island in the Sun 57; Battle of the VI 58; Third Man on the Mountain 59; Subterfuge 68.

424 RICE Joan (1930–   ) Actress. B: Derby. Waitress. Brief stardom. Blackmailed 50; One Wild Oat, The Story of Robin Hood 51; Curtain Up, The Gift

Horse 52; *The Steel Key, A Day to Remember* 53; *His Majesty O'Keefe, The Crowded Day, One Good Turn* 54; *Police Dog* 55; *Women Without Men* 56; *The Long Knife* 58; *Operation Bullshine* 59; *Payroll* 61.

425 RICHARD Cliff (1940–   )
Actor. B: India. RN: Harry Webb. Pop singer, records and TV: 58. Top British box-office for his musicals. *Serious Charge* 59; *Expresso Bongo* 60; *The Young Ones* 61; *Summer Holiday* 63; *Wonderful Life* 64; *Finders Keepers* 66; *Two a Penny* 67.

426 RICHARDSON Sir Ralph (1902–   ) Actor. B: Cheltenham. Stage: 21. Character stardom despite, or because of, his basic theatricality. Also Hollywood. *The Ghoul, Friday the 13th* 33; *The Return of Bulldog Drummond, Java Head, The King of Paris* 34; *Bulldog Jack* 35; *Things to Come, The Man Who Could Work Miracles* 36; *Thunder in the City* 37; *South Riding, The Divorce of Lady X, The Citadel, Smith* (short) 38; *Q Planes, The Four Feathers, The Lion Has Wings, On the Night of the Fire* 39; *The Day Will Dawn, The Silver Fleet* 42; *The Volunteer* 43; *School for Secrets* 46; *Anna Karenina, The Fallen Idol* 48; *Outcast of the Islands, Home at Seven* (also dir.) 51; *The Sound Barrier, The Holly and the Ivy* 52; *Richard III* 55; *Smiley, The Passionate Stranger* 56; *Our Man in Havana* 59; *Oscar Wilde* 60; *Woman of Straw* 64; *The Wrong Box, Khartoum* 66; *Oh! What a Lovely War* 68.

427 RICHARDSON Tony (1928–   ) Director (also producer). B: Shipley. RN: Cecil Antonio Richardson. Stage producer: 49. Films via *Free Cinema*. Some striking if stylised features. Also Hollywood (for one film) and France. *Momma Don't Allow* (short) (co-

dir.) 55; *Look Back in Anger* 59; *The Entertainer, Saturday Night and Sunday Morning* (prod.) 60; *A Taste of Honey* 61; *The Loneliness of the Long Distance Runner* 62; *Tom Jones* 63; *The Girl With Green Eyes* (prod.) 64; *Mademoiselle* 66; *The Sailor from Gibraltar* 67; *Red and Blue, The Charge of the Light Brigade* 68.

428 RIDGWELL George (18 –1935)
Director. B: Woolwich. Soldier, singer; playwright: 97. Script ed. then dir. for Vitagraph, 10. *Sword of Damocles, A Gamble in Lives* 20; *The Four Just Men, Greatheart, The Amazing Partnership* 21; *The Further Adventures of Sherlock Holmes* series (15); *The Eleventh Hour, The Pointing Finger, Knight Errant, A Lost Leader, The Missioner, The Crimson Circle* 22; *The Romance of British History* series; *The Last Adventures of Sherlock Holmes* series (15), *Becket, One Colombo Night* 23; *The Notorious Mrs. Carrick* 24; *Lily of Killarney* 29.

429 RILLA Wolf (1920–   ) Director. B: Germany. Father: Walter Rilla. Radio 42; TV producer. Several small gems. *Marilyn, Glad Tidings, Noose for a Lady, The Large Rope* 53; *The Black Rider, End of the Road* 54; *Stock Car, The Blue Peter* 55; *Pacific Destiny* 56; *The Scamp* 57; *Bachelor of Hearts* 58; *Witness in the Dark* 59; *Village of the Damned, Piccadilly Third Stop* 60; *Jessy* (doc.), *Watch It Sailor* 61; *Cairo* 62; *The World Ten Times Over* 63; *Money-go-Round* (doc.) (sc. only).

430 RISDON Elizabeth (1887–1958)
Actress. B: Wandsworth. Stage: 10. Early star of silents, wed her U.S director George Loane TUCKER. Long career in Hollywood. *Bridegrooms Beware* (short), *Maria Marten* 13; *The Cup Final Mystery, Finger of Destiny, Inquisitive Ike* (short), *Black-eyed Susan, The Suicide*

Club, The Loss of the Birkenhead, Beautiful Jim, The Bells of Rheims, It's a Long Long Way to Tipperary, Her Luck in London, The Courage of a Coward (short), The Sound of Her Voice (short), Idol of Paris 14; There's Good in Everyone (short), Honeymoon for Three, Gilbert Gets Tiger-itis (short), Midshipman Easy, London's Yellow Peril, Florence Nightingale, From Shopgirl to Duchess, Another Man's Wife, Her Nameless Child, Grip, Home, The Christian, A Will of Her Own, Charity Ann, Fine Feathers, Love in a Wood 15; Meg the Lady, Esther, Driven, The Morals of Weybury, Motherlove, The Princess of Happy Chance, A Mother of Dartmoor, A Mother's Influence, The Manxman 16; Smith 17.

431 ROBESON Paul (1898–) Actor. B: Princeton. Lawyer; 24: stage singer. Negro star who made his best pictures in Britain. Sanders of the River 35; Song of Freedom 36; Big Fella, King Solomon's Mines, Jericho 37; The Proud Valley 40.

432 ROBEY Sir George, C.B.E. (1869–1954) Actor. B: London. RN: Wade. Engineer; music halls 1891. 'The Prime Minister of Mirth' who made several good silent and sound comedies. George Robey Turns Anarchist (short) 14; £66.13.9¾ for Every Man Woman and Child, Blood Tells 16; Doing His Bit 17; George Robey's Day Off (short) 18; The Rest Cure, One Arabian Night, Don Quixote 23; The Prehistoric Man 24. Sound: (shorts) And Very Nice Too, Good Queen Bess 13; (shorts) The Barrister, Safety First, The Bride, Mrs. Mephistopheles 28; The Temperance Fete, Marry Me 32; Don Quixote 33; Chu Chin Chow 34; Royal Cavalcade, Birds of a Feather 35; Men of Yesterday, Calling the Tune, Southern Roses 36; A Girl Must Live 39; Salute John Citizen 42; Variety Jubilee, They Met in the Dark 43; Waltz Time, Henry V, The Trojan Brothers 45; The Pickwick Papers 52.

433 ROBSON Dame Flora, C.B.E. (1902–) Actress. B: South Shields. Stage: 21. Character star. Also Hollywood. Gentleman of Paris 31; Dance Pretty Lady 32; One Precious Year 33; Catherine the Great 34; Fire Over England, Farewell Again, I Claudius 37; Poison Pen, The Lion Has Wings, Smith (short) 39; 2,000 Women 44; Great Day 45; The Years Between, Caesar and Cleopatra 46; Black Narcissus, Frieda, Holiday Camp 47; Good Time Girl, Saraband for Dead Lovers 48; The Tall Headlines 52; Malta Story 53; Romeo and Juliet 54; High Tide at Noon, No Time for Tears 57; The Gypsy and the Gentleman, Innocent Sinners 58; Murder at the Gallop 63; Guns at Batasi 64; Young Cassidy, Those Magnificent Men in Their Flying Machines, A King's Story (voice) 65; Eye of the Devil 66; The Shuttered Room 67.

434 ROC Patricia (1918–) Actress. B: Hampstead. RN: Felicia Riese. 37: stage. Beautiful star of the 40s. Also Hollywood. Rebel Son, The Gaunt Stranger 38; The Missing People, A Window in London 39; Dr. O'Dowd, Pack Up Your Troubles, Gentleman of Venture, Three Silent Men 40; The Farmer's Wife, My Wife's Family 41; Let the People Sing, Suspected Person, We'll Meet Again 42; Millions Like Us 43; 2,000 Women, Love Story, Madonna of the Seven Moons 44; Johnny Frenchman, The Wicked Lady 45; The Brothers, So Well Remembered, Jassy, Holiday Camp, When the Bough Breaks 47; One Night With You 48; The Perfect Woman 49; Circle of Danger 51; Something Money Can't Buy 52; The Hypnotist, The House in the Woods 57; Bluebeard's Ten Honeymoons 59.

435 ROGERS Maclean (1899–1962) Director, former writer. B: Croydon. 18: publicist British Empire Films; ed. First National. Middle to low budget films, especially comedies. Scripting: *God's Clay* 28; sound: *Rookery Nook, The Loves of Robert Burns* 30; *Tons of Money, Mischief* 31. Directed: *The Third Eye* (also sc.) 28; sound: *The Mayor's Nest* 32; *Up for the Derby, Summer Lightning, Trouble, The Crime at Blossoms* 33; *It's a Cop, Scoop, Virginia's Husband, The Feathered Serpent* 34; *Marry the Girl, A Little Bit of Bluff, The Right Age to Marry, Old Faithful, The Shadow of Mike Emerald* 35; *Twice Branded, A Touch of the Moon, Not So Dusty, To Catch a Thief, Nothing Like Publicity, Busman's Holiday, The Heirloom Mystery, All That Glitters, A Wife or Two, The Happy Family* 36; *When the Devil Was Well, Farewell to Cinderella, The Strange Adventures of Mr. Smith, Fifty Shilling Boxer, Father Steps Out, Why Pick on Me, Racing Romance* 37; *Easy Riches, Merely Mr. Hawkins, Paid in Error, Darts Are Trumps, Romance a la Carte, If I Were Boss, His Lordship Regrets, Weddings Are Wonderful, His Lordship Goes to Press* 38; *Miracles Do Happen, Shadowed Eyes, Old Mother Riley Joins Up* 39; *Garrison Follies* 40; *Saving Saving* (short), *Facing the Music, Gert and Daisy's Weekend* 41; *Front Line Kids, Gert and Daisy Clean Up* 42; *Variety Jubilee, I'll Walk Beside You, Somewhere in Civvies* 43; *Heaven Is Round the Corner, Give Me the Stars* 44; *Don Chicago* 45; *The Trojan Brothers, Woman to Woman* 46; *Calling Paul Temple, The Story of Shirley Yorke* 48; *Dark Secret* 49; *Paul Temple's Triumph, Something in the City* 50; *Madame Louise, Old Mother Riley's Jungle Treasure* 51; *Salute the Toff, Hammer the Toff, Paul Temple Returns, Down Among the Z Men* 52; *Flannelfoot, Forces Sweetheart, Behind the Headlines* 53; *Calling All Cars, Johnny On the Spot* 54; *Song of Norway, The Love Match* (prod. only) 55; *Not So Dusty, Assignment Redhead, You Pay Your Money, Mark of the Phoenix* 56; *A Clean Sweep* (short), *Not Wanted on Voyage, Noddy in Toyland* 48; *Just Joe* 59; *Not a Hope in Hell* 60.

436 ROLFE Guy (1915–   ) Actor. B: Hendon. 36: Stage. Lean, handsome; missed steady stardom through illness. *Hungry Hill* 45; *Odd Man Out* 46; *Nicholas Nickleby, Meet Me at Dawn, Uncle Silas, Easy Money* 47; *Broken Journey, Saraband for Dead Lovers, Portrait from Life* 48; *Fools Rush In, The Spider and the Fly* 49; *The Reluctant Widow, Prelude to Fame* 50; *Home to Danger* 51; *Ivanhoe* 52; *Operation Diplomat* 53; *Dance Little Lady* 54; *You Can't Escape* 55; *It's Never Too Late* 56; *Girls at Sea* 58; *Yesterday's Enemy, The Stranglers of Bombay* 59; *The Alphabet Murders* 65.

437 ROME Stewart (1886–1965) Actor. B: Newbury. RN: Wernham Ryott. Stern hero of HEPWORTH and Broadwest films, mainly opposite Violet HOPSON. Mellowed into gentlemanly character player. Also Continental films. Main shorts: *A Throw of the Dice* 13; *The Whirr of the Spinning Wheel, Thou Shalt Not Steal, The Girl Who Played the Game, The Guest of the Evening, Stress of Circumstances, The Bronze Idol, Unfit, His Country's Bidding, Time the Great Healer, The Man From India, John Linworth's Atonement, Life's Dark Road, The Shepherd of Souls* 14. Features: *Justice, The Heart of Midlothian, Tragedy of Basil Grieve, Creatures of Clay, The Cry of the Captive, The Girl Who Lived in Straight Street, The Terror of the Air, The Grip of Ambition, The Schemers, The Chimes, Brothers* 14; *The Canker of Jealousy, Barnaby Rudge, A Lancashire Lass, The Curtain's Secret, The Incorruptible Crown, Courtmartialled, The*

Bottle, The Baby on the Barge, The Sweater, The Second String, Sweet Lavender, The Golden Pavement, The White Hope, The Nightbirds of London, The Recalling of John Grey, As the Sun Went Down, Iris 15; Face to Face, Trelawney of the Wells, The White Boys, Sowing the Wind, Annie Laurie, Partners, The Marriage of William Ashe, Grand Babylon Hotel, Comin' Thro' The Rye, The House of Fortescue, Molly Bawn 16; Her Marriage Lines, The Cobweb, The American Heiress, The Man Behind the Times, The Eternal Triangle, A Grain of Sand 17; The Touch of a Child 18; A Daughter of Eve, The Gentleman Rider, Snow in the Desert, A Great Coup 19; Her Son, The Romance of a Movie Star, The Case of Lady Camber, The Great Gay Road 20; Her Penalty, The Penniless Millionaire, Christie Johnstone, The Imperfect Lover 21; Dicky Monteith, When Greek Meets Greek, Son of Kissing Cup, The White Hope 22; The Prodigal Son, The Uninvited Guest, Fires of Fate, The Woman Who Obeyed 23; The Colleen Bawn, The Eleventh Commandment, The Stirrup Cup Sensation, Nets of Destiny 24; Thou Fool 26; Somehow Good 27; The Ware Case, The Passing of Mr. Quin, Zero, The Man Who Changed His Name 28; sound: Dark Red Roses 29; The Last Hour, The Price of Things, Kissing Cup's Race 30; Other People's Sins, Deadlock, The Great Gay Road, Rynox 31; The Marriage Bond, Betrayal, Reunion 32; Song of the Plough 33; Important People, Designing Woman, The Girl in the Flat, Lest We Forget 34; Temptation 35; Debt of Honour, Men of Yesterday 36; Wings of the Morning, The Squeaker, Dinner at the Ritz 37; Dance of Death 38; Confidential Lady, Shadowed Eyes 39; Banana Ridge 41; One of Our Aircraft Is Missing, Salute John Citizen 42; Tom's Ride (short) 44; The World Owes Me a Living, The Magic Bow 46; The White Unicorn, Jassy 47; My Sister and I, Woman Hater 48; Let's Have a Murder 50.

438 ROOKE Arthur H. Director. Stage actor: 94; film actor: 15. Actor/director silents principally for I. B. Davidson. Co-dir.: A Pitboy's Romance, The Village Blacksmith, For All Eternity, Holy Orders 17; Thelma, 18. Directed: A Game of Consequences (short), The Rugged Path 18; The Double Life of Mr. Alfred Burton, God's Clay, The Garden of Resurrection 19; Lure of Crooning Water, Duke's Son, Mirage 20; Brenda of the Barge, The Education of Nicky 21; The Sport of Kings, A Bachelor's Baby, A Sporting Double, The Sporting Instinct, Weavers of Fortune 22; Scandal, M'Lord of the White Road 23; Eugene Aram, Wine of Life, The Gay Corinthian, The Diamond Man, Nets of Destiny 24; The Blue Peter 29.

439 ROSMER Milton (1881–195) Actor and director. B: Southport. Stage: 99. Long film career as leading man, character player, and occasionally director. Acted: The Mystery of a Hansom Cab 15; Whoso Is Without Sin, Cynthia in the Wilderness, The Greater Need, Still Waters Run Deep, The Man Without a Soul, Lady Windermere's Fan 16; Little Women 17; The Chinese Puzzle, Odds Against Her 19; With All Her Heart, Colonel Newcome, Wuthering Heights, The Twelve Pound Look, The Golden Web, Torn Sails 20; The Diamond Necklace, The Will, Belphegor the Mountebank, Demos, The Amazing Partnership, A Woman of No Importance, General John Regan, A Romance of Wastdale 21; The Passionate Friends, David Garrick (short), The Pointing Finger 22; A Gamble With Hearts 23; Shadow of Egypt 24; The Woman Juror (short) 26; sound: High Treason 29; The W Plan 30; Grand Prix 34; The Phantom Light 35; South Riding 38; Beyond Our Horizon (short), Let's Be Famous, Goodbye Mr. Chips, The Lion Has Wings 39; The Stars

Look Down, Return to Yesterday, Dangerous Comment (short) 40; *Atlantic Ferry, Hatter's Castle* 41; *Frieda, Fame Is the Spur, End of the River, Daybreak* 47; *The Monkey's Paw, The Small Back Room, Who Killed Van Loon* 48. Directed: *Cash on Delivery* (short) 26; *Balaclava* (co-dir.) 29; sound: *Dreyfus* (co-dir.), *The Perfect Lady, Many Waters, P.C. Josser* 31; *After the Ball* (co-dir.) 320 *Channel Crossing* 33; *Secret of the Loch, What Happened to Harkness* 34; *Emil and the Detectives, The Guv'nor, Maria Marten* 35; *Everything Is Thunder* 36; *The Great Barrier* 37; *The Challenge* 38.

440 ROTHA   Paul   (1907–   ) Director, writer. B: London. Painter, critic. 29: asst. *Piccadilly*. A founder-father of the 'British Documentary School' at E.M.B., his fiction features are disappointing. Docs.: *Contact, The Rising Tide* 33; *Shipyard* 34; *The Face of Britain, Death on the Road* 35; *The Future's in the Air* 36; *New Worlds for Old* 38; *The Fourth Estate* 40; *World of Plenty* 43; *Land of Promise* 45; *Total War in Britain* 46; *A City Speaks* 47; *The World Is Rich* 48; *World Without End* 52; *Cradle of Genius* 61. Features: *No Resting Place* 51; *Cat and Mouse* 58.

S

441 SAMUELSON George Berthold (1888–1947) Director. 10: Birmingham film renter. 13: co-prod. with Will Barker *60 Years a Queen*. 14: own prod. co., Worton Hall studio. Later prods. with Sir William Jury, S. W. Smith, Gordon Craig, some of which he directed: *The Admirable Crichton, The Way of an Eagle* 18; *The Bridal Chair* 19; *The Winning Goal* 20; *The Game of Life* 22; *I Pagliacci* (co-dir.), *Afterglow* (co-dir.) 23; *Motherland* 27; *Two Little Drummer Boys, For Valour, The Forger* 28; *Valley of Ghosts* 29; sound: *Spanish Eyes* 30; *The Other Woman, Jealousy, The Wickham Mystery, Inquest* 31; *Collision, Threads, The Callbox Mystery* 32; *The Crucifix* 34.

442 SANDERS George (1906–   ) Actor. B: St. Petersburg. Textiles, tobacco. 22: stage. Suave star; main work in Hollywood. *Find the Lady, Strange Cargo, The Man Who Could Work Miracles, Dishonour Bright* 36; *So This Is London, The Saint in London, The Outsider* 39; *Ivanhoe* 52; *Bluebeard's Ten Honeymoons, A Touch of Larceny* 59; *Cone of Silence, Village of the Damned* 60; *The Rebel, Five Golden Hours* 61; *Operation Snatch, In Search of the Castaways* 62; *Cairo, The Cracksman* 63; *A Shot in the Dark* 64; *The Amorous Adventures of Moll Flanders* 65; *The Quiller Memorandum* 66; *The Best House in London* 68.

443 SAUNDERS Charles (1904–   ) Director. B: London. 27: asst. dir. *Ideal Cinemagazine*. 35: ed. Gaumont. B-bracket thrillers, often prod. by Guido Coen. *No Exit* 30; *Tawny Pipit* (co-dir.) 44; *Trouble in the Air, Fly Away Peter* 48; *Dark Interval* 50; *Chelsea Story, One Wild Oat* 51; *Blind Man's Bluff, Come Back Peter, Death of an Angel* 52; *Black Orchid, Love in*

Pawn 53; *Golden Link, Meet Mr. Callaghan, The Scarlet Web* 54; *One Jump Ahead, The Hornet's Nest, Time to Kill* 55; *The Narrowing Circle, Behind the Headlines, Find the Lady* 56; *There's Always a Thursday, The Man Without a Body, Murder Reported, A Date with Disaster, The End of the Line* 57; *Womaneater, Kill Her Gently* 58; *Nudist Paradise, Strictly Confidential, Naked Fury* 59; *Operation Cupid, The Gentle Trap* 60; *Dangerous Afternoon, Jungle Street* 61; *Danger By My Side* 62.

444 SAVILLE Victor (1897–)
Director and producer. B: Birmingham. 16: salesman Sun Exclusives. 21: Film Advertising Services with Michael Balcon. 23: prod co. Balcon Freedman & Saville (*Woman to Woman* etc.). 26: Gaumont prod. team ELVEY Saville & Gundrey; sc. *Mademoiselle from Armentieres*. Probably our best director of the 30s in the full Hollywood style; later went to the film capital. Produced: *Hindle Wakes, Roses of Picardy, The Glad Eye, A Sister to Assist 'Er, The Flight Commander, A Woman in Pawn* 27; *The Citadel* 38; *Goodbye Mr. Chips* 39. Directed: *Conquest of Oil* (doc.) 21; *The Arcadians* 27; *Tesha* (also prod.) 28; sound: *Kitty* (also prod.), *Woman to Woman, Me and the Boys* (short) (also prod.) 29; *The W Plan* (also prod.), *A Warm Corner* 30; *The Sport of Kings, Michael and Mary, Sunshine Susie, Hindle Wakes* 31; *The Faithful Heart, Love on Wheels* 32; *The Good Companions, Friday the Thirteenth, I Was A Spy* 33; *Evergreen, Evensong* 34; *The Iron Duke, The Love Affair of the Dictator, Me and Marlborough, First a Girl* 35; *It's Love Again* 36; *Dark Journey* (also prod.), *Storm in a Teacup* (also prod.), *Action for Slander* (also prod.) 37; *South Riding* (also prod.) 38; *Conspirator* 49; *Calling Bulldog Drummond* 51; *24 Hours of a Woman's Life* 52.

445 SCHLESINGER John (1926–)
Director. B: London. Amateur films; bit parts. 57: B.B.C. TV director. Exciting, stylish features in the modern school. *The Starfish* (short) 52; *Terminus* (short) 60; *A Kind of Loving* 62; *Billy Liar* 63; *Darling* 65; *Far From the Madding Crowd* 67.

446 SCOTT Janette (1938–) Actress. B: Morecambe. Mother: Thora Hird. Ex-child star; also Hollywood. *Went the Day Well* 42; *2,000 Women* 44; *No Place for Jennifer* 49; *The Galloping Major, No Highway, The Magic Box* 51; *Background* 53; *As Long As They're Happy* 54; *Now and Forever* 55; *The Good Companions* 56; *Happy Is the Bride* 57; *The Lady Is a Square* 58; *The Devil's Disciple* 59; *School for Scoundrels* 60; *His and Hers, Double Bunk* 61; *Two and Two Make Six, The Day of the Triffids* 62; *Paranoiac, The Old Dark House, The Siege of the Saxons* 63; *The Beauty Jungle* 64.

447 SCOTT Peter Graham (1923–) Director. 40: asst. dir. *Room for Two*. Popular comedies and adventures. Shorts: *C.E.M.A.* 42; *Vegetable Seed Growing* 43; *This Modern Age* series 47; Features: *Panic at Madame Tussauds* 49; *Sing Along with Me* 52; *Escape Route* (co-dir.) 53; *Hideout* 56; *Account Rendered, The Big Chance* 57; *Breakout* 58; *The Headless Ghost, Devil's Bait* 59; *Let's Get Married, The Big Day* 60; *The Pot Carriers, Captain Clegg, Bitter Harvest* 62; *The Cracksman, Father Came Too* 63; *Mr. Ten Per Cent* 67; *Subterfuge* 68.

448 SEARLE Francis (1909–)
Director. B: Putney. Chemist; cameraman, ed. Lower case crime thrillers. Shorts: *Ace Cinemagazines* 36; *War Without End* 38; *Sam Pepys Joins the Navy* 41; *They Keep the Wheels Turning* 42;

First Day on the Spot 43; Student Nurse 44; Day of Grace 57; Music With Max Jaffa 59; Miss MacTaggart Won't Lie Down 66; Gold is Where You Find It, Talk of the Devil 67. Features: Girl in a Million 46; Things Happen at Night 48; Celia 49; The Man in Black, Someone at the Door, The Lady Craved Excitement 50; The Rossiter Case, Cloudburst, A Case for P.C. 49 51; Never Look Back, Whispering Smith Hits London, Love's a Luxury 52; Murder at 3 a.m., Wheel of Fate 53; Profile 54; The Gelignite Gang 56; Undercover Girl 58; Murder at Site Three 59; In Walked Eve, A Ticket to Paradise 60; Freedom to Die 61; Emergency, Gaolbreak, Dead Man's Evidence, Night of the Prowler 62; The Marked One 63.

449 SEARS Heather (1935–   )
Actress. B: London. Attractive, sensitive star. Dry Rot 56; The Story of Esther Costello 57; Room at the Top 58; The Siege of Pinchgut 59; Sons and Lovers 60; Phantom of the Opera 62; Saturday Night Out, The Black Torment 64.

450 SELLERS Peter (1925–   )
Actor. B: Southsea. 45: variety and radio impersonator, comedian. Multi-voiced, then multi-faced, a world star of the 60s. Let's Go Crazy (short), London Entertains (doc.), Penny Points to Paradise 51; Super Secret Service (short) 53; Orders are Orders, John and Julie, The Ladykillers 55; The Case of the Mukkinese Battlehorn (short) 56; Dearth of a Salesman (short), Insomnia is Good for You (short), Cold Comfort (short), The Smallest Show on Earth, The Naked Truth 57; Up the Creek, Tom Thumb 58; Carlton-Browne of the F.O., The Mouse that Roared, I'm All Right Jack, Two Way Stretch, Battle of the Sexes 59; The Running Jumping and Standing Still Film (short), Never Let Go, The Millionairess 60; Mr. Topaze (also dir.), Only Two Can Play, Waltz of the Toreadors, The Road to Hong Kong, Lolita, The Dock Brief, The Wrong Arm of the Law 61; Heavens Above, Dr. Strangelove 63; Shot in the Dark 64; The Wrong Box 66; Casino Royale, The Bobo 67.

451 SEWELL Vernon (1903–   )
Director. B: London. 29: camera asst. Nettlefold Prods.; ed. Low-budget thrillers favouring a spooky twist. The Medium 34; Breakers Ahead 38; The Silver Fleet 42; The World Owes Me a Living, Latin Quarter 45; Appointment with Crime (sc. only) 46; Ghosts of Berkeley Square 47; Uneasy Terms 48; Jack of Diamonds 49; Trek to Mashomba 50; The Dark Light, Black Widow 51; Ghost Ship 52; Counterspy, The Floating Dutchman 53; Dangerous Voyage, Radio Cab Murder 54; Where There's a Will 55; Home and Away, Johnny You're Wanted, Soho Incident 56; Rogue's Yarn 57; Battle of the VI 58; Wrong Number 59; Urge to Kill 60; Wind of Change, House of Mystery, The Man in the Back Seat 61; Strongroom 62; Strictly for the Birds, A Matter of Choice 63; Some May Live 67; Blood Beast Terror, Crimson Altar 68.

452 SHARP Don (1922–   ) Director, formerly writer. B: Australia. 45: stage actor. From children's films to stylish Hammer horror. Scriptwriting: Ha'penny Breeze 49; Child's Play 52; Background, Conflict of Wings 53; Blue Peter 54. Directed: The Stolen Airliner (also sc.) 55; The Adventures of Hal 5 (also sc.), The Golden Disc, The Changing Years (short) 58; The Professionals, Linda 60; Kiss of the Vampire 62; It's All Happening 63; Devil Ship Pirates, Witchcraft 64; The Face of Fu Manchu, The Curse of the Fly, Rasputin the Mad Monk 65; Our Man in Marrakesh, Brides of Fu Manchu 66; Jules Verne's Rocket to the Moon 67; Taste of Excitement 68.

453 SHAW Harold M. Director. B: Tennessee. 1893 stage actor. 09: actor, Edison, 11: director. To England as top U.S. director for London Films, starring wife Edna Flugrath. *Clancarty* (short), *The House of Temperley* 13; *Beauty and the Barge* (short), *Lawyer Quince* (short), *The Bosun's Mate* (short), *The Ring and the Rajah* (short), *Duty* (short), *Branscombe's Pal* (short), *Child o' My Heart* (short), *England's Menace, Trilby, For the Empire, Bootle's Baby, The King's Minister, A Christmas Carol, Two Columbines* (short), *Two Little Britons, V.C.* 14; *Lil o' London, The Incomparable Bellairs, Liberty Hall, Brother Officers, The Heart of a Child, Ashes of Revenge, A Garret in Bohemia, The Third Generation, The Derby Winner, Mr. Lyndon at Liberty, The Firm of Girdlestone* 15; *Two Roads, The Heart of Sister Anne, You* (short), *Me and Me Moke, The Last Challenge* 16; *The Pursuit of Pamela, London Pride, True Tilda, Land of Mystery, Love and the Whirlwind* 20; *Kipps, A Dear Fool, The Woman of his Dreams, General John Regan* 21; *Wheels of Chance, False Evidence* 22.

454 SHAW Sebastian (1905–) Actor. B: Holt. 14: stage. Handsome star of the 30s. *Caste* 30; *Taxi to Paradise, Little Miss Nobody* 33; *Four Masked Men, Get Your Man, Adventure Ltd:, The Way of Youth* 34; *Brewster's Millions, The Lad, Ace of Spades, Three Witnesses, Department Store, Jubilee Window, Birds of a Feather* 35; *Jury's Evidence, Tomorrow We Live, Men Are Not Gods* 36; *Farewell Again, The Squeaker* 37; *Too Dangerous to Live, The Spy in Black* 39; *Now You're Talking* (short), *The Flying Squad, Bulldog Sees It Through, Three Silent Men* 40; *East of Piccadilly* 41; *Journey Together* 45; *The Glass Mountain* 48; *Landfall* 49; *Laxdale Hall* 52; *It Happened Here* 64.

455 SHAW Susan (1929–) Actress. B: Norwood. RN: Patsy Sloots. M: (1) Albert Lieven; (2) Bonar COLLEANO. Rank Charm School star, ex-photographer's model. *London Town* 45; *Walking On Air* 46; *The Upturned Glass, Holiday Camp, Jassy, It Always Rains on Sunday* 47; *To the Public Danger, My Brother's Keeper, London Belongs to Me, Quartet, Here Come the Huggetts, Vote for Huggett* 48; *It's Not Cricket, The Huggetts Abroad, Marry Me, Train of Events* 49; *Waterfront, The Woman in Question, Pool of London* 50; *There Is Another Sun* 51; *Wide Boy, The Killer Walks* 52; *The Intruder, Small Town Story* 53; *The Large Rope, The Good Die Young, Time Is My Enemy* 54; *Stolen Time, Stock Car* 55; *Fire Maidens From Outer Space* 56; *Davy, The Diplomatic Corpse* 57; *Chain of Events* 58; *Carry On Nurse* 59; *The Big Day* 60; *Stranglehold* 62; *The Switch* 63.

456 SHELLEY Barbara (1923–) Actress. B: London. Model; films in Italy 54. Attractive star of horror films. *Cat Girl, End of the Line, The Solitary Child, Camp on Blood Island* 57; *Blood of the Vampire* 58; *Deadly Record, Bobbikins* 59; *Village of the Damned, A Story of David* 60; *Shadow of the Cat* 61; *Postman's Knock, Death Trap, Stranglehold* 62; *Blind Corner* 63; *The Gorgon, Secret of Blood Island* 64; *Dracula Prince of Darkness, Rasputin the Mad Monk* 65; *Quatermass and the Pit* 67.

457 SHERIDAN Dinah (1920–) Actress. B: Hampstead. M: (1) Jimmy HANLEY; (2) John Davis. Photographer's model, fresh young star, executive's wife. *Irish and Proud of It* 36; *Landslide, Behind Your Back, Father Steps Out* 37; *Merely Mr. Hawkins* 38; *Full Speed Ahead* 39; *Salute John Citizen* 42; *Get Cracking* 43; *For You Alone, 29 Acacia Avenue, Murder in Reverse* 45; *Hills of*

Donegal 47; *Calling Paul Temple* 48; *The Huggetts Abroad, The Story of Shirley Yorke, Dark Secret* 49; *No Trace, Blackout* 50; *Paul Temple's Triumph, Where No Vultures Fly* 51; *The Sound Barrier, Appointment in London* 52; *Genevieve, The Story of Gilbert and Sullivan* 53.

458 SHINER Ronald (1903–1965)

Actor. B: London. Mountie; stage 28; films 34: *Doctor's Orders*. Comic cockney in very many films until he became star in the 50s. *Worm's Eye View* 51; *Reluctant Heroes, Little Big Shot, Top of the Form* 52; *Innocents in Paris, Laughing Anne* 53; *Up to His Neck, Aunt Clara* 54; *See How They Run* 55; *Keep It Clean, Dry Rot, My Wife's Family* 56; *Carry On Admiral, Not Wanted on Voyage* 57; *Girls at Sea* 58; *Operation Bullshine, The Navy Lark* 59; *The Night We Got the Bird* 60.

459 SHOTTER Winifred (1904–   )

Actress. B: London. Stage: 18. Petite star who came to the screen with the Aldwych farce team. *Rookery Nook, On Approval* 30; *Plunder, Chance of a Night Time, Mischief* 31; *A Night Like This, Jack's the Boy, The Love Contract* 32; *Just My Luck, Night of the Garter, Summer Lightning, Up to the Neck, Sorrell and Son* 33; *Lillies of the Field* 34; *D'Ye Ken John Peel, The Rocks of Valpre, Marry the Girl* 35; *His Lordship Regrets* 38; *John and Julie* 55.

460 SIM Alastair, C.B.E. (1900–   )

Actor. B: Edinburgh. Tailor, playwright; stage 30. Expert in eccentrics. *Riverside Murder, The Private Secretary, A Fire Has Been Arranged, Late Extra* 35; *Troubled Waters, Wedding Group, The Big Noise, Keep Your Seats Please, The Man in the Mirror, The Mysterious Mr. Davis* 36; *Strange Experiment, Clothes and the Woman, Gangway, The Squeaker, A Romance in Flanders, Melody and Romance* 37; *Sailing Along, The Terror, Alf's Button Afloat, This Man Is News, Climbing High* 38; *Inspector Hornleigh, This Man in Paris, Inspector Hornleigh on Holiday* 39; *Law and Disorder, Her Father's Daughter* (short) 40; *Inspector Hornleigh Goes to It, Cottage to Let* 41; *Let the People Sing* 42; *Waterloo Road* 44; *Green for Danger* 46; *Hue and Cry, Captain Boycott* 47; *London Belongs to Me* 48; *The Happiest Days of Your Life* 49; *Stage Fright* 50; *Laughter in Paradise, Scrooge, Lady Godiva Rides Again* 51; *Folly to be Wise* 52; *Innocents in Paris* 53; *An Inspector Calls, The Bells of St. Trinians* 54; *Escapade, Geordie* 55; *The Green Man* 56; *Blue Murder at St. Trinians* 57; *The Doctor's Dilemma, Left Right and Centre* 59; *School for Scoundrels, The Millionairess* 60.

461 SIMMONS Jean (1929–   ) Act-

ress. B: Crouch Hill. Child star to world star. M: Stewart GRANGER (1950–60). *Give Us the Moon* 43; *Kiss the Bride Goodbye, Meet Sexton Blake, Mr. Emmanuel* 44; *Caesar and Cleopatra, The Way to the Stars, Sports Day* (short) 45; *Great Expectations, Hungry Hill* 46; *Black Narcissus, Uncle Silas, The Woman in the Hall* 47; *The Blue Lagoon* 48; *Adam and Evelyne, Hamlet* 49; *So Long at the Fair, Trio, Cage of Gold, The Clouded Yellow* 50; *Footsteps in the Fog* 55; *The Grass is Greener* 61; *Life at the Top* 65.

462 SINCLAIR Hugh (1903–1962)

Actor. B: London. Stage 22. Handsome leading man; also Hollywood. *Escape Me Never* 35; *The Marriage of Corbal, Strangers on a Honeymoon* 36; *A Girl Must Live* 37; *The Four Just Men* 39; *The Saint's Vacation, The Saint Meets the Tiger* 41; *Alibi, Tomorrow We Live* 42; *Flight From Folly, They Were Sisters* 45; *Corridor of Mirrors* 48; *Don't Ever Leave Me, Trottie*

True, The Rocking Horse Winner 49; No Trace 50; Circle of Danger 51; Never Look Back, Judgement Deferred, Mantrap 52; Three Steps in the Dark 53; The Second Mrs. Tanqueray 54.

463 SINDEN Donald (1923–)
Actor. B: Plymouth. Stage: 41. Slightly stolid star. The Cruel Sea 52; A Day to Remember, You Know What Sailors Are, Doctor in the House 53; The Beachcomber, Mad About Men, Simba 54; Above Us the Waves, An Alligator Named Daisy, Josephine and Men 55; The Black Tent, Eyewitness, Tiger in the Smoke, Doctor at Large 56; Rockets Galore, The Captain's Table 58; Operation Bullshine, Your Money or Your Wife 59; The Siege of Sidney Street 60; Twice Round the Daffodils, Mix Me a Person 62; Decline and Fall 68.

464 SLAUGHTER Tod (1885–1956)
Actor. B: Newcastle. RN: N. Carter Slaughter. Stage: 05. Last exponent of Victorian melodrama in almost literal screen versions by George KING. Maria Marten 35; Sweeney Todd, The Crimes of Stephen Hawke 36; Song of the Road, Darby and Joan, It's Never Too Late to Mend, Ticket of Leave Man 37; Sexton Blake and the Hooded Terror 38; The Face at the Window 39; Crimes at the Dark House 40; Bothered by a Beard (short), The Curse of the Wraydons 46; The Greed of William Hart 48; King of the Underworld, Murder at Scotland Yard 52.

465 SMART Ralph (1908–)
Director. B: London. 27: asst. ed. B.I.P. 28: screenplays (The Sacrifice, etc.). 34: dir. shorts at Merton Park. 40: dir. propaganda shorts Australia. 45: Asst. dir. The Overlanders. A few fair features but busier as TV film producer. The Woodpidgeon Patrol (short) 30; Bush

Christmas 46; Quartet (co-dir.) 48; A Boy a Girl and a Bike 49; Bitter Springs 50; Never Take No for an Answer 51; Curtain Up 52; Always a Bride 53.

466 SMITH Sir C. Aubrey, C.B.E. (1863–1948) Actor. B: London. Cricketer; stage 92. Tall silent star before becoming Hollywood's fine old English gentleman. Red Pottage 18; The Face at the Window, Castles in Spain, The Bump (short), The Shuttle of Life 20; The Bohemian Girl, Flames of Passion 22; The Temptation of Carlton Earle 23; The Unwanted 24. Sound: Birds of Prey, Such Is the Law 30; Contraband Love 31; The Tunnel 35; The Story of Papworth (short) 36; Sixty Glorious Years 38; The Four Feathers 39; An Ideal Husband 47.

467 SMITH George Albert (1864–1959) Inventor, director. B: Brighton. Portrait photographer. 96: builds cine camera. 97: makes trick films, patents double exposure. 00: develops cut-in close-ups; joins Charles Urban's Warwick Trading Co.; builds studio in St. Anne's Well Garden. 06: patents Kinemacolour 2-colour system. Main shorts: The Miller and the Sweep, X-rays, Tipsy Topsy Turvey, The Haunted Castle 97; The Baker and the Sweep, The Corsican Brothers, Cinderella, Faust and Mephistopheles, Photographing a Ghost, Santa Claus 98; The Legacy, A Good Joke, The Haunted Picture Gallery, Aladdin and the Wonderful Lamp 99; The Two Old Sports series, Grandma Threading her Needle, The House that Jack Built, Grandma's Reading Glass 00; The Little Doctor and the Sick Kitten 01; At Last that Awful Tooth, After Dark, Mother Goose Nursery Rhymes 02; Mary Jane's Mishap, John Bull's Hearth, Dorothy's Dream 03; A Visit to the Seaside 08; Natural Colour Portraiture, Kinemacolor Puzzle 09.

468 SMITH Herbert (1901–   )
Director. B: London. Asst. dir. SAM-
UELSON. Musicals and comedies for
British Lion before turning assoc. prod.
for Two Cities. *British Lion Varieties*
series, *On the Air* 34; *Equity Musical
Revue* series; *In Town Tonight, Night Mail*
35; *Soft Lights and Sweet Music, They
Didn't Know* 36; *It's a Grand Old World,
Calling All Stars, Leave It to Me* 37;
Around the Town, I've Got a Horse 38;
Home From Home, All at Sea 39.

469 STAMP Terence (1940–   )
Actor. B: Stepney. Handsome young star
of the modern school. Also Hollywood,
Italy. *Term of Trial, Billy Budd* 62; *Modesty
Blaise* 66; *Far From the Madding Crowd,
Poor Cow* 67.

470 STAMP TAYLOR Enid (1904–
1946) Actress. B: Monkseaton. Beauty
contest winner; stage 21. Elegant
blonde. *Easy Virtue, Remembrance, Land
of Hope and Glory* 27; *A Little Bit of Fluff,
Yellow Stockings, Cocktails* 28; *Broken
Melody* 29; sound: *Meet My Sister* 33; *A
Political Party, Gay Love, Virginia's
Husband, The Feathered Serpent* 34; *Radio
Pirates, So You Won't Talk, Mr. What's His
Name, Jimmy Boy, While Parents Sleep,
Two Hearts in Harmony* 35; *Queen of
Hearts, Blind Man's Bluff, Housebroken* 36;
*Take a Chance, Underneath the Arches,
Feather Your Nest, Okay for Sound, Talk-
ing Feet, Action for Slander* 37; *Blondes
for Danger, Stepping Toes, Old Iron,
Climbing High* 38; *The Lambeth Walk, The
Girl Who Forgot* 39; *The Farmer's Wife,
Spring Meeting, Hatter's Castle, South
American George* 41; *Alibi* 42; *Candle-
light in Algeria* 43; *The Wicked Lady* 44;
Caravan 46.

471 STANNARD Don (1916–1949)
Actor. B: Westcliff. Hollywood films 37.

Handsome hero with brief fame as
screen version of radio's Dick Barton.
*Caesar and Cleopatra, They Were Sisters,
Don Chicago, Pink String and Sealing Wax*
45; *I'll Turn to You* 46; *Death in High
Heels* 47; *Dick Barton Special Agent, The
Temptress* 48; *Dick Barton Strikes Back* 49;
Dick Barton at Bay 50.

472 STEEL Anthony (1920–   )
Actor. B: Chelsea. Stage 45. Handsome
hero. *Portrait from Life, Saraband for Dead
Lovers, A Piece of Cake, Christopher
Columbus* 48; *Once Upon a Dream, Helter
Skelter, Marry Me, Poet's Pub, Don't Ever
Leave Me, Trottie True, The Chiltern
Hundreds* 49; *The Blue Lamp, The Wooden
Horse, The Mudlark* 50; *Laughter in Para-
dise, Another Man's Poison, Where No
Vultures Fly* 51; *Emergency Call, Something
Money Can't Buy, The Planter's Wife* 52;
*Malta Story, Master of Ballantrae, Albert
R.N.* 53; *West of Zanzibar, The Sea Shall
Not Have Them, Out of the Clouds* 54;
Passage Home, Storm Over the Nile 55;
The Black Tent, Checkpoint 56; *Harry
Black, A Question of Adultery* 58; *The
Switch, A Matter of Choice* 63.

473 STEELE Tommy (1936–   )
Actor. B: Bermondsey. RN: Thomas
Hicks. Seaman. 56: pop singer. Also
Hollywood. *Kill Me Tomorrow, The Tommy
Steele Story* 57; *The Duke Wore Jeans* 58;
Tommy the Toreador 59; *Light Up the Sky*
60; *It's All Happening* 63; *Half a Sixpence*
67; *Where's Jack* 68.

474 STEIN Paul L. (1892–   )
Director. B: Vienna. Stage actor, direc-
tor. 20: dir. U.F.A., 28: Hollywood.
Musicals and romances with a woman's
angle. *Lily Christine* 32; *The Song You Gave
Me* 33; *Red Wagon, Blossom Time* 34;
Mimi, Heart's Desire 35; *Faithful* 36; *Café
Colette* 37; *Just Like a Woman, Jane Steps*

Out, Black Limelight 38; Poison Pen, The Outsider 39; Gentleman of Venture 40; The Saint Meets the Tiger 41; Talk About Jacqueline 42; Kiss the Bride Goodbye, Twilight Hour 44; Waltz Time 45; Lisbon Story, Laughing Lady 46; Counterblast 48; The Twenty Questions Murder Mystery 50.

475 STEPHENS Robert (1931–   ) Actor. B: Bristol. Stage: 44. Stage star repeating his success in films. Also Hollywood. Circle of Deception 60; A Taste of Honey, The Queen's Guards 61; The Inspector, Lunch Hour 62; The Small World of Sammy Lee 63; Morgan a Suitable Case for Treatment 66; Romeo and Juliet, The Prime of Miss Jean Brodie 68.

476 STEVENSON Robert (1905–   ) Director, formerly writer. B: London. M: Anna LEE. Gainsborough scenarist who became a top Hollywood-style director; later went to U.S. Scripting: Greek Street 30; The Ringer, Michael and Mary, The Calendar, Sunshine Susie 31; The Faithful Heart, Love on Wheels, Lord Babs, Case of the Frightened Lady 32; FP-1, The Only Girl, Early to Bed 33; The Battle 34; Paradise for Two 37. Directed: Happy Ever After 32; Falling for You 33; Jack of All Trades, Tudor Rose (also sc.), The Man Who Changed His Mind, King Solomon's Mines, Nonstop New York 36; Owd Bob 38; The Ware Case, Young Man's Fancy 39; Return to Yesterday 40; Kidnapped 60; In Search of the Castaways 62.

477 STOCKFELD Betty (1905–1965) Actress. B: Sydney. Stage: 24. Cool blonde beauty. City of Song, Captivation, 77 Park Lane 31; Money for Nothing, Life Goes On, The Impassive Footman, The Maid of the Mountains 32; King of the Ritz, Lord of the Manor, Anne One Hundred 33; The Man Who Changed His Name, The Battle, Brides to Be 34; The Lad, Runaway Ladies

35; Under Proof, Beloved Vagabond, Dishonour Bright 36; Who's Your Lady Friend? 37; I See Ice 38; Hard Steel, Flying Fortress 42; The Girl Who Couldn't Quite 50; Guilty 56; True as a Turtle 57.

478 STUART John (1898–   ) Actor. B: Edinburgh. RN: Croall. 19: Stage. 20 years a star, silent and sound, still playing character cameos. Her Son, The Great Gay Road, The Lights of Home 20; Land of My Fathers, Film Song Album series, Leaves From My Life series 21; Sinister Street, Little Mother, A Sporting Double, If Four Walls Told, The Extra Knot (short) 22; This Freedom, The Mistletoe Bough (short), Little Miss Nobody, School for Scandal, The Reverse of the Medal (short), Constant Hot Water (short), The Loves of Mary Queen of Scots 23; Claude Duval, Her Redemption, His Grace Gives Notice, Alley of Golden Hearts, The Gayest of the Gay 24; We Women, Daughter of Love, Parted (short), Venetian Lovers 25; Baddesley Manor (short), Kenilworth Castle (short), Tower of London (short), The Pleasure Garden, London Love, Mademoiselle from Armentieres, Curfew Shall Not Ring Tonight (short), Back to the Trees (short), The Woman Juror (short) 26; Hindle Wakes, Roses of Picardy, The Glad Eye, The Flight Commander, Woman in Pawn 27; Sailors Don't Care, Mademoiselle Parley Voo, Smashing Through 28; sound: Kitty, High Seas, Taxi for Two, Memories (short), Atlantic 29; Eve's Fall, No Exit, Children of Chance, Kissing Cup's Race, The Nipper 30; Midnight, The Hound of the Baskervilles, Hindle Wakes 31; In a Monastery Garden, Number 17, Men of Steel, Verdict of the Sea, Little Fella, Women Are That Way (short) 32; Naughty Cinderella, Mr. Quincy of Monte Carlo, The Lost Chord, This Week of Grace, Love's Old Sweet Song, Head of the Family, Mayfair Girl, Home Sweet Home, Enemy of the Police,

Top: Terence Stamp, Anthony Steel, Tommy Steele, Robert Stephens
Centre: John Stuart, Eric Sykes, Sylvia Syms, Alma Taylor
Bottom: Terry-Thomas, Richard Todd, Wendy Toye, Rita Tushingham

Top: Jack Warner, Chrissie White, Michael Wilding
Centre: Norman Wisdom, Googie Withers, Tony Wright
Bottom: Susannah York, Mario Zampi, Mai Zetterling

The Wandering Jew, House of Trent, The Pointing Finger 33; The Black Abbot, Four Masked Men, Grand Prix, Bella Donna, The Blue Squadron, Blind Justice, The Green Pack 34; D'Ye Ken John Peel, Abdul the Damned, Royal Cavalcade, Lend Me Your Husband, Once a Thief 35; The Secret Voice, Reasonable Doubt 36; The Elder Brother, Pearls Bring Tears, The Show Goes On, Talking Feet 37; The Claydon Treasure Mystery 38; Old Mother Riley in Society 40; Old Mother Riley's Ghosts, Ships With Wings, The Seventh Survivor, Penn of Pennsylvania, The Big Blockade 41; Banana Ridge, Hard Steel, The Missing Million, Women Aren't Angels, Headline 42; Candles at Nine, Madonna of the Seven Moons 44; Camera Reflections 45; Mrs. Fitzherbert, Mine Own Executioner, The Phantom Shot 47; House of Darkness, Third Time Lucky, Escape from Broadmoor 48; The Temptress, Man on the Run, The Man from Yesterday 49; The Magic Box, Mr. Denning Drives North 51; The Ringer, Mantrap, To the Rescue (short) 52; Street Corner, Four Sided Triangle, Front Page Story, Mysterious Bullet (short) 53; Men of Sherwood Forest 54; The Gilded Cage, John and Julie, Johnny You're Wanted, Tons of Trouble 55; It's a Great Day, Alias John Preston, Eyewitness, The Last Man to Hang, Reach for the Sky 56; Quatermass II, The Secret Place, The Naked Truth 57; Chain of Events, Further Up the Creek, The Revenge of Frankenstein, The Secret Man, Blood of the Vampire 58; The Mummy, Too Many Crooks 59; Sink the Bismarck, Bottoms Up, Village of the Damned 60; Paranoiac 63; The Scarlet Blade 64; Son of the Sahara 66.

479 SUMMERS Jeremy (1931–)
Director. B: St. Albans. Father: Walter SUMMERS. Depth Charge 60; Highway Holiday (short) 61; Suddenly It's Jazz (short), The Punch and Judy Man 62;

Crooks in Cloisters 63; Ferry Cross the Mersey 64; San Ferry Ann, Dateline Diamonds 65; The Ghost of Monk's Island 66; The Vengeance of Fu Manchu, Five Golden Dragons 67; House of a Thousand Dolls, Face of Eve 68.

480 SUMMERS Walter, M.C., D.C.M., M.M. (1896–) Director and writer. B: Barnstaple. Stage as boy. 13: asst. dir. Prisoner of Zenda. 18: scenarist HEPWORTH. Scripted most of his own films; famed for realism. Scripting: Stable Companions, Brown Sugar, The Faithful Heart, If Four Walls Told, Let's Pretend 22; Royal Divorce, The Right to Strike, The Cause of All the Trouble (short), The Knockout, Married Love, Hotel Mouse, Should a Doctor Tell 23; She 25; sound: Mutiny of the Elsinore 37; Queer Cargo, Black Limelight 38. Directed: I Pagliacci (co-dir.), Afterglow (co-dir.), A Couple of Down and Outs 23; The Unwanted, The Cost of Beauty, Who Is the Man, The Perfect Crime (short) 24; Ypres (doc.) 25; Mons (doc.), Nelson 26; The Battles of Coronel and Falkland Islands (doc.) 27; Bolibar 28; The Lost Patrol, Chamber of Horrors 29; sound: Raise the Roof, Suspense, The Man from Chicago 30; The Flying Fool, Men Like These 31; The House Opposite 32; Timbuctoo 33; The Warren Case, The Return of Bulldog Drummond, What Happened Then 34; McGlusky the Sea Rover, Music Hath Charms (co-dir.) 35; Ourselves Alone (co-dir.), The Limping Man 36; The Price of Folly 37; Premiere 38; At the Villa Rose, Dark Eyes of London 39; Traitor Spy 40.

481 SWINBURNE Nora (1902–)
Actress. B: Bath. RN: Elinore Johnson. Stage: 12. Attractive silent star, later character actress. Branded, Saved From the Sea 20; The Fortune of Christina McNab, Autumn of Pride 21; Wee McGregor's

Sweetheart 22; Hornet's Nest 23; Unwanted, His Grace Gives Notice 24; A Girl of London 25; One Colombo Night 26. Sound: Alf's Button, Caste 30; Potiphar's Wife, These Charming People, Man of Mayfair 31; A Voice Said Goodnight, Mr. Bill the Conqueror, Whiteface 32; Perfect Understanding, Too Many Wives 33; Boomerang, The Office Wife 34; Lend Me Your Husband 35; Jury's Evidence, The Gay Adventure, The Lonely Road 36; Dinner at the Ritz 37; Lily of Laguna, The Citadel 38; Gentleman of Venture 40; The Farmer's Wife 41; They Flew Alone 42; The Man in Grey, Dear Octopus 43; Fanny by Gaslight 44; They Knew Mr. Knight 45; Jassy 47; Good Time Girl, The Blind Goddess, Quartet, The Bad Lord Byron 48; Fools Rush In, Marry Me, Christopher Columbus, Landfall 49; My Daughter Joy 50; Betrayed, The End of the Affair 54; The Strange Awakening 58; Third Man on the Mountain 59; Conspiracy of Hearts 60.

482 SYKES Eric (1924–   ) Actor. B: Oldham. Radio ; TV writer turned comedian 48. Own TV series gained him cameos and stardom. Orders Are Orders 55; Watch Your Stern 60; Very Important Person, Invasion Quartet 61; Village of Daughters, Kill or Cure 62; Heavens Above 63; The Bargee, One Way Pendulum 64; Those Magnificent Men in Their Flying Machines, Rotten to the Core, The Liquidator 65; The Spy with a Cold Nose, The Plank (also dir. and sc.), Shalako 68.

483 SYMS Sylvia (1934–   ) Actress. B: Woolwich. Attractive blonde star. My Teenage Daughter 56; No Time for Tears, Woman in a Dressing Gown, The Birthday Present 57; The Moonraker, Ice Cold in Alex, Bachelor of Hearts 58; No Trees in the Street, Ferry to Hong Kong, Expresso Bongo 59; Conspiracy of Hearts, The World of Susie Wong 60; Flame in the Streets, Victim 61; The Quare Fellow, The Punch and Judy Man 62; The World Ten Times Over 63; East of Sudan 64; Operation Crossbow, The Big Job 65; Danger Route 67; Hostile Witness 68.

T

484 TAUBER Richard (1893–1948) Actor. B: Linz. Singer, stage: 12. Many German films before becoming Britain's favourite screen singer. Blossom Time 34; Heart's Desire 35; Land Without Music 36; Pagliacci 37; Waltz Time 45; Lisbon Story 46.

485 TAYLOR Alma (1896–   ) Actress. B: London. Grew up in Hepworth films from child star via Tilly the Tomboy series to top the 1915 Pictures & Picturegoer popularity poll. Main shorts: The Story of a Picture, The Little Milliner and the Thief, The Burglar and Little Phyllis, Tilly the Tomboy goes Boating 10; Evicted, The Veteran's Pension, A Fight With Fire, The Smuggler's Stepdaughter, For a Baby's Sake 11; Curfew Must Not Ring Tonight, The Dear Little Teacher, King Robert of Sicily 12; The Mill Girl, Tried in the Fire, Adrift on Life's Tide, The Girl at Lancing Mill, A Little Widow is a Dangerous Thing 13; Blind Fate, The Whirr of the Spinning Wheel, The Quality of Mercy, The Hills Are Calling, His Country's Bidding, Time the Great Healer, Morphia the Death Drug 14; The Refugee, Tares 18; Broken in the Wars 19. Features: Oliver Twist 12; The Old Curiosity Shop 13; Justice, The Heart of Midlothian, By Whose Hand, The Girl Who Lived In Straight Street, The Schemers, The Basilisk, In the Shadow of Big Ben 14; The Canker of Jealousy, A Lancashire Lass, Courtmartialled, The Bottle, The Baby on the Barge, The Man Who Stayed at Home, Sweet Lavender, The Golden Pavement, The Outrage, Iris 15; Trelawny of the Wells, Sowing the Wind, Annie Laurie, The Marriage of William Ashe, The Grand Babylon Hotel, Comin' Thro' The Rye, Molly Bawn 16; The Cobweb, The American Heiress, Merely Mrs. Stubbs, Nearer My God to Thee 17; The Touch of a Child, Film Tags series, Boundary House The Nature of the Beast, Sunken Rocks, Sheba, The Forest on the Hill 19; Anna the Adventuress, Alf's Button, Helen of Four Gates, Mrs. Erricker's Reputation 20; The Tinted Venus, The Narrow Valley, Dollars in Surrey, Tansy 21; The Pipes of Pan, Mist in the Valley, Strangling Threads, Comin' Thro' The Rye 23; The Shadow of Egypt 24; The House of Marney 26; Quinneys 27; Two Little Drummer Boys, A South Sea Bubble 28; sound: Deadlock 31; Bachelor's Baby 32; Things Are Looking Up 35; Everybody Dance 36; Lilacs in the Spring 54; Stock Car, Lost 56; Blue Murder at St. Trinian's 57.

486 TEARLE Sir Godfrey (1884–1953)

Actor. B: New York. Stage: 93. Stage star with a long career in and out of films. Romeo and Juliet (short) 08; The Fool 13; Lochinvar 15; Sir James Mortimer's Wager (short), The Real Thing at Last (short) 16; A Sinless Sinner, The March Hare, Fancy Dress, Nobody's Child, Queen's Evidence 19; Kenilworth Castle (short), One Colombo Night, If Youth But Knew 26; sound: Infatuation 30; These Charming People, The Shadow Between 31; Puppets of Fate 33; Jade (short) 34; The 39 Steps, The Last Journey 35; East Meets West, Tomorrow We Live 36; One of Our Aircraft is Missing 42; Undercover, The Lamp Still Burns 43; Medal for the General 44; The Rake's Progress 45; Private Angelo 49; White Corridors, I Believe in You 51; Mandy, Decameron Nights, The Titfield Thunderbolt 52.

487 TENNYSON Penrose (1912–1941)

Director. B: London. 32: asst. dir. The Good Companions. M: Nova PILBEAM. His three features helped set the Ealing Style before his early death. There Ain't No Justice 39; The Proud Valley, Convoy 40.

488 TERRY-THOMAS (1911–)

Actor. B: London. RN: Thomas Hoare-Stevens. 38: radio. Moustached, gap-toothed, upper-class comic. Also Hollywood. Helter Skelter, Melody Club 49; The Queen Steps Out (short), Cookery Nook (short) 51; Private's Progress 56; The Green Man, Brothers In Law 56; Lucky Jim, The Naked Truth, Happy Is the Bride, Blue Murder at St. Trinians 57; Tom Thumb, Too Many Crooks 58; Carlton-Browne of the F.O., I'm All Right Jack 59; School for Scoundrels, Make Mine Mink 60; His and Hers, A Matter of WHO 61; Operation Snatch, Kill or Cure 62; Mouse on the Moon, The Wild Affair 63; Those Magnificent Men in Their Flying Machines, You Must Be Joking 65; Our Man in Marrakesh, The Sandwich Man 66; Jules Verne's Rocket to the Moon 67; Don't Raise the Bridge Lower the Water 68.

489 THATCHER Heather Actress.

B: London. Attractive blonde now remembered for her vague characters in

Hollywood films. *The Prisoner of Zenda* 15; *Altar Chains* 16; *Key of the World* 18; *The First Men in the Moon, Pallard the Punter, The Green Terror* 19; *Will o' the Wisp* series, *The Little Hour of Peter Wells* 20; *The Flag Lieutenant* 26; *Express Love* (short) 29; sound: *Comets, A Warm Corner* 30; *Stepping Stones* 31; *Loyalties, It's a Boy* 33; *The Private Life of Don Juan* 34; *The Love Affair of the Dictator* 35; *Anna Karenina* 48; *Trottie True, Dear Mr. Prohack* 49; *Encore* 51; *Father's Doing Fine, The Hour of 13* 52; *Will Any Gentleman* 53; *Duel in the Jungle* 54; *The Deep Blue Sea, Josephine and Men* 55.

490 THOMAS Gerald (1920–   )
Director. B: Hull. Brother: Ralph THOMAS. 46: asst. ed. 50: ed. *Tony Draws a Horse*. After a few thrillers, has carried on successfully with producer Peter Rogers. *Circus Friends* 56; *Time Lock, Vicious Circle* 57; *Chain of Events, The Solitary Child, The Duke Wore Jeans, Carry On Sergeant* 58; *Carry On Nurse, Carry On Teacher, Please Turn Over* 59; *Carry On Constable, Watch Your Stern, No Kidding* 60; *Carry On Regardless, Raising the Wind* 61; *Carry On Cruising, Twice Round the Daffodils, The Iron Maiden, Nurse on Wheels* 62; *Carry On Cabby, Carry On Jack* 63; *Carry On Spying, Carry On Cleo* 64; *The Big Job, Carry On Cowboy* 65; *Carry On Screaming, Don't Lose Your Head* 66; *Follow That Camel* 67; *Carry On Doctor, Carry On Up the Khyber* 68.

491 THOMAS Jameson (1892–1939)
Actor. B: London. Stage: 10. Moustached star of late silents. Also Hollywood. *Chu Chin Chow* 23; *The Drum* (short), *The Cavern Spider* (short), *The Decameron Nights, The Sins Ye Do, Chester Forgets Himself* (short) 24; *Daughter of Love, Afraid of Love, The Apache, The Gold Cure* 25; *The Brotherhood* (short), *Jungle Woman,*

Pearl of the South Seas 26; *Blighty, Roses of Picardy, Poppies of Flanders* 27; *The White Sheik, The Farmer's Wife, Tesha, The Rising Generation, Weekend Wives* 28; *Piccadilly, Power Over Men, The Feather* 29; sound: *As We Lie* (short) 27; *High Treason, Memories* (short), *Hate Ship* 29; *Elstree Calling, Night Birds* 30.

492 THOMAS Queenie (1900–   )
Actress. B: Cardiff. Blonde star of Bertram PHILLIPS productions. *John Halifax Gentleman* 14; *The Angels of Mons* (short), *The Vengeance of Allah* 15; *Frills* (short), *Won by Losing, The Chance of a Lifetime* 16; *Ye Wooing of Peggy* (short), *A Man the Army Made* 17; *Meg o' the Woods, What Could a Gentleman Do, Rock of Ages, It's Happiness That Counts* 18; *A Little Child Shall Lead Them* 19; *Trousers* 20; *Rainbow Comedies* 22; *Syncopated Picture Plays* series, *School for Scandal* 23; *Her Redemption, Straws in the Wind, The Alley of Golden Hearts, The Gayest of the Gay* 24; *The Last Witness, The Gold Cure* 25; *Safety First* 26; *Warned Off* 28.

493 THOMAS Ralph (1915–   )
Director. B: Hull. Brother: Gerald THOMAS. Journalist; 32: clapper boy Sound City. 34: asst. ed. British Lion. 46: Rank trailers. Good all-round maker of commercial cinema with producer Betty Box. *Helter Skelter, Once Upon a Dream, Traveller's Joy* 49; *The Clouded Yellow* 50; *Appointment with Venus* 51; *The Venetian Bird* 52; *The Dog and the Diamonds, A Day to Remember* 53; *Doctor in the House, Mad About Men* 54; *Doctor at Sea, Above Us the Waves* 55; *The Iron Petticoat, Checkpoint* 56; *Doctor at Large, Campbell's Kingdom* 57; *A Tale of Two Cities, The Wind Cannot Read* 58; *The 39 Steps, Upstairs and Downstairs* 59; *Conspiracy of Hearts, Doctor in Love* 60; *No Love for Johnnie, No My Darling Daughter* 61; *A Pair of Briefs, The Wild and*

the Willing 62; Doctor in Distress, Hot Enough for June 63; The High Bright Sun 64; Doctor in Clover 65; Deadlier Than the Male 66; Some Girls Do, Nobody Runs Forever 68.

494 THORNTON F. Martin Director. B: U.S.A., to England 06. Stage magazine art ed., then actor. 09: film actor. Long career from Kinemacolor to Stoll. Main shorts: An Indian's Recompense, The White Man's Way, An Outlaw Yet a Man, The Society Playwright, Santa Claus 12; A Christmas Spirit 13. Features: In the Days of Robin Hood, The Fish and the Ring, The Tempter, Love and War in Toyland, The World the Flesh and the Devil 13; Little Lord Fauntleroy 14; Jane Shore (co-dir.), New Adventures of Baron Munchausen, The Faith of a Child, The Vengeance of Allah 15; Diana and Destiny, The Man Who Bought London 16; Love's Old Sweet Song, If Thou Wert Blind, A Man the Army Made (sc. only), The Happy Warrior 17; The Splendid Coward, The Great Impostor, A Romany Lass, Nature's Gentleman 18; The Power of Right, The Warrior Strain, The Knave of Hearts, The Man Who Forgot 19; The Iron Stair, Flames, Bars of Iron 20; My Lord Conceit, Frailty, The River of Stars, Gwyneth of the Welsh Hills, Prey of the Dragon 21; Melody of Death, Lamp in the Desert, Belonging, Little Brother of God, The Sailor Tramp 22; The Romany 23; Women and Diamonds, Mutiny 24.

495 TODD Ann (1909–   ) Actress (recently director of docs.). B: Hartford. Stage: 28. Several times a star, but especially in the 40s. Also Hollywood. M: David LEAN (1949–57). Keepers of Youth, These Charming People, The Ghost Train 31; The Water Gypsies 32; The Return of Bulldog Drummond 34; Things to Come 36; Action for Slander, The Squeaker 37; South Riding 38; Poison Pen 39; Danny

Boy, Ships With Wings 41; Perfect Strangers, The Seventh Veil 45; Gaiety George 46; Daybreak 47; So Evil My Love, The Passionate Friends 48; Madeleine 49; The Sound Barrier 52; The Green Scarf 54; Time Without Pity 57; Taste of Fear 61. Docs.: Thunder in Heaven (prod. & sc.) 64; Thunder of the Gods (dir. & sc.) 66; Thunder of the Kings (dir. & sc.) 67.

496 TODD Richard (1919–   ) Actor. B: Dublin. RN: Palethorpe-Todd. Stage: 37. Popular pocket-size star with two major performances. Also Hollywood. For Them That Trespass 48; The Last Journey, The Hasty Heart 49; Stage Fright, Portrait of Clare 50; Flesh and Blood, The Story of Robin Hood 51; 24 Hours of a Woman's Life, The Venetian Bird, Elstree Story (doc.) 52; The Sword and the Rose, Rob Roy the Highland Rogue 53; The Dambusters 55; Saint Joan, Yangtse Incident, Naked Earth, Chase a Crooked Shadow 57; Intent to Kill, Danger Within 58; Never Let Go 60; The Long and the Short and the Tall, Don't Bother to Knock (also prod.), The Hellions 61; The Boys 62; The Very Edge, Death Drums Along the River 63; Coast of Skeletons 64; Operation Crossbow, Battle of the Villa Fiorita 65; Subterfuge 68.

497 TOYE Wendy (1917–   ) Director. Dancer. 37: stage producer. Has not quite repeated her stage success in films. The Stranger Left No Card (short) 53; The Teckman Mystery 54; Three Cases of Murder (co-dir.), Raising a Riot, All for Mary 55; On the Twelfth Day (short) 56; True as a Turtle 57; We Joined the Navy 62; The King's Breakfast (short) 63.

498 TRAVERS Linden (1913–   ) Actress. B: Houghton-le-Spring. RN: Florence Lindon-Travers. Stage: 31. Brunette beauty. Children of the Fog 35; Wednesday's Luck 36; Double Alibi,

Against the Tide, Brief Ecstasy, The Last Adventurers 37; Bank Holiday, Almost a Honeymoon, The Terror, The Lady Vanishes 38; Inspector Hornleigh on Holiday 39; The Stars Look Down 40; The Ghost Train, The Seventh Survivor, South American George 41; The Missing Million 42; Beware of Pity 46; Master of Bankdam, Jassy 47; No Orchids for Miss Blandish, Quartet 48; The Bad Lord Byron, Christopher Columbus 49.

499 TRIMBLE   Larry / Lawrence (1885–1954) Director. B: U.S.A. Farmer. Vitagraph director who came to England with John Bunny and again with Florence TURNER, making some of the best British pictures of the period. Shorts: Bunny at the Derby, Michael McShane Matchmaker, Bunny Blarneyed, The Pickwick Papers series 12; Rose of Surrey, Jean's Evidence, The Younger Sister, The Lucky Stone 13; The Awakening of Nan, Creatures of Habit, Flotilla the Flirt, Film Favourites, One Thing After Another, Polly's Progress, Snobs, Daisy Doodad's Dial 14. Features: The Harper Mystery 13; The Murdock Trial, For Her People, Through the Valley of Shadows, Shepherd Lassie of Argyle 14; Shopgirls, As Ye Repent, Alone in London, My Old Dutch, Lost and Won, Caste, Far From the Madding Crowd, The Great Adventure 15; Sally In Our Alley, A Place in the Sun, Grim Justice 16.

500 TRINDER Tommy (1909–   ) Actor. B: Streatham. Cockney music hall comic who convinced as a character star for Ealing. Almost a Honeymoon, Save a Little Sunshine 38; She Couldn't Say No 39; Laugh It Off, Sailors Three 40; Eating Out (short), The Foreman Went to France 41; The Bells Go Down 42; Champagne Charlie, Fiddlers Three 44; Bitter Springs 49; You Lucky People 55; Make Mine a Million 58; The Beauty Jungle 64.

501 TRONSON Robert (1924–   ) Director. B: Chilmark. 47: stage mgr. 55: TV producer. Second feature crimes. Man at the Carlton Tower, Man Detained, Never Back Losers 61; Number 6, The Traitors 62; Ring of Spies, On the Run, Farewell Performance 63; All in Good Time (short) 64.

502 TRUMAN Michael (1916–   ) Director. B: London. 34: asst. ed. Sound City. 37: ed. The Return of the Scarlet Pimpernel. Army training films. The Lavender Hill Mob (prod.) 51; Touch and Go 55; Go to Blazes 62; Girl in the Headlines 63; Daylight Robbery 64.

503 TUCKER George Loane (1881–1921) Director. B: U.S.A. Railway clerk; films with Biograph. To England as a top director to work with Harold SHAW at London Film Co. M: Elizabeth RISDON. The Third String (short), She Stoops to Conquer, The Black Spot (short), The Cage (short), A Bachelor's Love Story (short), The Difficult Way, England Expects, On His Majesty's Service, Called Back, The Fringe of War, The Revenge of Mr. Thomas Atkins 14; 1914, The Middleman, The Prisoner of Zenda, Rupert of Hentzau, Sons of Satan, The Shulamite, Jelfs, The Christian, His Lordship (short), Her Uncle (short), Mixed Relations (short), An Odd Freak (short) 15; The Morals of Weybury, The Game of Liberty, Arsene Lupin, The Man Without a Soul, The Manxman 16; A Mother of Dartmoor, A Mother's Influence 17.

504 TULLY Montgomery (1904–   ) Director (also writer). B: Dublin. Author, playwright. 29: docs. Crime thrillers, mostly for Anglo-Amalgamated and Grand National. Behind the Guns (short) 40; Salute to the Farmers (short) 41; For You Alone (sc. only), Waltz Time (sc. only), *Murder in Reverse* 45; *Lisbon Story* (sc. only), *Spring Song* 46; *Mrs. Fitzherbert* 47; *Boys in Brown* 49; *A Tale of Five Cities* (co-dir.) 51; *Girdle of Gold* 52; *Small Town Story* 53; *The Diamond* (3D), *Five Days, 36 Hours, Devil's Point, Late Night Final* (short) 54; *The Glass Cage, Dial 999* 55; *Wall of Death* (short), *Case of the River Morgue* (short), *Destination Death* (short) 56; *The Lonely House* (short), *Inside Information* (short), *Case of the Smiling Widow* (short), *Night Crossing* (short), *The White Cliffs Mystery* (short), *The Counterfeit Plan, The Hypnotist, The Key Man, Man in the Shadow, No Road Back, Print of Death* (short) 57; *Crossroad Gallows* (short), *Crime of Honour* (short), *Escapement, The Strange Awakening, The Long Knife, Man With a Gun, The Diplomatic Corpse, I Only Arsked* 58; *Man Accused* 59; *Jackpot, The Price of Silence, Dead Lucky, The House in Marsh Road, The Man Who Was Nobody* 60; *The Middle Course, Two Wives at One Wedding, The Third Alibi* 61; *She Knows Y'Know, Out of the Fog* 62; *Clash By Night, Master Spy* 63; *Boy With a Flute* (short) 64; *Who Killed the Cat* 66; *Battle Beneath the Earth* 68.

505 **TURNER Florence** (1888–1946) Actress. B: New York. 00: Stage; films 07, world fame as The Vitagraph Girl. To England with Larry TRIMBLE her dir. to form own co. assoc. with Cecil HEP-WORTH. Shorts: *The Rose of Surrey, Jean's Evidence, The Younger Sister, The Lucky Stone* 13; *Creatures of Habit, Flotilla the Flirt, Daisy Doodad's Dial, Polly's Progress, One Thing After Another, Film Favourites, Snobs* 14; *Lights o' London, The Street Tumblers* 22; *The Boatswain's Mate, Film Favourites* 24. Features: *The Harper Mystery* 13; *The Murdock Trial, For Her People, Through the Valley of Shadows, Shepherd Lassie of Argyle, Shopgirls* 14; *As Ye Repent, Alone in London, My Old Dutch, Lost and Won, Far From the Madding Crowd, A Welsh Singer, Doorsteps, Grim Justice, East Is East* 15; *The Ugly Duckling* 20; *The Old Wives' Tale* 21; *The Little Mother, Was She Justified?* 22; *Hornet's Nest, Sally Bishop* 23; *Women and Diamonds* 24.

506 **TUSHINGHAM Rita** (1942–) Actress. B: Liverpool. Pert, wide-eyed young star of the realist school. *A Taste of Honey* 61; *The Leather Boys, A Place to Go* 63; *The Girl with Green Eyes* 64; *The Knack* 65; *The Trap* 66; *Smashing Time* 67; *Diamonds for Breakfast* 68.

507 **TWIST Derek** (1905–) Director. B: London. 31: asst. ed. Gainsborough. 33: ed. *Waltz Time. End of the River* 47; *All Over the Town* 49; *Green Grow the Rushes* 51; *Police Dog* 55; *Family Doctor* 58.

U

508 USTINOV Peter (1921–)
Actor (also director and writer). B: London. Stage: 38; playwright. Character star, at his best in comedy. Also Hollywood. *Hullo Fame, Mein Kampf My Crimes* 40; *One of Our Aircraft Is Missing, The Goose Steps Out* 42; *The Way Ahead* (also sc.), *Carnival* (sc.) 44; *School for Secrets* (dir. & sc.) 46; *Vice Versa* (dir. & sc.) 47; *Private Angelo* (also co-dir. & sc.) 49; *Odette* 50; *Hotel Sahara, The Magic Box* 51; *Beau Brummell* 54; *School for Scoundrels* (sc.) 60; *The Sundowners* 61; *Billy Budd* (also dir. & sc.) 62; *Peaches* (short) (voice) 64; *Hot Millions* 68.

V

509 VARNEL Marcel (1894–1947)
Director. B: Paris. Stage actor/director; 25 to U.S.A. 31: dir. films for Fox. Son: Max VARNEL. Made some of the best British comedies despite or because of being French. (HAY, CRAZY GANG, ASKEY, FORMBY.) *Freedom of the Seas, Girls Will Be Boys* 34; *Dance Band, I Give My Heart, No Monkey Business* 35; *All In, Public Nuisance No. I* 36; *Good Morning Boys, Okay for Sound, Oh Mr. Porter* 37; *Convict 99, Alf's Button Afloat, Hey Hey U.S.A., Old Bones of the River* 38; *Ask A Policeman, The Frozen Limits, Where's That Fire* 39; *Band Waggon, Neutral Port, Gasbags, Let George Do It* 40; *I Thank You, Hi Gang, The Ghost of St. Michaels, South American George, Turned Out Nice Again* 41; *Much Too Shy, King Arthur Was a Gentleman* 42; *Get Cracking, Bell Bottom George* 43; *He Snoops to Conquer* 44; *I Didn't Do It* 45; *George in Civvy Street, This Man Is Mine* 46.

510 VARNEL Max (1925–)
Director. B: Paris. Father: Marcel VARNEL. Films 47; asst. dir. *Father Brown* (54). Lowercase thrillers mainly for Danzigers. *A Woman Possessed, Moment of Indiscretion, Links of Justice* 58; *The Great Van Robbery, The Child and the Killer, Web of Suspicion, Top Floor Girl, No Safety Ahead, Crash Drive* 59; *Sentenced for Life, A Taste of Money* 60; *A Question of Suspense, Murder in Eden, Part Time Wife, Return of a Stranger* 61; *Fate Takes a Hand, Enter Inspector Duval, Mrs. Gibbons' Boys* 62; *The Rivals, The Silent Invasion* 63.

511 VAUGHAN Frankie (1928–)
Actor. B: Liverpool. RN: Abelson. Pop singer; also Hollywood. *Ramsbottom Rides Again* 56; *These Dangerous Years* 57; *Wonderful Things, The Lady is a Square* 58; *Heart of a Man* 59; *It's All Over Town* 64.

512 VEIDT Conrad (1893–1943) Actor. B: Berlin. Stage: 13. German films: 17. Magnetic character star; also Hollywood. *Rome Express* 32; *I Was a Spy, The Wandering Jew, Bella Donna, Jew Suss* 33; *The Passing of the Third Floor Back* 35; *King of the Damned* 36; *Dark Journey, Under the Red Robe* 37; *The Spy in Black* 39; *Contraband, The Thief of Bagdad* 40.

513 VICTOR Henry (1898–1945) Actor. B: London. Stage. Tall star of silents whose German accent spoiled his sound career. Also Hollywood. *Revolution* 15; *She, The Picture of Dorian Gray* 16; *Ora Pro Nobis* 17; *The Secret Woman* 18; *Heart of a Rose, Lass o' the Looms, Call of the Sea* 19; *Calvary, As God Made Her, John Heriot's Wife, Beyond the Dreams of Avarice* 20; *The Old Wives' Tale, Sheer Bluff* 21; *Bentley's Conscience, A Romance of Old Baghdad, Diana of the Crossways, A Bill of Divorcement, The Crimson Circle* 22; *The Prodigal Son, Scandal, Royal Oak* 23;

The Colleen Bawn, The White Shadow, Henry King of Navarre, Slaves of Destiny, His Grace Gives Notice, The Love Story of Aliette Brunton, The Sins Ye Do 24; *A Romance of Mayfair* 25; *Luck of the Navy* 27; *The Guns of Loos, Tommy Atkins* 28; *After the Verdict, Down Channel, The Hate Ship* 29; sound: *Song of Soho* 30; *I Spy, Tiger Spy* 33; *The Scotland Yard Mystery, The Way of Youth* 34; *Murder at Mont Carlo, Handle With Care, Can You Hear Me Mother* 35; *The Secret Voice, Fame, Conquest of the Air* 36; *Holiday's End, Our Fighting Navy, Fine Feathers* 37.

514 VORHAUS Bernard Director. Good quota pictures for Twickenham; to Hollywood. *Camera Cocktales* series 32; *On Thin Ice, Money for Speed, Crime on the Hill, The Ghost Camera* 33; *Night Club Queen, The Broken Melody, Blind Justice* 34; *Street Song, The Last Journey, Ten Minute Alibi, Dark World* 35; *Dusty Ermine* 36; *Cotton Queen* 37.

W

515 WALBROOK Anton (1900–1967) Actor. B: Vienna. RN: Adolf Wohlbruck. Stage: 16. Charming Continental star. *Victoria the Great, The Rat* 37; *Sixty Glorious Years* 38; *Gaslight* 40; *Dangerous Moonlight, 49th Parallel* 41; *The Life and Death of Colonel Blimp* 43; *The Man from Morocco* 44; *The Red Shoes, Queen of Spades* 48; *Oh Rosalinda!* 55; *Saint Joan* 57; *I Accuse* 58.

516 WALKER Norman (1892–   ) Director. B: Bolton. 12: stage. 20: asst.

dir. Straightforward style, since 39 making religious films. *Oxford Bags* (short) 26; *Tommy Atkins, Widecombe Fair* 28. Sound: *Hate Ship, Loose Ends, A Romance of Seville, The Middle Watch* 30; *Uneasy Virtue, The Shadow Between* 31; *Mr. Bill the Conqueror, Fires of Fate* 32; *The Fortunate Fool, The Flaw, House of Trent, Forging Ahead* 33; *Lilies of the Field, Dangerous Ground, The Way of Youth* 34; *Key to Harmony, Turn of the Tide* 35; *Debt of Honour* 36; *Sunset in Vienna, Our Fighting Navy* 37; *Beyond Our Horizon* (short)

39; *The Man at the Gate* 41; *Hard Steel, The Great Mr. Handel* 42; *They Knew Mr. Knight* 45; *The Promise* 52; *John Wesley* 55; *Shield of Faith* 56; *Supreme Secret* 57.

517 WALLS Tom (1883–1949) Actor, previously director. B: Kingsthorpe. Policeman, jockey. Stage: 05. Star and producer of Aldwych Theatre farces which he brought to the screen for Herbert WILCOX, later turning into a brilliant character actor. Actor-director: *Rookery Nook, On Approval, Canaries Sometimes Sing* 30; *Tons of Money, Plunder* 31; *A Night Like This, Thark, Leap Year* 32; *The Blarney Stone, Just Smith, A Cuckoo in the Nest, Turkey Time* 33; *A Cup of Kindness, A Lady in Danger, Dirty Work* 34; *Fighting Stock, Stormy Weather, Foreign Affaires* 35; *Pot Luck, Dishonour Bright* 36; *For Valour* 37; *Second Best Bed, Old Iron* 38. Actor: *Me and Marlborough* 35; *Strange Boarders, Crackerjack* 38; *Undercover, They Met in the Dark* 43; *Halfway House, Love Story* 44; *Johnny Frenchman* 45; *This Man is Mine* 46; *Master of Bankdam, While I Live* 47; *Spring in Park Lane* 48; *Maytime in Mayfair, The Interrupted Journey* 49.

518 WALSH Kay (1914–   ) Actress. B: London. Dancer. Attractive leading lady and character actress. *How's Chances, Get Your Man* 34; *Smith's Wives, Luck of the Irish* 35; *If I Were Rich, Secret of Stamboul, All That Glitters* 36; *Keep Fit, The Last Adventurers* 37; *I See Ice, Meet Mr. Penny* 38; *The Mind of Mr. Reeder, The Missing People, All at Sea, The Middle Watch* 39; *Sons of the Sea, The Chinese Bungalow, The Second Mr. Bush* 40; *In Which We Serve* 42; *This Happy Breed* 44; *The October Man, Vice Versa* 47; *Oliver Twist* 48; *Last Holiday, Stage Fright, The Magnet* 50; *Encore, The Magic Box, Hunted* 51; *Meet Me Tonight* 52; *The Rainbow*

Jacket, Lease of Life 54; *Cast a Dark Shadow* 55; *Now and Forever* 56; *The Horse's Mouth* 58; *Tunes of Glory* 60; *Greyfriars Bobby* 61; *Reach for Glory, Lunch Hour* 62; *80,000 Suspects, Dr. Syn Alias the Scarecrow* 63; *The Beauty Jungle* 64; *He Who Rides a Tiger* 65; *The Witches* 66.

519 WARD Warwick (189 –1967) Actor. B: St. Ives. RN: Mannon. Stage. Suave moustached hero/villain of the 20s who turned prod. in the 30s for A.B.P.C. Also Continent and U.S.A. *The Silver Lining* 19; *Mary Latimer Nun, Wuthering Heights, Call of the Road, Build Thy House, The Manchester Man* 20; *The Diamond Necklace, Handy Andy, Belphegor the Mountebank, Demos, Corinthian Jack, The Golden Dawn, Mayor of Casterbridge, Little Meg's Children* 21; *The Lilac Sunbonnet, Tell Your Children, Call of the East, Petticoat Loose* 22; *Bulldog Drummond, The Lady Owner, The Hotel Mouse* 23; *The Money Habit, The Great Turf Mystery, Southern Love, Hurricane Hutch in Many Adventures, The Prude's Fall, Human Desires* 24; *The Woman Tempted* 26; *The White Sheik, Maria Marten* 28; *After the Verdict, The Three Kings, The Woman He Scorned* 29; sound: *The Informer* 29; *The Yellow Mask, Birds of Prey* 30; *To Oblige a Lady, Number Please, Deadlock, Stamboul, Man of Mayfair* 31; *The Callbox Mystery, Life Goes On, Blind Spot* 32; *FP One* 33; *Elstree Story* (voice) (doc.) 52.

520 WARNER Jack (1900–   ) Actor. B: Bromley-by-Bow. RN: John Waters. Engineer; radio: 34. Comedian who became a warmly human character star in films. *The Dummy Talks* 43; *The Captive Heart* 45; *Hue and Cry* 46; *Dear Murderer, Holiday Camp, It Always Rains on Sunday, Easy Money* 47; *Against the Wind, My Brother's Keeper, Here Come* the Huggetts, Vote for Huggett 48; The Huggetts Abroad, Train of Events, Boys in Brown, The Blue Lamp 49; Talk of a Million, Valley of Eagles, Scrooge 51; Emergency Call, Meet Me Tonight, Those People Next Door 52; The Final Test, The Square Ring, Albert R.N., Bang You're Dead 53; Forbidden Cargo 54; Quatermass Xperiment, The Ladykillers, Now and Forever 55; Home and Away 56; Carve Her Name With Pride 57; Jigsaw 62.

521 WATT Harry (1906–   ) Director. B: Edinburgh. 31: E.M.B. 34: asst. dir. Man of Aran. Made some of our finest docs. plus good location features for Ealing. Shorts/docs.: Night Mail (co-dir.) 36; The Saving of Bill Blewitt, Big Money 37; North Sea 38; Squadron 992, The First Days (co-dir.) 39; London Can Take It, The Front Line, Britain at Bay 40; Target for Tonight (also sc.), Christmas Under Fire 41; Dover Revisited, 21 Miles 42. Features: Nine Men (also sc.) 43; Fiddlers Three, For Those In Peril (sc. only) 44; The Overlanders (also sc.) 46; Eureka Stockade (also sc.) 49; Where No Vultures Fly 51; West of Zanzibar 54; The Siege of Pinchgut 59.

522 WEBSTER Ben (1864–1947) Actor. Barrister. Stage: 87. Also characters in Hollywood. The House of Temperley 13; Bootles' Baby, V.C., Lil o' London, Liberty Hall, Enoch Arden 14; In the Blood, A Garret in Bohemia, Two Roads 15; His Daughter's Dilemma, Cynthia in the Wilderness, The Vicar of Wakefield 16; Masks and Faces, The Profligate, The Gay Lord Quex, If Thou Wert Blind 17; Because 18; 12–10, Nobody's Child 19; The Call of Youth 20; Miriam Rozella 24; The Only Way 25; Downhill 27; sound: The Lyons Mail 31; Threads 32; One Precious Year 33; The Old Curiosity Shop 34; Drake of England 35; Eliza Comes to Stay, Conquest of the Air 36.

523 WEST Walter Director. B: London. M: his star Violet HOPSON. Made sporting silents for own prod. co. Broadwest. Full Up (short), Thick and Thin (short) 14; A Bold Adventuress, The London Flat Mystery, By the Hand of a Brother, The Woman Who Did 15; Burnt Wings, The Hard Way, The Answer, The Merchant of Venice 16; The Ware Case, The Ragged Messenger, Missing the Tide 17; A Fortune at Stake 18; Not Negotiable, Under Suspicion, Daughter of Eve, The Gentleman Rider, Snow in the Desert 19; A Dead Certainty, Her Son, The Case of Lady Camber 20; Kissing Cup's Race, A Sportsman's Wife, Vi of Smith's Alley, The Imperfect Lover 21; The Scarlet Lady, When Greek Meets Greek, Son of Kissing Cup, Was She Justified 22; Hornet's Nest, The Lady Owner, Beautiful Kitty, What Price Loving Cup, In the Blood 23; The Great Turf Mystery, The Stirrup Cup Sensation 24; Trainer and Temptress, Daughter of Love 25; Steve Donoghue series, Woodcroft Castle (short), The Brotherhood (short) 26; Maria Marten, Sweeney Todd 28; Warned Off 29; sound: Aura (short) 31; Hundred to One 33; Bed and Breakfast 36; We Do Believe in Ghosts (short) 47.

524 WESTON Charles H. (18 – 1917) Director, writer, actor. B: U.S.A. 12: Punch films. To England with actor Arthur Finn for B. & C., then together in own co. Regent Films. Wrote, directed and appeared in sensational features. The Battle of Waterloo, Through the Clouds, The Broken Chisel, Tragedy in the Alps, In Fate's Grip, To Save Her Dad, The Master Crook, A Son of Japan (short), The Little Snow Waif (short), The Ragged Prince (short), Lieut. Daring and the Mystery of Room 41, Lieut. Daring Aerial Scout 13; The Seventh Day, Detective Finn, The King of Seven Dials, The Great Python Robbery, Detective Finn and the Foreign Spies,

Called to the Front, Saving the Colours, What a Woman Will Do, Mother in Exile, Master Spy, Wife of a Thief, Through the Firing Line, The Bishop's Silence, For King and Country, Facing the Enemy, The Bugle Boy of Lancashire 14; The Road to Calais, Battling Brown of Birmingham, Vice and Virtue, The Underworld of London, Dungeon of Death, The Port of Missing Women, Vengeance of Nana, The Life of an Actress, The Woman Without a Soul, The Hand at the Window, Pimple series 15.

525 WESTON Harold Director. B: Australia. 05: stage producer; author, playwright, actor. The Call of the Drum 14; The War Cloud, Admiral's Orders, Another Man's Wife, Shadows, Strategy, The Mystery of a Hansom Cab 15; The Climax, The Green Orchard, The Black Knight, Honour in Pawn, Cynthia in the Wilderness 16; All the World's a Stage 17.

526 WHELAN Tim (1893–) Director. B: Indiana. Stage actor/producer. 20: films. Main work in Hollywood but many good, fast British films. Adam's Apple 28; When Knights Were Bold 29; sound: It's a Boy, Aunt Sally 33; The Camels Are Coming 34; Two's Company 36; Smash and Grab, The Mill on the Floss, Farewell Again, Action for Slander 37; The Divorce of Lady X, Saint Martin's Lane 38; Q Planes (co-dir.), Ten Days in Paris 39; This Was a Woman 48.

527 WHITE Chrissie (1895–) Actress. B: London. Grew up in HEPWORTH films from child star via Tilly the Tomboy series to top star of 20s. Wed co-star/director Henry EDWARDS. Main shorts: For the Little Lady's Sake 08; The Cabman's Good Fairy, The Girl Who Joined the Bushrangers, The Sheriff's Daughter 09; Tilly the Tomboy Goes Boating 10; Gipsy Nan, The Fireman's Daughter 11; A Curate's Love Story, The Mermaid, The Lieutenant's Bride, Plot and Pash 12; At the Foot of the Scaffold, Blood and Bosh, Drake's Love Story, Held for Ransom, Her Crowing Glory, Captain Jack V.C., Lieut. Pie's Love Story 13. Features: Kissing Cup, The Vicar of Wakefield, Shadows of a Great City, The Cloister and the Hearth 13; David Garrick, The Girl Who Lived In Straight Street, Dr. Fenton's Ordeal, The Basilisk, Time the Great Healer 14; Barnaby Rudge, The Curtain's Secret, The Sweater, The Second String, The Man Who Stayed At Home, Sweet Lavender, The Nightbirds of London, The Recalling of John Grey, As The Sun Went Down 15; Face to Face, Trelawny of the Wells, A Bunch of Violets, The White Boys, Partners, Sowing the Wind, Comin' Thro' the Rye, Molly Bawn 16; Exploits of Tubby series, Her Marriage Lines, The Man Behind The Times, Carrots, The Eternal Triangle, A Grain of Sand, Dick Carson Wins Through, The Blindness of Fortune, Broken Threads 17; The Hanging Judge, Film Tags series, The Refugee (short), Broken in the Wars (short), Towards the Light 18; His Dearest Possession, The City of Beautiful Nonsense 19; A Temporary Vagabond, Aylwin, The Amazing Quest of Mr. Ernest Bliss, John Forrest Finds Himself 20; The Lunatic at Large, Wild Heather, The Bargain 21; Simple Simon, Tit for Tat 22; Lily of the Alley, Boden's Boy, The Naked Man 23; The World of Wonderful Reality 24; sound: The Call of the Sea 30; General John Regan 33.

528 WILCOX Herbert, C.B.E. (1892–) Director. B: Cork. 19: film renter, Astra; producer, scenarist, then director using German studio. Brought over big Hollywood stars for lavish silents. 26: Founded Elstree with J. D. Williams. 28: dir. of production British & Dominions. Made international star of Anna NEAGLE and wed her. Very basic directorial style but probably more box-office hits than any other producer. *Chu Chin Chow* 23; *Southern Love, Decameron Nights* 24; *The Only Way* 25; *Nell Gwyn* 26; *London, Tiptoes, Mumsie* 27; *Dawn, The Bondman* 28; *The Woman in White* 29; sound: *The Loves of Robert Burns* 30; *Chance of a Night Time* (co-dir.), *Carnival* 31; *The Blue Danube, Goodnight Vienna* 32; *Yes Mr. Brown, The King's Cup, Bitter Sweet, The Little Damozel* 33; *The Queen's Affair, Nell Gwyn* 34; *Peg of Old Drury* 35; *Limelight, The Three Maxims, This'll Make You Whistle* 36; *London Melody, Victoria the Great* 37; *Sixty Glorious Years* 38; *They Flew Alone* 42; *The Yellow Canary* 43; *I Live in Grosvenor Square* 45; *Piccadilly Incident* 46; *The Courtneys of Curzon Street* 47; *Spring in Park Lane, Elizabeth of Ladymead* 48; *Maytime in Mayfair* 49; *Odette* 50; *Into the Blue, The Lady With the Lamp* 51; *Derby Day, Trent's Last Case* 52; *Laughing Anne* 53; *Trouble in the Glen, Lilacs in the Spring* 54; *King's Rhapsody* 55; *My Teenage Daughter* 56; *These Dangerous Years* 57; *The Man Who Wouldn't Talk, Wonderful Things* 58; *The Lady Is a Square, Heart of a Man* 59.

529 WILDING Michael (1912–   ) Actor. B: Westcliff. 33: art dept. B.I.P. Charming star; also Hollywood. *Wedding Group* 35; *There Ain't No Justice* 39; *Tilly of Bloomsbury, Sailors Don't Care, Sailors Three, Convoy* 40; *The Farmer's Wife, Kipps, Cottage to Let, Ships With Wings, Spring Meeting* 41; *The Big Blockade, Secret Mission, In Which We Serve* 42; *Undercover, Dear Octopus* 43; *English Without Tears* 44; *Piccadilly Incident, Carnival* 46; *The Courtneys of Curzon Street, An Ideal Husband* 47; *Spring in Park Lane* 48; *Maytime in Mayfair, Under Capricorn* 49; *Stage Fright, Into the Blue* 50; *The Lady With the Lamp* 51; *Derby Day, Trent's Last Case* 52; *Zarak* 56; *Danger*

Within, Hello London 58; *The World of Suzie Wong* 60; *The Naked Edge* 61.

530 WILLIAMS Emlyn, C.B.E. (1905–   ) Actor (also writer and director). B: Mostyn. Stage: 27. Playwright. Stylish star. Also Hollywood. *The Frightened Lady, Men of Tomorrow, Sally Bishop, Friday the Thirteenth* (also sc.) 32; *Evergreen* (sc.), *My Song For You, Evensong, Roadhouse, The Man Who Knew Too Much* (sc.) 33; *The Iron Duke, The Love Affair of the Dictator, City of Beautiful Nonsense, The Divine Spark* (sc.) 35; *Broken Blossoms* (also sc.) 36; *I Claudius* (uncompleted) 37; *Dead Men Tell No Tales* (also sc.), *A Night Alone, The Citadel* (also sc.), *They Drive By Night* 38; *Jamaica Inn* 39; *The Stars Look Down, Mr. Borland Thinks Again* (short), *Girl in the News, You Will Remember* 40; *This England* (also sc.), *Major Barbara, Hatter's Castle* 41; *The Last Days of Dolwyn* (also dir.) 49; *Another Man's Poison, The Magic Box* 51; *Ivanhoe* 52; *The Deep Blue Sea* 55; *I Accuse* 58; *Beyond This Place* 59; *The L-shaped Room* 62; *Night Must Fall* (sc.) 64; *Eye of the Devil* 66.

531 WILLIAMS Hugh (1904–   ) Actor. B: Bexhill. RN: Brian Williams. Stage: 21; playwright. Smooth, well-groomed hero; also Hollywood. *A Night in Montmartre, Gentleman of Paris* 31; *In a Monastery Garden, Whiteface, Down Our Street, Insult, After Dark, Rome Express* 32; *Bitter Sweet, The Jewel, Sorrell and Son, This Acting Business* 33; *Lieut. Daring R.N., The Last Journey, Her Last Affaire* 35; *The Amateur Gentleman, The Man Behind the Mask, The Happy Family* 36; *Gypsy, Side Street Angel, The Windmill, The Perfect Crime, Brief Ecstasy* 37; *The Dark Stairway, Bank Holiday, Dead Men Tell No Tales, His Lordship Goes to Press, Premiere* 38; *Inspector Hornleigh, Dark Eye of*

London 39; *Ships With Wings* 41; *One of Our Aircraft Is Missing, The Day Will Dawn, Talk About Jacqueline* 42; *Girl in a Million* 46; *Take My Life, An Ideal Husband* 47; *The Blind Goddess, Elizabeth of Ladymead* 48; *Paper Orchid, The Romantic Age* 49; *The Gift Horse, The Holly and the Ivy* 52; *The Fake, Twice Upon a Time, The Intruder, Star of My Night* 53; *Khartoum* 66.

532 WILLIAMSON James A. (1855–19) Director; producer. B: Scotland. Chemist; founded Hove Camera Club. 96: bought projector, converting it to camera, 97. 98: filmed local events and with family enacted short scenes in back garden. 00: rented house as studio. 02: built Wilbury Road studio. First dir. to achieve true cinematic technique with *Attack on a China Mission Station* (00) and *Fire* (01). Main shorts: *Two Naughty Boys Upsetting the Spoons, Sloper's Visit to Brighton* 98; *The Jovial Monks, Courtship Under Difficulties* 99; *Attack on a China Mission Station* 00; *The Big Swallow, Stop Thief, Are You There, Fire* 01; *A Day in Camp with the Volunteers, A Reservist Before and After the War* 02; *The Deserter, The Dear Boys Home for the Holidays* 03; *Two Brave Little Japs, Gabriel Grub* 04; *Our New Errand Boy, Two Little Waifs* 05; *Mrs. Brown Goes Home to her Mother, The Miner's Daughter* 06; *The Village Fire Brigade, The Brigand's Daughter* 07; *Still Worthy of the Name, Raised from the Ranks* 08; *Tower of London, Peeps into Nature's Realm* series 09.

533 WILSON Frank (1873–19) Director; actor. B: Norfolk. Stage 1892. 08 joined HEPWORTH as actor with FITZHAMON, stayed to 17 as dir. Main shorts: *The Pneumatic Policeman* 08; *Mr. Mugwump* series 10; *Tilly Works for a Living* 12. Features: *A Cigarette Maker's Romance, The Vicar of Wakefield, Shadows of a Great City* 13; *Justice, The Heart of Midlothian, The Tragedy of Basil Grieve, Creatures of Clay, The Terror of the Air, The Cry of the Captive, The Grip of Ambition, The Schemers, The Hunchback, The Breaking Point, The Stress of Circumstance, Dr. Fenton's Ordeal, In the Shadow of Big Ben, Life's Dark Road* 14; *A Lancashire Lass, The Curtain's Secret, The Incorruptible Crown, The Sweater, The Second String, The Golden Pavement, Her Boy, The White Hope* 15; *The Recalling of John Grey, Partners, A Bunch of Violets, The White Boys, Face to Face, Nightbirds of London, The Grand Babylon Hotel* 16; *Exploits of Tubby* series, *Her Marriage Lines, The House of Fortescue, The Man Behind the Times, The Eternal Triangle, Carrots, As the Sun Went Down, A Grain of Sand, The House Opposite, A Munition Girl's Romance, A Gamble for Love, The Adventures of Dick Dolan* (short) 17; *The Snare, A Turf Conspiracy, The Woman Wins* 18; *A Soul's Crucifixion, The Irresistible Flapper* 19; *With All Her Heart* 20; *The White Hope* 22; *Dr. Fu Manchu* series (sc.) 24.

534 WILSON Rex (18 –1951) Director. RN: George Wilson. Interesting silent films, mostly for SAMUELSON. *Tom Brown's Schooldays* 16; *Ora Pro Nobis, The Life of Lord Kitchener* 17; *Tinker Tailor Soldier Sailor, God Bless Our Red White and Blue, Onward Christian Soldiers, Lead Kindly Light* 18; *In Bondage, Sweethearts, Some Artist, The Man Who Won, Quinneys, Mrs. Thompson, The Right Element* 19; *Pillars of Society, Unmarried* 20; *Tilly of Bloomsbury* 21; *Saint Elmo* 23.

535 WINNER Michael (1936–) Director (also writer). B: London. 51: film critic. 55: shorts. Gimmicky style. *Man With a Gun* (sc.) 58; *Climb Up the Wall* (also sc.), *Shoot to Kill* (also sc.) 60;

Old Mac, Some Like It Cool (also sc.), *Out of the Shadow* (also sc.), *Haunted England* (short) 61; *Play It Cool, Behave Yourself* (short) 62; *The Cool Mikado* (also sc.), *West 11* 63; *The System* 64; *You Must Be Joking* (also sc.) 65; *The Jokers* (also sc.), *I'll Never Forget What's'isname* 67; *Hannibal Brooks* (also prod.) 68.

536 WISDOM Norman (1920–   )

Actor. B: London. Stage, TV: 48. Phenomenally successful slapstick comic with a sentimental streak. *Trouble in Store* 53; *One Good Turn* 54; *As Long As They're Happy, Man of the Moment* 55; *Up in the World* 56; *Just My Luck* 57; *The Square Peg* 58; *Follow a Star* 59; *The Bulldog Breed, There Was a Crooked Man* 60; *The Girl on the Boat* 61; *On the Beat* 62; *A Stitch in Time* 63; *The Early Bird* 65; *The Sandwich Man, Press for Time* 66.

537 WITHERS Googie (1917–   )

Actress. B: Karachi. Cabaret 31. Attractive star of comedy and drama. M: John McCallum. *The Girl in the Crowd, The Love Test* 34; *Windfall, Her Last Affaire, All at Sea, Dark World* 35; *Crown v. Stevens, King of Hearts, She Knew What She Wanted, Accused, Crime Over London* 36; *Pearls Bring Tears, Paradise for Two* 37; *Paid in Error, If I Were Boss, Kate Plus Ten, Strange Boarders, Convict 99, The Lady Vanishes, You're the Doctor* 38; *Murder in Soho, Trouble Brewing, The Gang's All Here, She Couldn't Say No* 39; *Bulldog Sees It Through, Busman's Honeymoon* 40; *Jeannie, Back Room Boy* 41; *One of Our Aircraft Is Missing, The Silver Fleet* 42; *On Approval, They Came to a City* 44; *Dead of Night, Pink String and Sealing Wax* 45; *The Loves of Joanna Godden, It Always Rains on Sunday* 47; *Miranda, Once Upon a Dream* 48; *Traveller's Joy* 49; *Night and the City* 50; *White Corridors, The Magic Box* 51; *Derby Day* 52; *Devil on Horseback* 54; *Port of Escape* 56.

538 WONTNER Arthur (1875–1960)

Actor. B: London. Stage 97. Silent star who found new fame as the sound 'Sherlock Holmes'. *Frailty, Lady Windermere's Fan, The Bigamist* 16; *Bonnie Prince Charlie, Jose Collins series* 23; *Eugene Aram, The Diamond Man* 24; *The Infamous Lady* 28; sound: *The Message* (short) 30; *The Sleeping Cardinal, Gentleman of Paris* 31; *Condemned to Death, The Missing Rembrandt, The Sign of Four* 32; *The Triumph of Sherlock Holmes, Line Engaged* 35; *Dishonour Bright, Second Bureau* 36; *Thunder in the City, Storm in a Teacup, Silver Blaze, The Live Wire* 37; *Just Like a Woman, Kate Plus Ten, The Terror, Thirteen Men and a Gun, Old Iron* 38; *The Life and Death of Colonel Blimp* 43; *Blanche Fury* 47; *The Elusive Pimpernel* 50; *Brandy for the Parson* 52; *Sea Devils, Genevieve* 53.

539 WOODS Arthur (1904–1942)

Director, previously writer. B: Liverpool. 26: ed. *Secrets of Nature* series. 30: asst. dir. B.I.P. Made some of the best middle-budget movies of the 30s. Scripting: *Pride of the Force, I Spy, A Southern Maid* 33. Directed: *Timbuctoo* (co-dir.), *On Secret Service* 33; *Give Her a Ring, Radio Parade of 1935* 34; *Music Hath Charms* (co-dir.), *Drake of England* 35; *Once in a Million, Rhythm in the Air, Where's Sally, Irish for Luck* 36; *Mayfair Melody, Don't Get Me Wrong, The Windmill, The Compulsory Wife, You Live and Learn* 37; *The Dark Stairway, The Singing Cop, Mr. Satan, Glamour Girl, Thistledown, Dangerous Medicine, The Return of Carol Deane* 38; *Q Planes* (co-dir.), *They Drive By Night, The Nursemaid Who Disappeared, Confidential Lady* 39; *Busman's Honeymoon* 40.

540 WRIGHT Basil (1907–)
Director. B: London. 27: asst. John
GRIERSON at E.M.B. 43: prod. Crown
Film Unit. A founder-father of British
Documentary School. Main docs.: *Windmill in Barbados* 30; *O'er Hill and Dale* 31;
The Country Comes to Town 32; *Cargo
from Jamaica* 33; *Song of Ceylon* 34; *Night
Mail* (co-dir.) 36; *Children at School* 37;
The Face of Scotland 38; *This Was Japan* 45;
The Story of Omolo 46; *Waters of Time* 51;
World Without End 53; *The Immortal Land*
58; *A Place for Gold* 60.

541 WRIGHT Tony (1925–)
Actor. B: London. Father: Hugh E.
Wright. M: Janet MUNRO (57–60).
Husky he-man hero popular in French
films. *The Flanagan Boy* 53; *Jumping for
Joy* 55; *Jacqueline, Tiger in the Smoke* 56;
Seven Thunders 57; *The Spaniard's Curse,
Broth of a Boy* 58; *The Rough and the
Smooth, In the Wake of a Stranger* 59;
*And the Same to You, Faces in the Dark,
House in Marsh Road* 60; *Attempt to Kill*
61; *The Liquidator* 65.

Y

542 YATES Peter (1929–)
Director. 48: stage. 53: dubbing asst.
Summer Holiday 63; *One Way Pendulum*
64; *Robbery* (also sc.) 67.

543 YORK Susannah (1941–)
Actress. B: London. Engaging blonde star.
Tunes of Glory, There Was a Crooked Man
60; *The Greengage Summer* 61; *Tom Jones*
63; *The Seventh Dawn, Scene Nun Take One*
(short) 64; *Sands of the Kalahari* 65;
*Kaleidoscope, A Game Called Scruggs, A
Man For All Seasons* 66; *Sebastian* 67;
Duffy, Lock Up Your Daughters 68.

544 YOUNG Terence (1915–)
Director, previously writer. B: Shanghai.

36: films. Spectacular stuff in the Hollywood style. Scriptwriting: *On the Night
of the Fire* 39; *Dangerous Moonlight* 41;
Secret Mission 42; *On Approval* 44; *Hungry
Hill, Theirs Is the Glory* (doc.) 46. Directed: *Men of Arnhem* (doc.) (co-dir.) 44;
*Corridor of Mirrors, One Night With You,
Woman Hater* 48; *They Were Not Divided*
50; *Valley of the Eagles* 51; *Tall Headlines*
52; *The Red Beret* 53; *That Lady* 54; *Storm
Over the Nile* (co-dir.) 55; *Safari, Zarak*
56; *Action of the Tiger, No Time to Die* 57;
Serious Charge 59; *Too Hot to Handle* 60;
Dr. No 62; *From Russia With Love* 63;
*The Amorous Adventures of Moll Flanders,
Thunderball* 65; *Triple Cross* 66.

Z

545 ZAMPI Mario (1903–1963)
Director, producer. B: Rome. 20: actor
Cines Films; 22: to England; 30: ed.
Warners; 37: prod. Two Cities. At his
best with comedy. *Thirteen Men and a Gun*
38; *Spy for a Day* 40; *The Phantom Shot* 47;
The Fatal Night 48; *Shadow of the Past,
Come Dance With Me* 50; *Laughter in
Paradise* 51; *Top Secret* 52; *Happy Ever
After* 54; *Now and Forever* 56; *The Naked
Truth* 57; *Too Many Crooks* 59; *Bottoms Up*
60; *Five Golden Hours* 61.

546 ZETTERLING Mai (1925–   )
Actress, now director. B: Sweden.
Beautiful blonde star of Swedish films:
44. Novelist. *Frieda* 47; *Quartet, Portrait
from Life* 48; *The Bad Lord Byron, The Lost
People, The Romantic Age* 49; *Blackmailed*
50; *Desperate Moment* 53; *A Prize of Gold*
55; *Seven Waves Away* 57; *The Truth
About Women* 58; *Jet Storm, Faces in the
Dark* 59; *Piccadilly Third Stop* 60; *Offbeat*
61; *Only Two Can Play, The War Game
(dir.) (short), The Man Who Finally Died*
62; *The Main Attraction, The Bay of St.
Michel* 63.

How to use the Index

An alphabetical index to every feature film listed in the preceding filmographies.

Space limitations have made it impossible to include shorts and documentaries in this index, but generally these would have only one text reference: to the director.

Where a director is not featured in the filmography section, as with many foreign directors who have worked in England, his name is given in brackets immediately following the film title. The numbers following the film titles refer to the preceding filmographies, which are arranged alphabetically and given progressive numbers. Those in bold type refer to directors.

Where more than one film has the same title, versions are identified by the last two digits of the year, i.e. 09, 36, etc., given in brackets immediately following the title. For quick location and as a space saver, all articles (A, An, The) are omitted where they form the first word of the title.

Downstream (G. G. Glavany) 49, 258
Dracula 115, 155, 301, 329
Dracula Has Risen from the Grave 164, 301
Dracula Prince of Darkness 155, 301, 456
Dragon of Pendragon Castle 32
Drake of England 31, 290, 522, **539**
Drake's Love Story 404
Dream Doctor (R. W. Lotinga) 173
Dreaming 32, 104, 112, 275
Dreaming Lips 117, 335
Dreams Come True 127
Dreyfus 211, 366, 439
Drink 358, 359
Driven 142, 371, 430
Drop Dead Darling 250
Drum 173, 236, 283, 284, 310, 335
Dry Rot 142, 151, 395, 449, 458
Dual Alibi (Alfred Travers) 313
Duchess of Seven Dials 396
Duel in the Jungle (George Marshall) 148, 489
Duffy (Robert Parrish) 334, 543
Duke Wore Jeans 473, 490
Duke's Son 135, 371, 438
Dumb Dora Discovers Tobacco (Charles Hawtrey) 174, 274
Dummy Talks 251, 352, 520
Dungeon of Death 524
Dunkirk 15, 112, 351, 378
Durant Affair 187
During One Night 170, 207
Dusty Bates (Darrell Catling) 314, 373
Dusty Ermine 31, 66, 514
D'Ye Ken John Peel 172, 237, **138**, 459, 478

Early Bird 11, 536
Early to Bed (Ludwig Berger) 197, 202, 476
Earth Dies Screaming 135, 411
East Is East **138**, 144, 505
East Lynne 201
East Lynne on the Western Front 167, 294, 310, **399**
East Meets West 333, 486
East of Ludgate Hill 223
East of Piccadilly **138**, 258, 304, 454
East of Sudan (Nathan Juran) 412, 483
Easy Money (34) 122, 372, 414
Easy Money (48) 51, 84, 198, **282**, 411, 436, 520
Easy Riches 435
Easy Virtue 52, 107, 234, 253, 254, 262, 470
Ebb Tide (Arthur Rosson) 28, 49, 127, 299, 382
Echo Murders 148, **214**, 411
Echo of Barbara 222
Echo of Diana 362
Edge o' Beyond (Fred Durrant) 141, 367
Edge of the World 82, **409**
Edge of Youth 70
Educated Evans 34, 292, 349
Education of Nicky 281, **438**
Edward My Son (George Cukor) 254, 277

Eight O'Clock Walk 15, **95**, 147, 254, 279
18 Minutes 23, 253, 312
80,000 Suspects 45, **193**, 269, 518
Elder Brother (Frederick Hayward) 478
Elder Miss Blossom 141, 367, 368
Elephant Boy (Robert Flaherty) 283, 284
Eleventh Commandment (24) 2, 96, **101**, 203, 235, 437
Eleventh Hour 428
Eliza Comes to Stay 21, 229, **138**, 522
Elizabeth of Ladymead 263, 369, 529, 531
Elstree Calling 60, 106, 171, 213, **234**, 252, 314, 366, 491
Elusive Pimpernel (20) **142**
Elusive Pimpernel (50) 220, 283, 306, 314, 376, **409**, 538
Embezzler 180
Emerald of the East (Jan de Kuharski) 383
Emergency 448
Emergency Call 176, 472, 520
Emil and the Detectives 292, **439**
Enchantment (Einar J. Bruun) 383
Encore 167, 261, 267, 360, 394, 400, 489, 518
End of the Affair (Edward Dmytryk) 115, 277, 351, 365, 481
End of the Line 443, 456
End of the River 409, 439, **507**
End of the Road (36) **61**
End of the Road (54) **429**
Enemy of the Police 279, 478
England Expects 503
England's Menace 5, **453**
English Rose 396
English Without Tears 114, **167**, 389, 529
Englishman's Home (14) **30**
Englishman's Home (39) **129**, 197
Enoch Arden 368, 522
Enter Inspector Duval 510
Enter the Queen (Arthur Varney-Serrao) 49
Entertainer 60, 151, 154, 310, 386, **427**
Ernest Maltravers (Jack Denton) 203
Escapade 296, 351, 353, 460
Escape (30) 40, 76, **124**, 213, 254, 408
Escape (48) (Joseph Mankiewicz) 114, 216, 218
Escape by Night 180
Escape from Broadmoor 180, 239, 478
Escape in the Sun (George Breakston) 38
Escape Me Never 117, 462
Escape Route 186, 447
Escape to Danger **95**, 208, 407
Escapement 504
Escort for Hire 187
Esther 142, 371, 430
Esther Redeemed 359
Esther Waters 46, 96, 118
Eternal Feminine (A. Varney-Serrao) 371
Eternal Triangle 240, 437, 527, **533**
Eugene Aram (14) **93**
Eugene Aram (24) 283, **438**, 538
Eureka Stockade 153, 378, **521**
Evening with the Royal Ballet 13

142

144

148

154

156

Q 'Planes 118, 236, 283, 314, 386, 426, **526**, 539
Qualified Adventurer 231, 290
Quare Fellow (Arthur Dreifuss) 340, 483
Quartet 8, 43, 46, 89, **108**, **167**, 138, 455, **465**, 481, 498, 546
Quatermass and the Pit 19, 456
Quatermass II 160, 193, 314, 478
Quatermass Xperiment 160, **193**, 520
Queen Mother 381
Queen of Hearts 23, 124, 152, 312, 470
Queen of Spades 130, 144, 244, 353, 515
Queen Was in the Parlour 107, 116
Queenie of the Circus 316, 358, **415**
Queen's Affair 369, 529
Queen's Evidence (James McKay) 486
Queen's Guards 254, 263, 335, 409, 475
Queer Cargo (Harold Schuster) 273, 480
Question of Adultery 80, 241, 472
Question of Suspense 256, 510
Question of Trust 142, 231
Quiet Wedding 13, 147, 311, 345
Quiet Weekend 147, **167**, 398
Quiet Woman 47, 180
Quiller Memorandum 7, 195, 442
Quinneys (19) 3, 141, **534**
Quinneys (27) **142**, 263, 314, 485

Racing Romance 435
Radio Cab Murder 210, **451**
Radio Lover (Austin Melford) 118
Radio Parade (Archie de Bear) 251
Radio Parade of 1935 99, 119, 221, **539**
Radio Pirates 72, 167, 186, 470
Rag Doll 95
Ragged Messenger 5, 177, 240, **523**
Raiders of the River (John Haggarty) 314
Rainbow Jacket 43, **125**, 361, 518
Raise the Roof 21, 480
Raising a Riot 118, 283, 356, **497**
Raising the Wind 490
Rajah's Tiara 331
Rake's Progress 178, 216, 276, 389, 486
Ramsbottom Rides Again 12, 32, 511
Rank Outsider (Richard Garrick) 327
Rasp 409
Rasputin the Mad Monk 301, **452**, 456
Rat (25) 116, 262, 380
Rat (37) 173, 380, 414, **416**, 515
Rattle of a Simple Man **51**, 83, 102
Reach for Glory 296
Reach for the Sky **176**, 356, 395, 398, 478, 518
Real Bloke 32
Reasonable Doubt 279, 478
Rebel 123, 411, 421, 442
Rebel Son 66, **126**, 310, 345, 434
Recalling of John Grey 240, 437, 527, **533**

Reckless Gamble 374
Recoil (22) 325, 379
Recoil (55) 180, 354
Red and Blue 418, 427
Red Beret 20, 66, 173, 241, **544**
Red Ensign 22, 409
Red Pearls 161
Red Pottage (Meyrick Milton) 5, 466
Red Shoes 409, 515
Red Wagon 66, 210, 474
Redemption of His Name 355
Reluctant Bride 78
Reluctant Heroes 147, 377, **416**, 458
Reluctant Widow 276, 282, 436
Rembrandt 86, 177, 283, 288, 291, 310
Remembrance (Bert Wynne) 240, 279, 470
Reptile 180
Repulsion 225, 405
Rest Cure 90, 432
Return from the Ashes 139, **304**, 313
Return of a Stranger (37) 148, **208**
Return of a Stranger (61) 5 510
Return of Bulldog Drummond 426, 480, 495
Return of Carol Deane 49, 539
Return of Mr. Moto 362
Return of the Frog 142, 213, 414
Return of the Rat 116, 159, 213, 262, 380, 408
Return of the Scarlet Pimpernel (Hans Schwartz) 26, 60, 66, 283, 334
Return to the Desert (Denis Kavanagh) 241
Return to Yesterday 58, 299, 439, **476**
Reunion 72, 375, 437
Reveille 21, 399
Revenge of Frankenstein 115, **155**, 478
Revenge of Mr. Thomas Atkins 5, **503**
Revolution 30, 513
Rhodes of Africa (Berthold Viertel) 10
Rhythm in the Air **539**
Riccochet 363
Rich and Strange 28, 234, 274, 328
Richard III 20, 45, 66, 175, 211, 283, 386, 426
Ride of the Valkyrie 59
Riders of the New Forest 296
Riders to the Sea 256
Riding High 119, 172, 323, 344
Right Age to Marry 435
Right Element 534
Right to Live (21) 90
Right to Live (33) 390, 393
Right to Strike 203, 396, 480
Ring 56, 203, 213, **234**, 254
Ring of Spies 501
Ringer (28) (Arthur Maude) 37
Ringer (31) 161, 213, 314, 476
Ringer (52) 140, 198, **205**, 218, 283, 313, 478
Ringing the Changes 233, 138
Rising Generation (Harley Knoles) 5, 28, 112, 491
Rising of the Moon (John Ford) 295
Rivals 5 10
River Beat 38, 188, 208

162

164

169

170

173